CW01638388

Disclaimer

Although I am a registered health professional, this book is a self-help guide for health and general well-being so I am obliged to write a legal disclaimer.

This book contains information regarding medical, nutritional, psychological and exercise rehabilitation for health care. The information is not meant to be a substitute for medical, nutritional, physical or psychological treatment. It is strongly recommended that you seek help and advice from a medical professional or registered health professional before participating in any of the suggested information within this book. Please seek help from your doctor or registered health professional if you suspect that you may have an injury. The publisher, author and editor of this book should not be held responsible for injury or other medical outcomes that may result from the advice, methods and suggestions contained within this book.

Copyright © 2018 by Heather Pearson

Photographs copyright © 2018 The Pearson Method

ISBN 978 1 5272 2733 0

All rights reserved.

No part of this publication may be replicated in any way or means, stored in a retrieval system or transmitted in any form electronic, photocopying, mechanical or recording or otherwise without the permission of the author.

Cover image and stock illustrations used under licence from Shuttershock.com

Editing and proof reading: www.firstproof.co.uk

Cover design and layout by Keith Voles

Photography by Richard Hammerton

What people say about the Pearson Method

This book is a masterpiece. Heather has interned with me twice at my clinic in Ohio, she treated me and rehabilitated my glutes and lower back so I experienced the physical side of the Pearson Method. My back felt incredible afterwards. Back Pain Free has so much information on subjects like sleep, depression and gut function, all very important factors when coping with pain. I applaud Heather's 'ready to do' techniques; they are a must have. I highly recommend this book to anyone suffering with back pain.

Dr Eric Serrano, Medical Doctor, Hormone Specialist, Ohio, USA

As the owner of the only global personal training business, part of my job is knowing when and who we should refer out to. This is always a minefield because some people talk a good game and never deliver, whereas other therapists are one-trick ponies who get stuck in the rut of their first ever treatment modality and fail to appreciate that the more tools a therapist has in their toolbox the better they are equipped to help their patients. Over the past decade that I have known Heather Pearson, first as a patient and then as a business owner referring my own clients, I have seen her tirelessly bolster her knowledge from every single source possible, always keeping an open mind and bringing new skills to the treatment table that can help even the trickiest of cases – especially with back pain. However, anyone who has spent much time around great therapists will tell you that in addition to knowledge, the one non-negotiable factor that the best people bring is their passion for helping people and just how much they actually care. Heather has helped thousands of people across the world to live more pain-free lives and we are all the better for having access to her wonderfully compassionate and educated practice with this book. It is an absolute must have for anyone suffering back pain, who wants to live pain free and stay that way.

Nick Mitchell, Global CEO of Ultimate Performance Group, Los Angeles, USA, Author of *Your Ultimate Body Transformation Plan*

Before I went to see Heather, I had been experiencing increasing back pain for over six months. Previously I had been very active, from an earlier military career and participation in many sports. I had sports massages but slowly felt more uncomfortable so I went to an osteopath but there was no long-term benefit. I would walk around my flat at all hours of the night, trying to do something to ease the discomfort. I couldn't understand it: I hadn't had an accident or suffered an injury yet my back was getting increasingly worse. I used to swim 60 lengths three times a week, I couldn't even manage a length without pain; I had twinges in my groin and trying to lift anything heavier than a light shopping bag had become a real effort, so much so that I had to switch to online shopping. As my back worsened, I wondered what on earth life was going to be like going forward. I certainly had a lot more empathy for anyone who had experienced any degree of back pain. I attended my first session in December 2017, Heather assessed me, and determined immediately what the problem was, telling me straight away that she could help me and I would be pain free again. This was music to my ears – even knowing it wouldn't be a 'quick fix', there was suddenly light at the end of the tunnel.

Heather explained that it would take a few months because of the chronic weakness. Even after my first session I felt looser, I stopped experiencing the same nagging issues and it gave me some relief over the coming weeks. It took four months to become pain free. I clearly remember Heather saying to me on one of my latter appointments that I was so close to reaching that point, that I wouldn't believe it – and by continuing with the exercises she had given me that point arrived about five days later, so when I saw her next I arrived with the biggest smile on my face, which said it all. I know that I will need to continue with my exercises to rebuild strength in my glutes, back and core. I am now back swimming again, can lift heavier objects, can turn freely in bed without pain or discomfort – so I feel like a new woman. I highly recommend this book to anyone who has a back injury.

Julie Young, Company Director, UK, Former Army Officer

Playing and training for competitive sport in the UK and US at an elite level in the Seniors category means I have suffered back pain and various injuries. Heather has been fantastic in treating my back and, even more importantly, preventing it from being injured through regular treatment and her unique rehab strength exercises. She has also assisted me with health supplementation that has enabled me to sleep through the night and recover better for competitive games or training the following day. All of the aforementioned tools are in this book; the Pearson Method works!

John Prenn, CEO Bonsoir Limited, London, UK, Real Tennis World Champion Seniors 2015, 2017

I have been coming to see Heather on and off for over ten years with various mild injuries and for maintenance work. A few years ago I had a prolapsed disc, I was in a lot of pain and had a severe sharp pain in my lower back; I never thought I'd be able to return to my normal activities and I was suffering from anxiety too. I'd get terrible sciatic nerve pain in my legs even after just 10 minutes of swimming. It took a lot of perseverance to get my glutes working properly to support my back but with Heather's treatment, rehab and re-assurance my sciatica disappeared completely; so did my anxiety. Now I don't even feel the area where the disc was bulging. She's also been a brilliant personal trainer and has given me fantastic advice about nutrition and health supplements. Heather has had such extreme injuries herself and has had to overcome these by her own determination which I feel adds to her success in treating others – which is what this book is about. It describes everything you need to know to get you out of pain and back to enjoying your favourite physical activities and enjoying life again.

Lydia Marchione, Opera Singer, London, UK

I had a slipped disc for many years and it used to give me debilitating pain. I saw two doctors who gave me strong painkillers that made me worse, who then recommended surgery, which I refused. I started to work with a personal trainer who recommended Heather to help with my back pain. Her passion for her work and enthusiasm were contagious, and she gave me hope that I could be pain free with regular treatments and rehab exercises. Today, not only am I totally pain free, but I have started playing tennis again which I had not been able to do for many years. One of the consequences of my back pain was that my jaw was stuck and I could hardly open my mouth. Heather did a few treatments on my jaw and I was back to normal. I could also go on and on about how all my children have benefited from her skills, but it would take a whole book in itself! I strongly recommend the Pearson Method for any kind of back pain.

Isabelle Lemaignen, Nutritional Therapist & Naturopath, California, USA

Having visited a renowned osteopath and two highly recommended sports therapists I was still suffering from acute lower back pain. I'd given up hope of any form of respite and any sleep. I then met Heather. Twenty minutes later my back was 60% better and after a second session the pain had totally disappeared. I have not had back pain since. Heather has a phenomenal knowledge and understanding of the human body and uses both professional and personal experience to extraordinary effect. For anyone who has suffered any form of back pain I highly recommend they read this truly life-changing book.

Grant Parsons, Director, Curtis Brown Group Ltd, London, UK

As a full time, working mother of three running two companies I can't afford to be incapacitated for any period of time; with a vast array of tools and knowledge at her disposal Heather has kept me, not just going, but strong. I first saw Heather for chronic neck and back pain 11 years ago. Within a short space of time I was completely pain free for the first time in years. Her thirst for knowledge and continuous drive to learn new techniques and add to her ever-more impressive arsenal of treatment methods leaves me in continual admiration and this book is justification of that. Back Pain Free can not only help people return to a pain free status, but it also teaches you the specific preventative rehab exercises to stay pain free.

Anita Bindra, Managing Director, Catalyst Cameras, London, UK

After a combination of working as an international director of photography and doing a lot of adventurous mountain biking and snowboarding for almost 30 years, my body has been pushed to extreme limits. My back has suffered numerous times from longs hours of work, long-haul flights and intense physical activities. If it weren't for Heather's incredible knowledge and understanding of the human body and her ever-expanding database of fast-working, effective treatments and rehab exercises, I would have missed a lot of work. Through her extensive knowledge of strength training she has kept me strong and mobile over the last 10 years. This book says it all!

Duane McClunie, Director of Photography, Documentary/Commercial/Drama, UK / International

I've been weight training for around 20 years at an elite level and competed at the British finals in both powerlifting and bodybuilding. Not only is it my hobby and passion but I'm also a strength coach so keeping myself injury free is vital. Over the years I've picked up my fair share of back injuries. I tried all the usual therapies such as sports massage but never really felt like they were the solution. My injuries kept coming back. Meeting Heather, in 2014, literally changed all of that. Her knowledge, experience, and practical skills are world class. I refer all of my clients to her and even took my 88 year-old granddad to her for his back pain. Why? Because the Pearson Method WORKS. I no longer worry about back injuries and my training keeps improving. In her book you'll discover everything you'll need to bulletproof your back and make those painful, frustrating days a thing of the past.

Phil Agostino, Strength Coach/Transformation Specialist, London, UK,
Author of *Lose the Flab Fast*

Over a 12-year period I suffered two Gilmore's groins (hernias), a pointless knee arthroscopy and groin strains. When those injuries occurred I had been playing football for an elite premiership academy team but had to stop due to injury. Heather told me all my injuries were caused by the same thing. Before seeing her I had been suffering with a completely dehydrated disc in my lumbar spine for 18 months. I tried massage, dry needling, pretty much every therapy out there but nobody could 'fix' me and the pain continued to worsen. The pain affected me to the point where I couldn't sit down for long periods of time and it had drastically affected my ability to work – it's hard to run two gyms when you're in agony. Heather explained that my glutes and lower back were in a mess but she could get me pain free. After seeing her only a few times and with a lot of rehab exercises, I am now walking around pain free.

Given how amazing my back is now I believe that if I had followed the Pearson Method 12 years ago I would have had a very good career in professional football. Heather's philosophy and methodologies are incredible. This book will give you your life back as Heather did for me.

Reece Mander, Owner RMF Gyms, Canary Wharf, London, UK

I was involved in a car accident ten years ago, which resulted in severe whiplash. I was in constant pain and had severely restricted movement with my neck and back. Everyday tasks like cooking and washing my hair had become extremely painful and difficult. I had gone from a healthy, active 25-year-old, to someone I did not recognise any more. I lost my independence and became anxious and depressed. I tried every treatment available including physiotherapy, osteopathy and acupuncture amongst others. Meeting Heather changed my life. I was drawn to her compassionate and empathetic nature and her vast knowledge of various subjects. Her combination of soft tissue work, specific rehab and strength training was invaluable and beyond any other therapist's capabilities I had ever encountered. Heather treated me, trained me in the gym and advised me on nutrition, diet and supplements which all aided my recovery; I became pain free. Today I am able to drive, work and do everyday tasks pain free. Heather is an amazing individual, determined and motivated, and the fact that she has been in the same position and overcome her own injuries is an inspiration. I would recommend this book to anyone suffering with back pain, as it gives real hope that you too can become pain free and stay that way.

Ouzma Shamsee, Family Lawyer, London

Contents

DEDICATION

This book is dedicated to YOU, the reader.

My hope is to provide you with all the elements that can enrich your life to live free of pain and suffering. I wish for each and every one of you to reach the end of your painful journey and enjoy life as it was supposed to be... *Back Pain Free.*

In fondest memory of my mentor Charles R. Poliquin who sadly passed away shortly before this book went to press.

Foreword by Dr Ken Kinakin DC

Author of Optimal Muscle Training - Founder of SWIS (Society of Weight-Training Injury Specialists)

Your life can change in an instant! It did for Heather Pearson. This is a true and transparent story of someone who experienced and survived a horrendous car crash which left them with an array of whole body injuries - the worst being excruciating back pain... 24 hours a day, 7 days a week.

In the medical field, there are 'tourists and natives' when it comes to pain. A 'tourist' is a doctor or therapist who studies the physiology of pain but never experiences what it is like to live with. A 'native' is a doctor or therapist who experiences pain continuously due to unfortunate circumstances. The 'natives' not only study pain, but they learn new ways to treat and rehabilitate themselves through advanced seminars, observing what works for themselves and seeing the success they can get with their patients in their clinic.

Back Pain Free is written in two parts. The first part is Heather's personal story of her car accident and an journey to help heal herself. She discusses the emotional, mental and physical roller coaster ride of being in incredible pain every day, the daily life restrictions and how it has an effect on you. A powerful quote taken from the book is "When you suffer pain day after day, it changes you". The book goes on to discuss how you start using unhealthy coping strategies such as taking too much medication, isolating yourself from friends and family, increasing your alcohol intake, thinking bad thoughts, and losing hope, because no one seems to know what is wrong or how to decrease your pain. Life then becomes a daily burden. That is how pain changes you.

Fortunately Heather didn't give up; she noticed small decreases in pain when she received advanced sports massage and cranial osteopathy. She also noticed a difference when she did gentle strength exercises and started to feel stronger. This inspired her to quit her job in the media field and start a journey to becoming a sports therapist and strength coach which eventually led to the end of her depression and being pain free.

The second part of the book is 'all about hands on'. The most effective treatment techniques Heather discovered that decreased her pain included Active Release Technique® (ART®), cranial osteopathy, and sports massage. Heather not only received these treatments but she became certified in these techniques and many, many more which she still uses every day on her patients. Plus, she also discusses other health strategies to help deal with back pain like tips on improving sleep, gut function, coping with depression, nutritional protocols, meditation and breathing techniques. Over a 10 year span Heather created her own diagnostic process to resolve back pain called the Pearson Method which includes tests like the 'Pearson Clam Test' and rehab strengthening exercise protocols to help rebuild your glutes, lower back and core in a step-by-step fashion that anyone can do in the privacy of their own home.

This book is written for the person who suffers chronic back pain every day. When you start reading it, you will find yourself nodding your head in agreement and saying to yourself, "that is me" when Heather describes what it is like to live with pain. It is also a guide for you to seek out the various advanced treatment techniques and see if they would be helpful, as well as coping strategies for the pivotal but less talked about subjects involved with back pain. And lastly, there is a progressive, gentle strengthening programme that has proven to be effective which can help your journey to decrease pain and strengthen your back, restoring your function back to normal. This book is the KEY to 'unlocking your door to freedom' – to being back pain free.

Why should you read this book?

Can you imagine life pain free? Well, I did and so far I'm living it but it's taken me many, many years to figure out that resolving back pain is a package. It's not just about doing a few exercises or some stretches every morning, it's a package compiled of multiple factors and it doesn't stop there. Once you are pain free you need to keep it that way. This book contains all the essential components for you to live a life free of pain; the intention is that it can change your life forever.

If you're reading this book I can only assume that you're experiencing pain or you know someone close to you that is suffering. If this is for you then you know what it's like to suffer back pain. Do you find it hard to stand upright first thing in the morning? I bet you can't turn over in bed without wincing in anguish? Is that first step out of bed like torture? Do you suffer in silence while experiencing pain ALL DAY LONG? Have you ever had the feeling that's it... that's your life now, you have to live with it forever? Do you find yourself fantasising what life would be like if you were pain free? If that's the case, this book is most definitely for you.

I was that person and boy did I suffer. I've been through a horribly challenging journey over the last 17 years, which I'd like to share with you. "Why should you listen to me?" I hear you ask? Who am I? I'm just an average member of the general public, I'm not a celebrity and I'm certainly not a well-known athlete but I am someone who went through a life-changing experience and as a result I changed career to become an injury specialist on a mission to heal anyone and everyone in pain. The first seven chapters of this book are the story of my car crash, one where I should have died; I still have no idea how I survived. I wish to tell you my story, how horribly messed up I was and then how I became back pain free. If I did it, so can you. However, if you don't want to read my story, feel free to jump straight to chapter 8 to learn about the tools of how to reach pain free status.

It's taken a long time to write this book although the intention has been there for many years. I'm now at a dependable stage of being 'pain free' in my lower, mid and upper back, hence I'm eager to share my personal success of recovery especially if you, or anyone you know, may be in the position that I once was... in absolute agony.

One of the most frustrating factors of being in pain is, it's invisible. Nobody knows you have it because they can't see it. I felt this was often worse than being in pain itself, always wondering if friends and colleagues actually believed me and getting frustrated because people would always forget. Another frustrating thing about pain is how much you are limited in your daily tasks – and you can forget about exercise. The perception of pain is different within each of us but there are a lot of common denominators. These may consist of activity inhibitions, depression and severe frustration to name just a few. Either way, the scope that these negative emotions manifest themselves is surprisingly, extremely broad which can leave a person helpless, severely depressed, feeling burdened and alone. If you've ever been in pain, albeit mild or severe, then you know exactly what I'm talking about.

Lower back pain is one of the most common issues for long-term sickness throughout the world but, contrary to belief, it isn't always caused by a specific incident or a sporting nature. Back pain can derive from giving birth or overusing muscles by doing too much of one thing such as DIY, or it can be caused by a postural issue from long drives in the car or sitting at a computer for many hours every week. I explain this in detail later in the book. Regardless of the reason, living with pain is soul destroying.

Personally, I was at rock bottom both physically and psychologically due to an exhaustive, long list of injuries after my car accident. Shortly after, I was in a position where I was in such horrendous pain, I couldn't walk even a few steps from my bedroom to my bathroom. I dreaded it every time I needed to visit the toilet. I feared going to bed at night, because turning over in bed was like torture. My body was in such horrific pain for years so I had to take a ridiculously large amount of medication that, in turn, led to even more issues. I had undiagnosed multiple broken bones and nerve entrapments as well as whole body muscular dysfunction. For many years I wasn't living, in any way shape or form; I had reached a point where I had no desire, motivation or focus to live life.

Pain is debilitating, it limits one's life and as a result it can change your personality. My journey has meant overcoming years of physical and emotional torment; agonising pain in my whole spine from the top of my neck down to my lower back, trying to fix a long list of excruciating muscular injuries in every joint (other than my wrists), nerve entrapments, learning how to deal with the daily limitations of normal life as well as emotional turmoil, dealing with the side effects of medication and discovering how to overcome the desperation of depression. Most significantly, the most important part of my journey was to see a small flicker of light at the end of a very long tunnel where I could explore the possibility of never having to live with pain again.

After many years of rehabilitation (rehab) exercises and various therapy modalities, I slowly began to understand my pain and accept what had happened to me. I knew that I could no longer perform my job in TV properly due to the long hours so I decided to change career and become a therapist devoting my life to help others become pain free. I started studying incessantly and eventually my studies sent me around the world so I could learn as much as possible from the most elite educators. I wanted to be the best therapist I could be, to help others. I didn't just learn about therapies but also about the values of nutrition, strength training, psychology and other tools that are encompassed within this book.

With the help of advanced treatments, good quality sleep, strength exercises and a healthy food regime I have been able to maintain pain free status in my whole spine. Since changing industries in 2005 I have become an established and successful sports therapist working with patients and athletes from all over the UK, Europe and the USA. I deliver voluntary lectures to sports schools and sports colleges and I teach an advanced soft tissue technique to elite therapists in medical teams, including those in the Premier League, the highest level of English football and most watched sports league in the world.

My story is like a 'rags to riches' journey, not in the context of money but rather one that has enriched my life with fulfilment from another source... helping others achieve their optimum goal of being pain free and teaching other therapists to do the same. I wish to tell my story about an outrageously tough, gruelling but successful voyage of reaching my desired goal of being pain free through hard work, discipline and sheer determination. I want to share with you how I got there so that you have all of the same tools in your box at your fingertips.

Of all the whole body injuries I suffered, back pain was by far the worst. My path to being pain free translates from conventional medicine to using alternative remedies towards natural medication and health supplementation, holistic healing, rehab strength exercises, psychology and more.

Having moved into the health and fitness industry after my life-changing experience, I can truly say I adore my profession and look forward to it every day, whether it be working with a 65-year-old female who's recovering from back pain or a professional athlete who needs to get back on the pitch within a given deadline. No amount of money can give you that buzz of exhilaration when you can help someone become pain free regardless of age, gender, background or injury – especially when you've been through hell yourself. There are certain symptoms and psychological emotions one just can't learn on a course or in a book, the only way you can possibly know it, is to experience it.

My daily intention is "I desire 100% pain free status with every patient as quickly and efficiently as possible" and my favourite motto is "the proof of the pudding is in the eating" because in terms of the outcome, results mean everything. I know what it really means to be in pure anguish on a daily basis and I'm now devoted to being the most successful therapist I can be with a constant pledge of continuing development towards my skills and knowledge. Research and technology evolves constantly so I have committed myself to a consistent regime of studying from the most elite therapists, strength coaches, psychologists and nutritionists around the world.

Recovering from back pain is a package that consists of a multitude of aspects, which you will learn throughout this book. That is what the Pearson Method is all about. There are truths I can tell you that you simply can't learn unless you've experienced them, where only dark and nasty sensations of any nature have a description. The reason for writing this book is to inspire you to use the tools within it and to provide you with a guide, an understanding, faith and hope that pain doesn't have to be forever and a belief that you can get there, you can be back pain free. I did it, so can you!

1
The Accident

"Are you alright love?"... "Love, are you OK?"... I could hear people shouting at me through the windscreen... I opened my eyes and realised my whole body was hanging forwards in my seatbelt. I had blacked out. It seemed to take forever to realise what had just happened, although it was probably seconds; actually I have no idea. I had been involved in a very severe car crash. Everything was happening in slow motion, it felt like I was in a movie. An eyewitness asked me if I was OK, I tried to nod, not really knowing if I was actually moving my head or not. I couldn't talk due to the immense amount of shock I was experiencing and before I knew it I was hyperventilating. My driver's door had completely caved in so an eyewitness came over to the passenger door and tried to help me move out of the driver's seat and into the passenger seat. He literally had to pull my legs over to the other seat; I was in so much shock that I had no use of my legs.

Let's go back a bit. By the late summer of 2001 life was fabulous! I was 31 years old and working as a Researcher/Assistant Producer for a TV company. I absolutely loved my job! I already had over eight years under my belt working in TV and I had numerous stories to tell about all the celebrities, actors and presenters I had worked with. That was during the daytime. In the evenings I would either be exercising with martial arts, weight training, running or horse riding which were passions or rather obsessions that I'd had since I was a very young age. At weekends I was a club DJ, in nightclubs around London. I was lucky to have started DJ'ing at the age of 17 and I got a huge buzz from it, the bigger the club, the bigger the buzz!

At that time my goals were to continue with my TV career into specialist directing and I was about to start training for my black belt in my martial art called Sun Kune Do. More importantly I was about to start training to compete in martial arts, something I'd wanted to do all my life. However, on 15th October 2001, I had no idea I would never fulfil any of my goals, my life was about to turn 180 degrees upside down overnight...

The week before, I had moved from West London (where I had lived all my life) to North London, to live with my boyfriend Sam. At the time, ironically, I had moved to his preferred side of London because I had a car and he didn't. In fact, he didn't drive at all so it seemed the more reasonable resolution to who would move where, after we decided to live together.

That particular Monday, I woke up feeling rather excited because I was about to start training for my black belt in Sun Kune Do and prepping to compete. Martial arts was my usual Monday evening hobby in East London. When I put my martial arts kit in the boot of my car that morning, I realised I'd left my records in the car having DJ'd on the Saturday night before. Back then, DJ's used vinyl records so the cases were extremely large and very heavy. Another reason for my excitement that day was that Sam was returning from Germany having been on a work trip for four days. All in all, it was a day to look forward to. I was so wrong.

About 8.15am, I drove out of my road in Highgate, on route to my work in West London. Although I had only moved into the area a week prior, I had already learnt some of the back roads, living up to my nickname, 'the back road queen!' Every morning I would pull out of a side road to cross the main Archway Road into another side road – it was a great way to save a lot of time. This particular morning traffic to my right was completely empty so I edged forward. At that time of the morning, traffic to my left was the usual, jam-packed solid. A man driving a MPV (multi-purpose vehicle) stopped to give way to me, so I thanked him by waving with a smile and then edged forward slowly to see if there were any cyclists in the bus lane... BANG... LIGHTS OUT...

"Are you alright love?"... "Love, are you OK?" ... I could hear people shouting at me through the windscreen... I opened my eyes, I realised my whole body was hanging forwards in my seatbelt... After the eyewitness had helped me move into the passenger seat, it was at that point that he explained what had happened. A lady in a large MPV had been speeding in the bus lane, most likely to avoid traffic, as people do sometimes even though it's illegal. Back then you could get away with it, now we have speed cameras everywhere around London which put a stop to that kind of irresponsible driving.

As I had edged forward into the bus lane to check for cyclists, the lady had driven straight into the passenger side of my car. The eyewitness suspected that she was driving at about 50 mph, too fast in a road with a 30 mph speed limit and clearly illegally. Nobody is allowed to drive in bus lanes at peak times of the day except buses. The lady was driving so fast that she didn't see me edge forward into the bus lane so I received the full impact, I was told this later on by the police officers. The impact was so intense that it spun my BMW 90 degrees to the right at such speed that my car knocked a huge, thick concrete pole clean out of the ground, which was the reason the driver's side door was totally smashed in. Hence, I had a double impact being hit from the left and then from the right with immense force. As I was taking this all in I noticed that my legs were shaking and things still seemed to be happening in slow motion.

I looked over at the front of a nearby building, which was also smashed in during the crash from the other car and saw a lady smoking a cigarette and talking to the passenger of the MPV involved in the accident. She calmly walked around the car, opened the boot of the car and walked back around to the front again as if looking for something. I assumed she was a kind bystander who had come to help out. After a few minutes she came over to my car, opened the passenger door and asked me if I was alright. I nodded my head, I definitely felt it move this time.

Shortly after, I heard sirens and before I knew it police cars (I can't remember how many) had arrived on the scene. All of a sudden that same lady turned around, stubbed out her cigarette very quickly and sat down on a step next to the MPV. She then appeared to make signs with her hands as if she was fainting and started making funny faces like she was in pain. It all seemed like she was acting out a scene from a car accident, a character of someone who was trying to feign suffering. I worked in TV, it was easy to spot a bad actor/actress. It was then that I realised she was the driver of the MPV.

A police officer came over and asked me if I was all right. I couldn't speak so I nodded my head and he told me he would interview me at the hospital; I nodded again. His colleague came over and I overheard him say that according to various eyewitnesses the other driver was clearly at fault and was driving illegally in the bus lane and, more than that, she was driving too fast. The officer also said that due to the nature of the skid marks on the road, or lack of them, I had received the full impact of the crash. In other words, the driver of the other car was driving so fast that she couldn't react quick enough to brake before the impact. He also added that with all due respect she seemed to be laying it on rather thick saying that she needed an ambulance. They had come to this conclusion from various eyewitness statements, saying that she was walking around straight after the crash and seemed absolutely fine, unlike myself who couldn't walk or talk. The officer further explained the possible reason for her behaviour was due to the fact that the tax disc on her MPV was out of date, so she was driving illegally.

What seemed like an hour later (again, probably only a few minutes) an ambulance arrived and a medic came over to assess me. He took my pulse, which was racing. I could hear and feel my heartbeat in my head it was so loud and fast. I remember feeling very calm in the presence of the medic, he was a very happy and relaxed man. Finally, I was able to talk but I was still in a high state of shock so I could only manage a few short spurts, I sounded like a robot with a low battery. Bizarrely, I joked with the medic that I sounded a Dalek from the Dr Who programme. The problem was the more I tried to laugh, the more I sounded like a Dalek! It was a rather delirious, comical moment in the midst of an extremely traumatic situation.

Eventually, my heart rate started to ease slightly so the medic tried to move me but I still had no use of my legs so he decided to wait. He explained that I was still experiencing symptoms of extreme acute shock and that I would be able to walk eventually. He waited for what seemed like an eternity then, finally, helped me get out of the car and into the ambulance. I was able to stand but I still didn't have full use of my legs so I was unable to walk unaided. The medic encouraged me to keep looking forward to help get me in the ambulance so I never looked back to see the messy situation that I had left behind me. Once in the ambulance, my first instinct was to call work to tell them I'd be late (I was in an ambulance on route to hospital, what on earth was I thinking, that's what shock does to you). My speech was almost normal by then so I did just that, I called work and explained that I'd been in a car crash and was on my way to hospital. The ambulance siren was going off in the background so my colleague who intercepted the answerphone message had a real shock!

Once at the hospital I was sent for a neck X-ray and soon after the police officer from the crash site came over to take my statement. I explained what had happened and he said he would be in touch. Before he left, he gave me the details of the garage where my car had been taken and also explained that it was highly likely that my car was a 'write off' and so I would need to pick up any possessions from my car. The other officer came over and told his colleague that the lady who had hit my car seemed fine but was still complaining of all sorts of pain. Both officers shook their heads and left. I waited over two hours to see a doctor who explained that the X-rays were clear so he examined me. At that time, I felt my heart rate had calmed down and I had no pain whatsoever. I had full range of movement in my neck, so I was discharged.

On the walk home from the hospital, all I could think about was calling the insurance company and getting a hire car as soon as possible so I could get back to work and then drive to my martial arts session later that evening. It's odd, the things you think about when you've just been involved in a serious accident. When I got home, I called Sam to let him know what had happened and then called the insurance company who gave me some bad news. Due to the nature of the accident i.e. driving across a main road and requiring another driver to give way, meant that liability was in question so they wouldn't give me a hire car. How frustrating? I was pretty angry that my morning had been so messed up. It's a very weird law that states, if the other person is to be fully liable for an accident, you have to wait for a busy road to be clear to drive across it which never happens in London in peak time traffic, let alone at night. In the meantime I called my sister to see if she could drive to my flat in North London and drive me to the car crash centre where my car had been taken so I could retrieve my possessions. I called work again to explain I probably wouldn't make it in that day. I was working on a very busy programme and we were just about to enter into the most hectic few weeks of that particular production. In the whole of my TV career, I was very conscientious about giving 100% in my job. In fact, I don't remember ever taking a sick day whilst working in TV prior to my accident.

At that stage, I felt absolute fine to deal with every procedure with speed and diligence. In fact, if anything, rationale was all I could think about. My sister drove over from West London and we departed for the crash centre in Tottenham about 25 minutes away from my flat. After crawling though horribly slow traffic we finally arrived and as we pulled into the car park of the rather large car crash centre, we drove past a garage which had two cars inside. My sister shouted, "OH MY GOSH, ******* *****, look at the state of your car. Oh my gosh, oh my..." She started crying, so I comforted her and explained that it was all right because that wasn't my car. I remember thinking how weird; that there was another black, 3 Series BMW in the same garage, except this one was so badly smashed up, it was totally crushed and I had no doubts that the driver would have ended up in hospital, if they had indeed got out alive. I felt very grateful.

We walked over to the reception desk and I stated my name and enquiry to the service receptionist who stared at me like he'd just seen a ghost. I was just about to ask him if he was OK when he quickly turned around, opened the door to the workshop and shouted to his colleagues. "Hey guys, you gotta come out and the see the driver of that black beemer, you're never gonna believe this!".

He then asked me again if I really was the driver of the black 'beemer' (BMW) that came in that morning. "Yes, I'm the driver of the black BMW, why all the drama? I'm just here to collect my possessions. I DJ'd on the weekend so I left my records in the boot of my car and my martial arts uniform is in there too."

He clearly wasn't listening to me and the next thing I knew, three men came rushing out of the workshop and into the reception. They were all staring at me like I was from outer space. They were looking me up and down making comments like "no way" and "she's not even scratched". Eventually they all went back into the workshop still muttering to each other, still looking shocked. I remember thinking: they are all so weird.

The service receptionist then explained that it was a miracle I had got out the car without any broken bones let alone got out alive. They were all in awe that I had survived and that I was on two feet, i.e. walking. One mechanic looked absolutely astonished. He said, "Listen love, do you know how lucky you are to be alive? No-one gets to even walk after a crash like that, you should be dead."

Bizarrely, by this time I felt quite annoyed, I didn't want to know how lucky I was, didn't they know I had phone calls to make? I just wanted to hurry up, get my belongings and get back on the phone to my car insurance company, again still thinking logically.

Eventually one of the mechanics walked us over to my car, still rambling on about all the wrecked cars he'd seen on a daily basis and how most drivers ended up dead if a car looked like mine. I had zoned out listening to him; all I could think about was the car insurance, the programme and what else I had to do when I got back to work.

All of a sudden I felt a huge rush of panic and shock. My heart started pounding so loud I thought I could hear it. I instantly felt like my legs were going to give way again. I realised that the car we'd seen when we first entered the garage was in fact mine. It was a complete and utter MESS. The number plate had been smashed to pieces, which is why I didn't recognise it. NO WAY. It simply couldn't be mine. REALLY? The mechanics were right: how on earth did I manage to be standing there, alive, with no broken bones? I felt like I was in a movie again, staring at my beautiful car all smashed up.

The passenger side wheel was actually facing the wrong way round, it was inside out, the impact of the other car had been so strong that the wheel had turned around 180° and as for my side of the car... the door had completely caved in, so much that it was concave, it must have been the concrete pole that was knocked straight out of the ground during the crash. I was very very lucky I hadn't lost my legs, I was told that by one of the mechanics and one of the police officers. The whole front of the car was shaped in a V, no wonder the police officer told me my car would be a complete write-off, but I had never looked back after I got out of the car. That's why the ambulance medic kept encouraging me to look forwards, it all made sense. My car was crushed so badly that it looked like it had been in one of those car crusher machines in scrap yards – it was literally half the size.

Blimey I thought, as my blood sugar started to crash, I've cheated death. What a horribly scary thought... I grabbed hold of my sister and told her we needed to get out of there asap. We collected my record boxes, my martial arts kit and a few other belongings and got back into my sister's car. As we drove past the reception, the mechanic waved for us to stop. He said "Listen love, I hope you realise how lucky you really are. Thank goodness for beemers being so sturdy, that car saved your life." I expressed my gratitude and finally, we drove away. I realised later that he was right.

My head was still swimming with shock as we drove back to my flat. I started getting waves of nausea and flashes of the accident; waking up from my unconscious state at the crash site. When we got back to my flat, I thanked my sister and insisted I was fine and that she should go home, as Sam would be returning later that day. After she left, even though I was clearly feeling sick, all I wanted to do was get straight back on the phone to the insurance company. Eventually, although I was still in 'sensible' mode, I finally started thinking "I nearly died today". The realisation was finally setting in.

2
The Aftermath

It was late afternoon on the day of the accident and I'd had no luck with the insurance company. It was one those situations where the question of liability was so up in the air that the insurance company of the lady who hit me wouldn't budge and so my insurance company said they would not provide me with a hire car so I would be 'car-less' for a while. I had to accept it. I didn't realise at that time that I wouldn't be allowed to drive anyway. I was told that my car would need to be assessed by an estimator and if it were a complete 'write-off' then I would be compensated in due course. So I called a few friends to tell them what had happened and that I was fine.

At around 5pm that day Sam came home, I was so happy to see him. I hugged him so tight. He said he got home as soon as he could. Sam made us both a cup of tea and we sat down and I told him all about the accident. He comforted me and told me not to worry about the car and that we'd get it sorted as soon as possible. He asked me if I was OK and I told him I was pretty freaked out when I saw the state of my totally smashed up car; otherwise I was fine. About five minutes later I started to feel an ache in my lower back, like when you've been on your feet all day and you need to sit down. I thought it was very weird that my lower back had started hurting and Sam suggested it was probably due to the stress of the whole day. However, within half an hour the ache had spread to my mid and upper back too. Within the hour my whole spine, from the top of my head to the base of my bum, felt as stiff as a plank of wood. By 6.30pm I had a headache from hell and my neck was in agony. It seemed like minutes had passed before my whole body was in complete anguish – even my knees and feet ached. I was in so much pain that Sam insisted we go to the hospital. I decided not to take painkillers as I was sure from previous first aid courses that I shouldn't take any medication until I'd seen a doctor.

We had only just moved into the area but I was thankful I had found out that morning that there was a local hospital. It was about 10 minutes' walk away although it felt more like 25 minutes, the way I was walking. The pain was so bad I was walking like a snail. By the time we got there I was in a really bad way. I was in so much agony I didn't know what to do with myself. I had never suffered an injury. I'd had the occasional headache from having a cold once or twice previously but in general I had always been extremely fit and healthy from a very young age.

We got to the hospital and registered at the Accident and Emergency reception and were told to wait. After an hour or so I told Sam the pain was getting worse, it was excruciating. My anxiety levels were increasing so I was extremely fidgety; the pain was so bad I couldn't sit still. I couldn't find a position that didn't hurt. By about 9pm the pain was so torturous that I was in floods of tears, Sam was really worried because he knew I never cried at anything. We used to joke that I was a 'cold hearted bitch' and had no emotions because he would cry at a sad movie and I would always sit there looking at him blankly. Sam practically begged a nurse to give me some painkillers. She told him she wasn't allowed to administer any medication until the doctor had seen me so I had to sit and suffer.

The wait was ridiculous. Within the next few hours, my whole back and neck felt like it was on fire, it was absolute AGONY, I felt like I was in hell. My left knee started to hurt a lot and I noticed when I went to the toilet I was limping because my feet hurt too. Through desperation I pestered Sam to ask the nurse for a painkiller and again he was denied. I had never known pain like this ever, I felt like someone had put a spell on me, it was so tiring. I remember thinking, "How can pain be this exhausting?" I was absolutely knackered. By the time I saw the doctor I had waited seven long, agonising hours in casualty. Even though I was in major anguish I almost ran into the room with glee at the thought of getting help for the dreadful pain.

The doctor started examining me and it was very clear that rotating my neck to the left and right, tilting my head forward and backward and leaning my ear to each shoulder left and right (this is called ranges of motion, ROM for short), were all very painful and extremely limited. The doctor hardly looked at me whilst he was talking and said, in a very blasé fashion, that he had finished his examination. I remember thinking "Is that it?", "Is that all you're going to do? But what about my mid and lower back and my knee and my feet?" The doctor said I had a mild case of whiplash and explained how I could help myself, not how he could help me. I was totally confused. I thought, "Hold on a minute, did he say mild whiplash?" The doctor went on to say that the old way of curing whiplash was to use a neck brace and administer painkillers. However, HIS 'new way' of resolving whiplash was to deal with the pain and not use any medication or a neck brace. I was speechless. I replied stating that I was in AGONY and would prefer medication but the doctor wouldn't budge. He repeated the same thing again, that pain was all in the mind and I could overcome it if I relaxed and went home and put my feet up and I would be OK for work the next day. "WHAT?", "Was he having a laugh?", I thought. I then became extremely angry and almost shouted at him that I'd waited seven hours in complete agony to be seen, only to be told there is nothing I can do but deal with it. Sam told me to calm down but how could I? I was in such a distressed state that I shouted at the doctor. "Seriously, what was the point in coming here and waiting seven hours to see you? What a ******* waste of my time." I then stormed out of the room in tears.

I was so furious and frustrated that I practically ran out of the hospital with Sam in tow. Once outside, I broke into hysterics, crying and shouting as the pain continued to worsen. Eventually Sam calmed me down and we walked home together very, very slowly. It was like I was in a ghastly nightmare and I'd wake up any minute... Once we got home Sam made me a cup of tea and told me that cups of tea always made everything better. I laughed at this, it's such a British thing. I took some paracetamol tablets, more than I should have. I was so exhausted that I fell asleep very quickly.

I woke up quite early the next day and was about to turn over and tell Sam about my nightmare dream when I realised that I couldn't move. I tried to turn over. "ARRRGGGHHHH". I screamed so loud that I woke Sam up. It felt like my whole spine was pinned to a plank of wood that had been burnt and that was as heavy as lead, almost like I could feel the nails everywhere, it was horribly painful and sore. I lay there for a while and spoke to Sam. The pain was horrific. I fought off tears and finally rose out of bed with Sam's help; it was a huge effort. It took a long time before I could stand up straight, every tiny movement hurt, even while I was standing, it was horrendous. I felt very very stressed.

We both decided that I needed to find a doctor who could help me properly, unlike the hospital doctor from the night before. I called work to tell them I couldn't come in as I needed proper medical attention. Sam got the telephone directory out and we both called around to find a local doctor's surgery. Most surgeries wouldn't accept new patients especially ones that were new to the area. I could feel my stress levels rising again but eventually Sam found one about 10 minutes' walk away.

I realised that my head was hurting really badly, I felt like I'd been hit over the head by a baseball bat. I also had severe pain in my left hip and knee, shoulders, jaw, feet, neck and back, basically my whole body hurt. We took a very slow walk over to the doctor's surgery. Walking was a real effort, my whole body hurt with every step especially my lower back and left hip and knee. I managed to see a doctor straight away. He was so empathetic and understanding about what had happened and he apologised for the doctor at the hospital the night before. He said that the hospital doctor should have given me some kind of medication to deal with the pain at the very least. This doctor was so friendly and compassionate that I got emotional. It was a tad embarrassing and surprising, especially as I'm not a very emotional person. The doctor finished his examination and diagnosed me with severe whiplash and secondary muscular trauma to my head, neck, shoulders, mid back, lower back, left hip, feet and left knee. He then gave me a prescription for some very strong anti-inflammatories and additional painkillers, a neck brace and also suggested I get some paracetamol for my headache too. That was a lot of medication but boy did I need it. He also referred me for physiotherapy at the local hospital and said he would put a rush on it. I was so thankful for this very helpful and caring doctor, I felt extremely grateful.

I spent the rest of the day being waited on by Sam and got back on the phone to chase the insurance company – again to no avail. I really don't know what possessed me to go to work the following day particularly as I was still in severe distress and I couldn't walk well at all. However, the medication had eased the pain a tad. The doctor had told me to rest up for a week or two, at least, he had written a doctor's note for me to take time off. However, working in television isn't a walk in the park and my current job deemed long and dedicated hours particularly in the run up to a transmission. So, stupidly, I trundled off to work the following day but this time on the bus and the train, not by car. I was told by my new doctor that I wasn't allowed to drive for 4-6 weeks. I hardly ever used London Transport so I didn't realise it would take so much longer than it would to drive and I quickly realised how many people wouldn't offer to give up their seat even though they could see I had a neck brace on and was blatantly in pain. My neck brace was huge, bright white and well, what can I say, you couldn't miss it! I also didn't realise how much it was going to hurt every time the train or bus driver stepped on the brakes. Every time the bus or train came to a halt I had another stab of pain, just to add insult to injury.

I was pleased that I'd made it into the office as it really lightened my mood to be around my colleagues especially my friend Christina, she was very understanding and supportive. I also felt a sense of self-worth being at work rather than moping around at home feeling sorry for myself. Due to all the medication I felt very light-headed in a spacey kind of way (I think some people would call this a 'space cadet') but I got on with it. The weird thing is, when you're at work, even with a neck brace on, people assume you're 100% healthy. I managed to get through most of the day but in the afternoon the pain had got worse so my friend told me to go home, she would cover for me.

The following day I slept through my alarm, I clearly wasn't used to the medication; my boss had a fit. She called me on the phone and absolutely tore into me about being so close to transmission and that we were under pressure with tight deadlines. She moaned and groaned for ages. I didn't manage to get a word in to defend myself or mention the amount of medication I was taking. I felt disappointed that I had overslept but also disappointed that my boss had been so non-empathetic even though I told her I had nearly died in the accident and that I was suffering a crazy amount of pain.

The next day, all I could think about was getting to work. It had already become a mission, within a day. It seemed to take forever and every time the train jerked I winced in pain. Soon after I arrived that day, I got emotional with my colleague Christina. I explained that I was totally out of my usual 'confident' comfort zone and I found myself in another place that I had no desire to be. I couldn't describe it. Christina was so lovely and made me feel so much better. Television could be a very pressurised environment at times, this being one of those times.

Over the next week I just got on with the job. Every day I dreaded the journey to and from work, knowing full well I would be in more pain during and after each journey but at least I wasn't moping around at home which made me feel a little bit better mentally, not physically. My friends had been amazing during that first week. My best friend from school, Heidi, was very worried especially as she was living in New York and couldn't come over to see me. She was also due to get married very soon and I was one of her bridesmaids so I assured her I'd be OK. Other friends of mine were very supportive too. My friend Sharma wouldn't stop texting me and my friend Peter called me every day. My brother Simon even offered to buy me a new car so I felt very comforted. I still had no luck with the insurance company; they were very inefficient.

On 26th October, 11 days after the accident, I was a bridesmaid at my best friend's wedding. Heidi had been my best friend since I was 10 years old so I wanted to do the best job possible. I still had to wear my neck brace with my bridesmaid outfit, which I joked about to no end, even though I was in absolute agony. I faked it for the whole weekend. I blatantly took way more medication than I should have just so I could smile properly in the wedding photographs. I did take the neck brace off for a few photographs but I put it straight back on during the reception. Some of the photographs looked very funny with my bridesmaid outfit, a neck brace and a big glass of champagne which I wasn't allowed to drink, it was just for show!

Heidi's dad Tom was so impressed that I had still gone through with my bridesmaid duties even though I had been in a traumatic car accident 11 days earlier. He must have told me this at least five times, probably more. Heidi's mum didn't stop hugging me the whole day, bless her. I had known Heidi all my life so I was as close to her family as I was to my own, her parents were like my second parents. Plus, my dad had died 10 years prior and my mum lived abroad. Heidi's parents always called me daughter no. 3 so I felt very emotional every time Tom mentioned how brave I was, he made me feel very special. I fought off tears a lot that day. Later on that evening, even though I knew I wasn't allowed to drink alcohol, I wanted to join in with the celebrations so I ended up having a couple of glasses of wine. It was then that I realised how much alcohol lessened my pain. I shouldn't have touched alcohol with the amount of medication I was taking but wow, what a difference, I almost felt normal for a couple of hours, it was amazing. My headache paid the price the following morning though, ouch.

The following week I started physiotherapy at my place of work. I was very lucky that we had in-house therapists. The physiotherapist taught me how to sit properly with my back arched against a chair. He lightly massaged my neck for a few minutes, which was very, very painful to touch (he could hardly apply any pressure) and he gave me two stretches to do. The session didn't last long but it was good to talk to someone who knew about these situations and the main thing was that I was doing something to help the pain.

A couple of days later something weird happened. I was in my flat and suddenly realised I didn't feel grateful any more about living. All my life I'd been the ultimate optimist, in fact my nickname was 'smiler' from the age of seven because I was always happy and smiling. I had always looked on the positive side of things especially when life was challenging even as a youngster. When I was 20 years old I'd lost my dad who I absolutely adored so my ability to remain positive regardless of the situation only got stronger. My motto had become 'life really is too short so make the most of it'.

My friend Jasmine called to check up on me.

"How are you?" she said.

"Do you know I'm actually not sure" I replied.

"Oh, what's happened?" she asked.

There was a short silence.

"Jas, you know I'm in a lot of pain but something's not right, I don't know what's wrong with me. This may sound silly but you know how I'm always a really positive person, well I feel really ungrateful and I don't understand why. I mean, I'm alive right? I've got my arms and my legs so why should I feel ungrateful? Even though I'm in a lot of pain, I didn't die so why don't I feel grateful that I'm alive?"

She started saying, "Well, do you..."

I cut her off. "... and another thing, I've been crying, like, a LOT and I don't know why, you know me, I never cry at anything, why do I feel so stressed and why am I bloody crying all the time?"

At this point my voice started to quiver and there was another silence.

Jasmine said, "Babe... maybe you're depressed?"

I was silent as this weird thought ticked over in my mind, Jasmine asked me if I was OK and I'd replied that I was fine and that maybe she was right although I didn't understand what depression was. I got off the phone and this thought stayed with me for the rest of the night. As I was mulling it over, I remembered how much my pain had eased when I was at Heidi's wedding after I'd had a couple of drinks so I wandered into the kitchen to find a bottle of wine and a very large glass.

3
The Depression

For those of you who have suffered with back pain you'll understand how much it can affect your emotional state. I had never experienced depression before my accident and I had always possessed an obstinate pride of always being happy, extremely positive and being in control so I had an extreme dislike of feeling unhappy and vulnerable. Hence, being in a position where I had to rely on friends, colleagues and family, made me feel helpless and weak... I detested it.

Within about six weeks' after the accident life couldn't be worse. I had acquired more physical issues. I had developed severe stomach cramps and shooting/stabbing pains in my vagina and anus area (it was like someone stabbing a knife up your bottom – well, up both holes). The stomach cramps would last for a few minutes and I had them about 30 times a day. I had also developed a stabbing pain in my right lower back and glutes (bum muscles) which seemed to coincide together with all the stabbing pains. My headache was still constant and it continued to worsen: sometimes it would turn into a migraine, other times it was a dull pain but it was there 24 hours a day. My whole spine was still incredibly painful particularly my lower back even though I was still on three lots of prescribed medication. My left knee still hurt and my right knee and feet had started hurting a lot. The strong ache in my shoulders had developed into pain and I had tingling in my hands, fingers and feet at random times. If I stood for too long I would limp when I walked. I was also suffering with nightmares from the accident. The caring doctor that I had seen the day after the accident had left the surgery so I saw a new lady who was equally as efficient and helpful. She thought that my stomach cramps were caused by an ovary problem so she referred me for a variety of tests at various hospitals. Due to the nature of my headaches my doctor changed my contraceptive pill and also referred me to a neurologist to be assessed.

I had seen an orthopaedic surgeon the previous day with regard to my insurance claim. He had barely touched me during his examination and when I received the report it was totally incorrect, all of my back pain complaints were missing. The orthopaedic surgeon completely left out that I had severe back pain as well as neck pain. After a few days of complaining to my solicitor I reluctantly signed the report and sent it off. I just didn't have the energy to put up more of a fight – I was too exhausted.

My smile gradually disappeared and I realised that deep down that I was putting on a front to everyone around me... I had become a different person in a very short space of time and I had begun to really dislike my life, a lot. Due to the pain I couldn't run or exercise in any way, in fact I couldn't partake in any physical activity. I couldn't DJ anymore and was absolutely gutted that I had to give up martial arts and any thoughts of competing. All my passions and hobbies were no longer and I had slipped into a kind of trance-like state where all I thought about was my past and how much I missed being pain free and 'normal'.

About eight weeks after the accident I started getting severe numbness in my legs when I sat down for long periods of time. My neck and back pain were still so bad that it didn't matter whether I was sitting, standing or even lying down, the pain was there regardless, it was exhausting. I still didn't understand: why was I so tired all the time? I was an extremely fit and healthy person so it didn't make sense. Another thing I didn't understand was that I had put on almost half a stone (3 kg) of weight too so most of my clothes were super tight; I couldn't fit into some of them. I assumed this was due to a lack of exercise. As a result, I had been crying myself to sleep every night with the assistance of alcohol. I had developed a very bad habit of drinking every evening to lessen my pain, both physical and emotional, plus I still couldn't drive so, in my eyes, it didn't really matter.

Just over 10 weeks after the accident I was finally allowed to take my neck brace off. I should have been really happy because it meant I was allowed to drive again but I couldn't find the energy to get excited. My motivation for life had significantly deteriorated and I found myself becoming a recluse outside of my work place, not wanting to socialise, not just because of the pain but also down to a sheer lack of desire with a big dose of anxiety. By this stage I realised I was extremely unhappy and sought help at work. I was very grateful that they had an in-house counsellor so I arranged a consultation.

As they say, it really is 'good to talk' and if I'm honest, seeing someone completely neutral in my life did help me to see the bigger picture, which was somewhat satisfying. The psychologist helped me see that I had generally set myself such high standards in life that now I couldn't physically uphold those expectations and so my emotional state couldn't deal with it. She also made me realise that the majority of my life limitations, physical pain and emotional distress was out of my control and when things are out of your control in life, you get frustrated; she was right about that. The counsellor asked if I'd talked to any of my friends and I said, "Absolutely not, I don't want to burden anyone with my problems." I said I had always been everyone else's agony aunt and I'd never suffered pain before or experienced any type of life change like this. The psychologist told me that this was normal for someone who was depressed. Although this made logical sense and our sessions lifted my mood a bit for that day, I was still a recluse outside of work and the pain was worse than ever.

In early December I visited my sister and decided, as I was allowed to drive again, I should get back in a car. I was insured on her car so I took it for a short drive around the corner. Within minutes my back pain increased every time I put my foot down on the clutch and changed gear. I headed straight back to my sister's house and decided I wasn't ready to drive just yet as it was too painful and I didn't want to make myself worse.

Christmas week arrived and Sam was working up north and visiting his family and friends. I had to travel to see my family via London Transport, it was usually a 35-minute drive but by bus and train it was a 90-minute journey from hell and to make matters worse, it was absolutely freezing. I soon realised that the cold affected me really badly and keeping warm was an absolute necessity; the more I shivered the worse the pain got especially my neck and lower back. It was the worst Christmas I'd ever encountered and I dowsed myself with too much medication and too much alcohol to feel better every night. My body was so de-hydrated from the alcohol that it was making my pain worse.

On my journey home I got to the train station and I had the worst thought ever... What if I didn't have these constant headaches? What if my back didn't hurt anymore? What if my nightmares disappeared? What if my neck didn't hurt anymore? What if my stomach cramps and shooting pains were no longer? What if I could make it all go away...? I suddenly realised that I was standing on the edge of the train platform and tears were rolling down my eyes. Was I just thinking about...? No, I couldn't have been, I'm an optimist... or was I? I wiped my tears away and put those silly thoughts miles away from my mind and started thinking about Sam coming home.

When I got home I told myself that I'm a happy person... yeah right. Of course then I told myself to buck up, life is the way it is, I've got my arms and my legs so I should count myself lucky to be alive. Although I was clearly unhappy, I told myself I needed to deal with it and that's that so I decided to have some more wine and completely disregard those silly thoughts I'd had earlier. Two major aspects of depression are denial and bargaining. I was experiencing both of those at the same time.

After Christmas came New Year's Eve, again, one of the worst I'd ever encountered. I spent it alone it my flat, in pain, depressed and having those silly thoughts again. Thankfully I drank far too much and completely conked out. I woke up on New Year's Day to the phone ringing; it was Sam calling me to wish me a Happy New Year. I feigned happiness and again went into the usual trance-like state thinking about the past. Later that night, once again, I overdid the medication and the alcohol dreaming about competing in martial arts, running along the River Thames and DJ'ing in front of a huge crowd... eventually I fell asleep Thankfully Sam was back the following day so I was back on the straight and narrow, or at least I thought I was.

During those first couple of weeks of the New Year I struggled with those silly thoughts again, it was like they were provoking me. I would be on my way to or from work, at the train platform, subconsciously crying and the thoughts would appear from nowhere but I forced myself to push them to the back of my mind and kept telling myself "I'm a strong woman".

It didn't work. Every day I tried and tried to pick myself up but the pain was so severe and exhausting and the physiotherapy didn't seem to be helping. In fact, I had used up all my physiotherapy sessions at work; they only allowed a few sessions so I was referred to physiotherapy at my local hospital. These sessions were even shorter than the ones at work. They didn't touch me either, they only gave me some exercises but they didn't help at all. I was also blatantly avoiding socialising. Other than the obvious fact that it was just too painful to sit or stand, I just couldn't face more pretence that I was happy when I clearly wasn't. I remember meeting my girlfriends who had asked me to come out one night and as soon as I walked in my friend Marcia quickly walked around the whole bar to find me a chair. They were all very sweet and supportive but I didn't have the heart to tell them how bad I was feeling, I didn't want to burden them, it was easier just to keep it to myself and suffer in silence.

There was one part of the counselling sessions that did seem to offer some understanding. When the psychologist asked if I talked about my emotions with anyone, I explained that I deliberately didn't talk about my feelings with friends and family, as I didn't want to feel like a burden on anyone. The feeling of being a burden to one's friends and family is one of the biggest problems with depression but I didn't know this back then. I further explained to my counsellor that this whole situation was my problem, nobody else's and so I had to deal with it alone. Why should I bring someone else down with me? The psychologist basically told me that it was good to talk and that I may feel more motivated after talking to friends and family. She explained that having a network of people who loved me was very important for me to move forward and would help me through this tough time especially through any 'unstable' periods. I nodded my head in acknowledgement and went away having no intention of talking about my pain or silly thoughts to any of my friends or family. They've known me all my life to be an extremely confident, outgoing optimist with a huge zest for life, if I told them the truth, they'd think I was stark raving mad... I thought I was a tad mad at that stage anyway and that was enough.

By late January I was struggling with my job. The long hours were taking their toll on my injuries especially my spine and I was taking medication like they were sweets. I hadn't realised that I was in total denial. I was trying to work through the immense pain by overdoing my medication; that was my way of attempting to gain control over my life.

Eventually my HR manager suggested I move into an assistant's role rather than working as a full time programme maker, as the hours and physical constraint would be better for me and it would still be in TV production. I was so aware of trying not to let my injuries affect my work, I could only see this as a demotion. My depressed state wouldn't let me see this as anything else so I saw this as a failure, which made my depression ten times worse. After work and at weekends I was dwelling far too much on the past and still drinking myself to sleep; I was stuck in a vicious circle.

In February, I finally received the insurance money for my car. I could drive my own car again! Alas, I wasn't excited at all; in fact, I was living life like a robot on autopilot. However, I did manage to get a good deal on another BMW, it was a much older car but as I had learned, driving a manual car was too painful so I settled for an automatic.

At work, I finally moved jobs to an assistant role in a new department and I found my new boss, Dave, to be very helpful, empathetic and funny. This department was very concerned about my physical state and all the members of staff were extremely friendly. Gradually I started to feel a bit more content, my work colleagues made me feel very 'at home' and they were genuinely very compassionate towards my pain on a regular basis, especially Geri and Fiona. I started to enjoy my job – well, it's not that I totally enjoyed it, but it was a whole lot better than the previous few months had been and the journey to and from work was easier as I was driving to work again.

Although I was still clearly depressed, I had given up on the counsellor. I guess at that time I hadn't realised just how depressed I actually was; I was in a state of complete denial. I told her I was happy again. Of course it was a complete lie and I'm not sure if she bought it but she signed me off anyway and that was that. I actually thought I was wasting her time as I had sunk into such a deep, dark and nasty hole that I honestly didn't know if and when I could bring myself back up again and I'd got to the point that I didn't care anymore. I faked smiles and nodded my head as and when it was deemed necessary, "Of course I'm fine, it's just a bit of back pain," I would tell everyone.

The psychologist's words had stuck in my mind about sharing my emotions and I had thought about talking to someone but had never come close. Then one day an opportune moment arose when my friend Monique asked me to tell her the truth about how I was feeling and it was OK to be open about it. It was the first time I had told anyone about how I had truly felt over the last six months. I explained that although I had pain all over my body, the pain in my back was the worst; it was debilitating and depressing. I also told her that I didn't think I could be more frustrated with my life in general. I told her how frustrated I was about having so many limitations and having to give up every hobby. I expressed my annoyance at other colleagues, outside of my department, who had obvious doubts about the severity of my pain. Many people find it hard to empathise with someone who has 'invisible' pain. I told Monique I found this infuriating especially as I was in such a bad way and I was still having the stomach cramps, headaches, stabbing pains, tingling in my hands and feet, numbness in my legs and pain and aches in my shoulders, knees and feet.

I was a bit nervous but Monique was extremely understanding and empathetic and she explained that she'd known other friends who had gone through depression and although they were different circumstances they had all felt better talking about it. Well, what can I say; Monique and the psychologist were both right! Talk about a weight off my shoulders, I couldn't believe how much relief I felt, to actually admit my feelings to someone. Monique was very caring and considerate towards my situation and I made her promise not to tell a soul. I may have opened up this time but that was enough for now.

I had started a very long but slow process of gradually pulling myself back out of the hole that I'd sunken into albeit with a few relapses. A flicker of hope ran through my mind just for a second but no matter how relieved I felt to finally talk about everything, I couldn't escape the physical pain as well the fact that my life was now completely boring and dull. My desire for life had disappeared altogether.

4

The Pain Rollercoaster

The next few months were a hard slog. I was still living in horrendous pain whilst taking a crazy amount of prescribed medication and extra painkillers just so that I could get through each day. Feeling psychologically and physically strong had become extremely difficult due to all of my symptoms so I was popping pills like they were sweeties to avoid feeling like a 'weakling' – not good. By that time my left knee was hurting a lot more when I walked and it was very painful when I sat down for long periods of time. My right knee and whole leg was hurting more too; it felt like concrete. I hadn't realised that I was leaning on my right leg all the time mostly because I had suffered a lot of atrophy (muscle wastage) on my left leg. I was shifting all my weight over to my right side. This is a very common scenario with back pain. My left calf was half the size of my right calf; it looked like a chicken leg. It's a typical scenario after having a serious trauma especially where your spine and hips are involved. Your body tends to lean to one side to help avoid more pain. The hospital physiotherapist had told me the reason for the pain in my glutes (bum muscles) which travelled down my leg, was most likely a sciatic nerve issue, I had it in both glutes but it was worse on the right leg. My legs were still going numb pretty much daily although it seemed a bit better since I had started cycling in the gym albeit for 15 minutes at a time. However, I had developed more numbness in my feet, it was worse when I sat for long periods and also came on towards the last five minutes of cycling which I didn't understand. I found out later it was because my sciatic nerve was trapped. My lower back pain was still by far the worst of all my symptoms and it was still atrocious.

I told the hospital physiotherapist about all of the other symptoms I was suffering and how bad my lower back pain was but they said my neck was more important. They said I needed to focus on my neck because the exercises would help heal everything and kind of filter down. I was extremely disciplined with doing my rehab exercises. I wanted to be normal again. The only annoying thing was that the physiotherapists kept changing every 2-3 months so within 10 months after the accident I had seen four physiotherapists at the same hospital. Each one gave me different exercises; the sessions were supposed to last for 30 minutes but I was usually out in 15 minutes. The exercises didn't help at all, if anything some of them made me worse but I trusted them as they knew best and I knew nothing so I kept at it.

I had started driving again which meant I had stopped drinking on weekdays, it was great to be mobile again although I was still very clearly depressed. Daily life had become a proper chore. Going to work in the car was way easier and less pain than using London Transport buses and trains but things like brushing my hair, tying my hair up in a ponytail, lifting a file out of a cabinet and carrying shopping bags, even light ones, really aggravated my back pain and turning over in bed was still torture. I was in too much agony to think about going back to martial arts, horse riding, running, weight lifting or DJ'ing but I had signed up at a local gym which was probably more for psychological reasons than anything else.

I couldn't do much. I tried to do some weight training but I'd lost too much strength, it was so frustrating. I had pain in so many movements and my ego got in the way so I gave up and just stuck to cycling, it was the one thing I could do without pain although my legs went numb during the last 5 minutes of a 15 minute cycle. Before my first visit to the gym I remember that one of my physiotherapists told me that I should use the recumbent bike, the one that leans backwards. He told me it was made for people with back pain. Well, I can assure you, that was the WORST thing I could have done. I tried it that weekend and after I got off the bike, my back pain went through the roof and it took 4-5 days to get back to the usual pain. So I stuck to the upright bike, really gently and only for 15 minutes plus a gentle stretch afterwards, though it was hard to get off the floor from a lying-down position. It was so boring but it was something and when you have nothing, something is great.

The following week the physiotherapist told me that I could get back on a horse because the movements would help my lower back. Wow, I was so excited, I couldn't wait to get back to horse riding! As soon as I got home I arranged a hacking session which is where you just walk, trot and canter on a horse in a beautiful surrounding. The place I used to visit was in a forest in Ruislip, it's a beautiful area full of woodland and fresh air. I turned up to my session bright eyed. Even though it was painful to get on the horse I felt amazing, it was the best thing ever! As we walked and trotted through the forest, the wind on my face made me feel so free and all of sudden I didn't care about the pain. However, half way through the ride, while we were trotting my back started to feel worse and by the end of the ride I was in a lot of distress, I got off the horse and into my car and I cried. It was horrid. What on earth was that physiotherapist thinking? I got home and ran a hot bath, I was in so much MORE pain, I was so, so gutted, I cried myself to sleep that night. When I woke up next day, I couldn't move, it was like the day after the car crash, I literally couldn't budge. I don't know how long it took me to get out of bed that day, thankfully it was a Sunday so I didn't have to go to work. By this time, I had cut down on drinking wine but I knew I'd need a few glasses that night.

Horse riding is the type of exercise that uses muscles in your whole body, so if you're weak and unstable it will make you worse. It was a terrible suggestion. I was in a worse state of pain for over a week. These are the kind of things you can only know if you have ever suffered back pain. I didn't have the energy to complain, I was too exhausted. It was well over 10 months since the accident and I was horribly bored with life, I was in constant pain everywhere, I couldn't sit, stand or lie down. I was still feigning happiness at work and with friends. I hardly socialised and I had no physical hobbies any more, which was how I used to get my kicks out of life. I wasn't living at all, I was plodding along living with pure distaste. Hate is a very strong word which I hardly ever use but I can honestly say I really hated life at that moment in time.

One thing had changed though: Sam and I had decided to go our separate ways. We both had our own stresses and it was too much for us to cope with so we decided to see out the end of the contract on our flat and part company. I decided to move back to West London to live with my sister Virginia and her husband Johnny. While I was still in North London I continued seeing my doctor to get my pain medication. My doctor was still investigating my headaches and migraines, stomach cramps, pelvic stabbing pains and foot/leg numbness. The tests came back all clear for ovary issues so she started looking into gastrointestinal (stomach) issues. My doctor was trying very hard to help me but she had absolutely no idea why I had the stomach cramps or the pelvic stabbing pains. I told her that I was moving back to West London so she said all my medical notes would be sent to my new doctor once I had found one. I found out six years later that the pelvic stabbing pain in my lower abdominal, vagina and anus area was a trapped nerve and the stomach cramps were due to extremely low stomach acid. More on that in chapter 13.

With two weeks to go before I moved back to West London, work had calmed down. It was August and most people were on summer holidays so I thought it would be a fairly easy transition with the house move. I attended the hospital for my last physiotherapy session. On that particular day, I had to get the train to work due to the later time of the appointment; the hospital was very close to the train station. Obviously I needed to continue my therapy so I wanted to ask if I could get referred to Ealing Hospital in West London, which was the local one near to my sister's house.

About 10 minutes into the session I asked about being referred. The physiotherapist walked over to her notes to read something. When she came back she asked me to perform a neck exercise one more time to finish up.

She then said, "Well, we're about done here, I can't refer you I'm afraid, that's all we can do for you, you've used up all of your sessions." I said, "I don't understand, you're telling me I can't get therapy any more even in West London?" She replied, "Yes that's right, you've had a lot of sessions in the last nine months so that's it now."

I was so confused. I could feel my heart beating faster and I started feeling extremely anxious and nauseous. I didn't understand, this was our health system, they provided therapy, why was I now being turned away when I was clearly in such a bad way?

So I said, "But I'm in so much pain, what will I do?" She replied, "Don't worry, time will heal you."

WTF?? WHAT??? "TIME WILL HEAL YOU?" I'm not sure I even said thanks when I got my bag and walked out in a haze, my mind was racing. All I could hear was her words over and over, "time will heal you", "time will heal you". Seriously? "Oh my goodness, what was I going to do?" I thought, "will time really heal me or is this my life now?" I was in just as much pain as I was the day after the accident and that was over 10 months ago AND I had developed a load more symptoms, would time heal all of those too? So many questions, my head hurt... more than normal.

As I walked to the train station I could feel my heartbeat in my head again, it was loud and strong. I was almost shouting thoughts in my head so fast that I started feeling lightheaded. I could feel myself welling up with tears out of pure anger and frustration. I was so emotional that I was bouncing between anger and fear at the same time. I thought, "How could they turn me away when I was in SO much pain? How dare they. What would I do now, how would I cope? Where would I get therapy now? Maybe I could talk to my new doctor but I have no doctor yet, I didn't know what therapy I would need or where to get it, I would need to find a new therapist." I couldn't stop ruminating.

I was on a rollercoaster, questioning everything. I was angry, frustrated and scared that this was it, this was my new life now. A life of pain, misery and boredom. I realised that I was standing on the platform of the train station and tears were streaming down my face. Those nasty thoughts came back. How easy would it be to just stop right now and step off the platform? No more pain, no more suffering, no more anxiety, no more fear... just peace, calm and serenity. I had reached breaking point.

Before I knew it the train had arrived at the platform and I was practically pushed onto it. A lady asked me if I was alright, she could see my tears. I told her I was OK and wiped my eyes. I had gone into a trance state again except this was worryingly deep, deeper than the norm. The rest of the day was a total haze, so many thoughts were swimming around my head of what life would be like now, no more physical exercise ever again, no more DJ'ing, no more horse riding, no more martial arts, I would never socialise properly again with my friends. I would become a recluse, a total hermit and live alone. When I got home I felt completely exhausted, I honestly didn't know if I could take any more. I was sinking, fast.

I'm not sure how I kept going over the next few weeks. I knew for sure I was still living in a daze but the pain kept me aware of life around me. I told my friends that I was moving back to West London.

They were still very concerned about me but really happy that I was going to be close by, I didn't share their motivation. I felt nothing, well, apart from the pain. I moved into to my sister's house. I was on autopilot and I transferred my gym membership from North London back to West London.

Within two weeks I had formed a routine at the gym, I attended twice on the weekend and once in the week. All I could do was sit on an upright bike and cycle gently. I'd lost every ounce of muscle in my arms and legs. I'd always had very muscular legs from a young age, from years of competitive gymnastics so my nickname was 'footballer's legs' at school when I was a teenager. Now I had pins for legs, they had no shape whatsoever, they were straight with absolutely no muscle. They were almost concave and not very lean. I had also put on more weight, I guess from lack of exercise and stress and I had developed a round tummy, my six-pack stomach was not even a one pack, I looked like a female version of Father Christmas. My huge love and passion for exercise had been crushed, it was torture watching gym members pushing weights, working so hard sweating and boasting about their great workouts. Gym instructors went around praising members on how hard they were working. Others would laugh and joke, everyone seemed so happy. After my bike session I would stretch and then go upstairs and cry in the shower, for ages. I would cry until I had no tears left. Then I would leave like nothing was wrong and go about my business, it wasn't the greatest routine but I was exercising a bit and keeping myself busy albeit feeling like crap at the end of it, it was a vicious circle.

A week later, a gym instructor called Rob came up to me and started asking questions about what my gym goals were. I honestly didn't want to talk to anyone but I was on a bike so I didn't really have a choice. Rob said he'd noticed I was in every Saturday and Sunday and all I would do was sit on the bike, do a stretch and then leave. I told him briefly that I'd been in a car accident and I was still in a lot of pain but I didn't go into detail. He mentioned he had a good friend called Neil who was a physiotherapist and so he offered his details. I politely declined and said I was fine.

Every time Rob saw me from then on he came over to talk to me. I was still very depressed and zoned out a few times while he was talking but he was so persistent. At times I felt quite annoyed but I didn't have the heart to tell him that I didn't want to talk to anyone and I'd prefer it if he'd left me alone. The third time he mentioned his physiotherapist friend I decided to take his details. Even though I didn't have the best impression of physiotherapists, I thought, what have I got to lose? Rob absolutely raved about him.

I went to see Neil and he spent a long time going over my case history. I had to explain everything from the medication I was taking to what my current symptoms were. He was very surprised that I'd never had an X-ray or MRI on my whole spine, especially my lower back. Neil then asked me to stand and he did a lot tests to observe my range of movement and strength. While I was standing he asked me if I had always leant to the right. I told him I didn't know what he was talking about so he asked me to stand and face the mirror. To my horror I was leaning to the right so badly that my right shoulder was about six inches lower than my left. How could I have not noticed this before? It was really bad. I told Neil I only looked in the mirror very briefly when I brushed my hair, which was still a huge effort because it hurt and I didn't own a full-length mirror. The mirror I used was only big enough to see my head and top of my neck. I looked very weird.

Neil continued testing me, twisting, turning and flexing my spine or trying to. It was all so painful and at the end he said he would massage me lightly to finish the session but he needed to be honest. Basically, he said my spine was in a very bad state and that my vertebrae (bones in my spine) were so excessively stiff in localised areas of my neck, mid and lower back that he thought it was likely I had suffered multiple fractures especially given the speed and nature of the car accident. He explained that even though I had an X-ray on the day of the accident, when you suffer trauma at such high speed your body undergoes a lot of inflammation so an X-ray won't always pick up hairline fractures until a few days after the event. He went on to say that it also depends who reads the X-rays, many of his patients had needed a second opinion to confirm their fractures. Either way he said as my spine had clearly suffered a LOT of damage, I was better off seeing a cranial osteopath. They specialised in spines when bones weren't moving properly. More on this in chapter 9.

Neil was extremely compassionate and very encouraging that I could be pain free one day. However, I felt quite disappointed that he couldn't help me as I was in a depressive bubble and all I could think about was being pain free and living a normal life. However, I discovered years later how important it is to refer a patient if you know they are better off seeing a therapist who has a speciality that you do not offer. It shows integrity, I have a lot of respect for therapists that know their limitations. Rob was right; Neil was awesome. It also made me realise that not all therapists are the same just because they have the same title, which is why I always suggest to go with a recommendation.

Thankfully my sister was already seeing a local cranial osteopath so I booked myself in with a lady called Amanda. Unfortunately, Amanda was very busy and couldn't fit me in for a couple of weeks so I panicked and immediately called Neil and practically begged him to see me one more time just to get some form of treatment – I was hooked. I had become completely disillusioned with physiotherapy at the hospital but I had found Neil to be so positive and reassuring. It gave me a good understanding that therapists differ and from that moment onwards, I would only stick to recommendations. It was only a few days after I'd seen Neil that I realized how comforted and secure I had felt for the first time in months. I saw Neil for a second time and it felt good just to be there, I was trying to help myself and he was very encouraging which made me feel like I was finally making progress, for the first time in over a year.

I finally saw Amanda and once again, the first session was entirely taken up by my very long case history. She was very kind and delayed her next patient just so she could give me at least five minutes of treatment, predominantly on my neck. She said, typically with my accident and symptoms she thought I would need six sessions but it was difficult to gauge until she'd given me a full treatment.

On my second visit Amanda assessed and treated my whole spine, she was shocked. Every few minutes she would say angrily "Goodness me!" or "Honestly!" Eventually she told me that my spine was exceptionally stiff and extremely tender in specific areas. She went on to say that my spine was in a complete mess and in her opinion it felt like I had suffered multiple fractures in my neck, mid and lower back. I told her Neil had said exactly the same thing. When I told her I had complained of back pain from the day of the accident she was shocked that I hadn't been sent for an X-ray or MRI for my whole spine. In layman's terms she said that it felt like all my vertebrae (bones of the spine) were not talking to each other, like they were totally separate entities so I had multiple blockages, everything was completely out of balance. Not surprisingly she said I would likely need way more than 6 sessions.

"It's no wonder you're in pain, tremendous pain I would imagine," she said. Amanda was extremely passionate about her job. Neil said I was in a mess and now Amanda was saying the same thing except she was angry, saying that I shouldn't have been in that state almost 18 months after the accident, questioning what kind of therapy had I been receiving. WOW, a HUGE rush of satisfaction consumed my whole body. I felt like someone had just slapped me round the face, in a good way! I felt exhilarated that two therapists understood me and more so they understood my pain which felt very, very satisfying. My emotions had been all over the place since the accident and I had turned from a depressive recluse into a hopeless wreck but then suddenly I felt a glimmer of hope. I felt like I had gained a teeny bit of control back in my life; maybe there was a light at the end of the tunnel? That was the first time I felt a hint of optimism but little did I know things were about to get a whole lot worse before they got better.

5
The Brink

I have to admit I found cranial osteopathy a very weird treatment; I say that in a good way. It feels like your therapist isn't really doing much. However, it is an exceptionally powerful technique. A cranial osteopath is a regular osteopath who performs a more refined approach to working on structures of your head and skull as well as the rest of your body. It's a very subtle and gentle treatment where the therapist's hands palpate different parts of your spine extremely softly and they treat whatever areas they find dysfunctional. This includes emotional issues as well as muscular/joint dysfunction. I remember feeling very relaxed during my sessions with Amanda and often chatted a lot while I was on the treatment table although she did tell me to be quiet sometimes!

Although it seemed like Amanda wasn't doing much I felt different sensations during the session and less stiff afterwards. I often felt better a few days later. At first, I had to see Amanda once a week; consistency is key with treatments. This is the same with most therapies. I wasn't doing any rehab exercises at that time because I hadn't felt any better by doing the exercises I was given by the hospital physiotherapists. However, I was cycling, which was something, and I had started using weights again, only very small light ones. There were a lot of exercises I still couldn't do but I did what I could and I was feeling a bit better about life although I was still far, far away from the happy, outgoing person that I used to be.

During every session with Amanda I would moan about not being able to run or do weight training and I whinged obsessively about having to give up martial arts and DJ'ing. That said, a friend of mine had offered to give me back my old residency space at the Spot Bar (now Jewel Bar) in Covent Garden which I later decided to start up again. Amanda had once been in the fitness industry so she understood why exercise was a huge passion of mine. We also both shared a passion for horses. I loved hearing her stories of riding horses. It was good to hear her stories for once, especially as she was very good listening to me bang on and on about how much I missed all my physical hobbies. I had built up a lot of trust in Amanda; it was an important part of my healing process.

Our sessions were mostly cranial osteopathy but occasionally Amanda would need to manipulate an area (known as adjustments or clicking bones) or massage another area. During one treatment she palpated my liver and released the sack of my liver which was stuck. Amanda explained that when you have a fall or accident where a large amount of force is involved, the sack (covering) around your liver can get stuck and may need releasing. Another time she palpated my stomach and suggested I do a detox as I appeared to be very constipated. I told her I had been constipated for over 18 months and as a result I had stopped eating bread, pasta and rice. I ate meat and vegetable soup a lot. Amanda told me this was a typical side effect of the NSAIDs (non-steroidal anti-inflammatory drugs) that I was taking. She said it was totally normal but nobody ever mentions how strong the medication is and how much it affects your bowels. I told her I couldn't come off them as I was still in far too much pain even though my stiffness had eased a bit since I'd been seeing her. Sometimes I only felt about a few percent better after our sessions but even 3 percent was progress, and progress meant everything.

I was lucky enough to move into my own place within a few months of being back in West London. It was great to have my own space but I missed being pampered by my sister, I had enjoyed my clothes being washed and having meals cooked for me – she was a good sister! I had signed up at a new doctor's surgery after I moved back so I could continue receiving all the pain medication. My new doctor was more than happy to continue giving me the NSAIDs and other prescribed painkillers on a regular basis. I thought it was weird that he never examined me, ever; I guess he trusted the notes. However, he did refer me to a gastrointestinal clinic for my stomach cramps, constipation and sharp pains in my anus and vagina areas.

A few weeks later I attended the gastrointestinal clinic. They were very helpful and arranged a lot of tests for me, the first one being an upper endoscopy which is where they insert an endoscope camera through your throat all the way through to your stomach. It was a horrible experience. While I waited for the results I was told the next test would be a lower endoscopy (where they insert a camera through your anus) but I would need to wait 4-5 months for an appointment as they were very busy.

After a few months Amanda told me that I no longer needed to see her every week and that I could cut our sessions to once every three weeks. Initially I panicked and insisted I still see her every week but she told me my spine was healing so it wasn't necessary to see her weekly any more. When you are receiving any form of treatment and you're making progress after being in such a horrid place, it's easy to become reliant on your therapist. So when they mention they don't need to see you as often, the first thing you do is panic because the thought of going back down that dark hole suddenly puts you on edge – it's inconceivable. This has happened with some of my own patients. I know how they feel instantly and explain that it's a good thing when treatment can be spread out; it's normal to have a fear of going backwards.

So I accepted it and gradually started getting into a routine. I was still in a crazy amount of pain but I had more movement and the numbness and stabbing pains had eased a little bit although I still suffered with them daily. I had to admit, even though I still had high levels of pain, I had started doing low impact aerobics classes at the gym and they seemed to make my headache better. They were a way of exercising with a group of people to music and the aerobics instructors, especially Dave Hoy, were really encouraging even though I had a sour face most of the time but I was content with doing some form of exercise. Work was good, I was enjoying it even though my back was in complete agony by the end of each day, and I was still taking painkillers like sweets. I was in preparation at work for a very well-known show which was full of a variety of events and competitions. Preparing for a live programme where we'd be filming a number of pre-recorded mini films as well as live TV was a big task and involved a lot of staff. The daily office hours increased and I had to work some weekends before I departed for the location, two hours away from London; I was in more pain than ever.

By now I was using a hot water bottle and a wheat-filled hot pack (I'd never heard of it, but thankfully my friend Chris bought it for me from his football physiotherapist) every day, it helped a lot. A hot pack is like a small scarf filled with scented wheat grains and herbs and is heated in a microwave; it stays hot for 15-20 minutes. Heat induces vasodilation of the blood vessels which means they expand so blood can flow more freely, which eases pain and stiffness in muscles. I took my hot pack with me on location so I could ease my back pain before going to bed; it also helped me to fall asleep. By the start of the seven-day location, I was already in a worse state so I thought I would increase the NSAIDs and painkillers to get me through the week.

After a week of being on location, working extremely long hours, my back pain was unbearable. Everything hurt. When I finally got home on a Monday afternoon I flaked out in bed. My boss reminded me that I didn't need to come into work the next day so I decided to have a lie in and then unpack my suitcase and do a load of washing. The only problem was that when I woke up I couldn't move. I felt like I'd been beaten up. The pain was excruciating, in fact my neck and back hurt more than normal. It took me quite a while to get out of bed and when I did I was bent over in pain. After what seemed like an hour, I finally stood up but I couldn't stand up straight. I took a step forward to go to the toilet and screamed "Argggghhhhhh", I stumbled and almost fell over. I grabbed the window ledge next to my bed. OMG the pain, I was panting and wincing. I didn't understand what was going on so I took another step. "Argggghhhhhh", I screamed again. There was SO MUCH PAIN. I couldn't walk. I was stuck two steps away from my bed and about 8 steps away from my bathroom. I really needed to use the toilet so I took another step fully expecting pain this time and boy did I get it – it was dreadful. I was confused. I had limped a lot after the accident but that was over 18 months ago; I didn't understand what was going on. I became very stressed and fearful; my heart was racing. I had to focus on the moment at hand. It seemed that if I took really tiny little steps, kind of dragging my feet a few inches whilst holding on to the wall I could move forward but really slowly. Each step was agony. Every time I put weight on each leg I got a nasty sharp, stabbing pain in my lower back and whole of my hip. If I stood still the pain wasn't as excruciating. I remember thinking: this must be what it's like to be electrocuted. It must have taken 20 minutes to finally get to the bathroom so by the time I had reached the toilet I was totally exhausted and in floods of tears. It hurt to sit down on the toilet, I felt like all my muscles had totally seized up

I realised many years later that I had suffered so much atrophy (muscle wastage) in so many muscles especially the whole of my left leg and around both hips, glutes and lower back that my lower body had become severely weak. By working ridiculously long hours for seven days on the go, and two weeks beforehand, I had used up whatever strength I had so I literally had nothing left; my body had completely shut down. Think of it like running two marathons every day for 14 days, having never run a day in your life or performed any type of training whatsoever. I explain this in more detail later in the book.

The rest of the day was just horrific. It took absolutely ages to get down the stairs because I had to keep stopping. The pain was nasty; on a scale of 0-10 where 10 is the worst, it was like a 30 out of 10, it was insane. When I finally got down the stairs I put the hot pack on and took another five minutes to get to the living room and eventually slumped onto the couch. I didn't really move much unless it was to heat up the hot pack in the microwave again which was a HUGE effort. I literally poured medication down my throat to help with the pain and then called my boss Dave to tell him I would have to take the next day off as I literally couldn't walk. Later on that Tuesday Dave came over to my house with some flowers, I was lucky that he lived close by. He is undoubtedly one of the most considerate men I have ever met and I was so grateful at that time that he was my boss! It took a while for me to open the door to let him in and then he had to help me to sit back down again. I remember his exact words, "Oh no chuck, you've got yourself in a bit of a pickle!" Typical Dave, he would always make light of a really horrid situation! We're still very close friends to this day.

Thankfully Dave told me not to worry, I had plenty of days in lieu from all of the Saturdays I had worked. That was fortunate because as it turned out I couldn't walk for three more days. I finally hobbled into work on the Friday, still taking three times the normal dose of NSAIDs and painkillers. I was so thankful it was a Friday, it was an easy day and I finished work early.

Only a few weeks later I was thrown into preparing for another large outside broadcast, which was the biggest one for the department in many years. I enjoyed working with the production team, my friends Geri and Fiona were very caring and regularly asked me if I was OK. My symptoms had worsened and due to the consistently longer working hours, I was now taking four times the normal dose of NSAIDs and painkillers on some days to help me get through the day. I had also developed more symptoms. The numbness had become so bad that both legs would go numb after sitting for only 20 minutes; I had to keep on getting up and walking around. This was definitely a result of working such long hours. The daily sharp pains around my anus and vagina had increased too. I had also developed a loud click in my mid back when I walked. I had noticed it on and off a year before but it had gradually increased and was now permanent. My jaw still hurt too.

My lower back had always been painful when I was sitting especially for long periods but now my bum, or what I thought was my bum muscles, were hurting too. It hurt a lot just to sit down. It felt like I was sitting on concrete with no cushion. I later learned that it was my hamstrings (muscles at the back of the upper leg) that were hurting. In fact, my quadriceps (muscles at the front of the thigh), hamstrings and lower back muscles were all overworking, even my calf muscles (back of your shins) ached a lot too as did my feet. This is called overcompensation – mine was immense.

By the time the live broadcast approached, my back pain was incredibly bad but I was enjoying the pressure of prepping for a huge live broadcast. We were on location for nine days, working very long hours and it was a lot of stress. I had started enjoying this type of stress, I guess because it was a major distraction from my pain and I felt involved. It made me feel quite special to be part of a team. Everyone was tense due to the nature of the broadcast – we had to get it right. There were over 150 staff members involved and the pressure was on. By the time the programme was over we were all relieved that it went very well and everyone was happy. I got home the next day and flaked out. The following day I woke up and realised how many hours I had worked over those nine days, we were at it night and day.

I couldn't move; I had overdone it yet again. I couldn't walk but this time the pain was worse. I had to go through all the same processes, holding on to the wall, tiny steps to move forward, stopping every step trying to get down the stairs and using heat constantly while popping painkillers like they were my favourite sweets. My boss came round again, this time with chocolates. I'm not a lover of chocolate but I had a few to be polite, I was so grateful for his company. He asked me about my treatments and why I wasn't getting any better. I said I would have to talk to my therapist Amanda.

Basically, I had been overdoing it really badly. If you only have 20% strength and you work 14 hours a day for nine days your body will use up every single bit of that 20% and more so that you have to stop, rest and recuperate in order for your body to catch up. The problem is that when you are trying to heal, your body uses up more energy in order for you to recover, so that 20% is really like 5% – which makes the situation ten times worse. People always ask me why they feel so tired at the end of the day even if they haven't done anything physical; even just sitting is tiring. Pain isn't tiring – it's exhausting.

The consequence of overworking in this type of situation is huge overcompensation and muscular pain. By the time I saw Amanda (it had been a few weeks because of working such long hours), I was in a very bad way. Amanda wasn't happy at ALL. In fact she was quite angry with me. She told me working such long hours was detrimental to my recovery and that I had regressed really badly. I was so disappointed in myself. I had got carried away with trying to live like a normal person even though I was still in such agony, I felt really stupid. Essentially, I was in denial.

Amanda suggested that I had my hours cut down at work so I could get back on track with my progress. The problem with TV is that non-production departments were the only ones that would work an 8-hour day. If you worked in production you might work 8-10 hour days in the office but typically working on location or in a studio were minimum 12-hour days, sometimes more. I decided to take Amanda's advice and talked to my boss. I was instantly removed from production and sent to another department. I didn't realise I would be sent to a non-production department and I quickly became very disheartened. It was my own fault, I had overdone it and been extremely irresponsible working crazy long hours and taking too many painkillers and NSAIDs just so I could try and feel normal; what an idiot. I started feeling more depressed instantly and it felt like I was thrown back down the rabbit hole yet again. It made me realise how far I had come with my depression. I hated the job. I was so bored and the stress of disliking my work situation wasn't helping my recovery at all. Little did I realise I was right: stress affects everything, ESPECIALLY the healing process. I moaned and groaned to Amanda again and told her that I was more unhappy than ever so she made a suggestion, one that would change my life forever.

6

The Positivity Equation: Acceptance + Self-Worth = Progress

Amanda said that I had always moaned (in a nice way!) about not being able to exercise, whether it be martial arts, running or weight training and so she suggested that I consider moving into the health and fitness industry. She said that training someone else wouldn't be very physical and that I could work a set amount of hours but, most importantly, I would be working in the industry that I love which could make up for the fact that I couldn't do much physical activity. I might not be able to physically perform a lot of exercises but at least I would be working in a fitness environment and I would get to learn a lot about my body. Furthermore, she said it would help my recovery tremendously to be away from the stress of working such long hours in TV. I told her I would go away and think about it.

When you experience an overnight life change, you have to accept things may never be the same. Most of us don't like change especially when it's not our choice. When ALL your life loves and desires have been taken away from you through no fault of your own, frustration sets in because you are not in control anymore. However, sometimes in life when you've had things taken away from you but then you have a glimpse of taking that control back, the thought of change is enlightening. I enjoyed my job in TV but it had become extremely difficult to adhere to the crazy hours and the new non-production role was really boring; I couldn't win. Eventually I was allowed back into my normal department but I was told to avoid working on programmes for a while. I worked as an assistant to my boss so I could try and progress my recovery. I thought about what Amanda had said about becoming a personal trainer and I started looking into it.

Firstly, I spoke to my friend Rob at my gym and then I spoke to every personal trainer and fitness instructor there. The course I decided to pursue was a full time, intensive, three-month personal trainer qualification, five times longer than any other personal trainer qualification in the country which also meant it was very expensive – thank goodness for credit cards! The reason it was labelled as 'intensive' meant that they crammed about 25 weeks of information into 12 weeks. The reason it was so good was because it included subjects like circuit training, pre- and post-natal training, holistic and sports massage and even sports therapy, how to fix injuries. The great thing was that you could split the course up into sections and do each subject separately. I was very tempted as I felt I needed some sort of focus to help with my depression. I decided I could do it because I had worked so many weekends that I had three weeks in lieu plus my annual five-week holidays so I could get eight weeks of the course done that year. I signed up and arranged to learn my first subject, anatomy and physiology.

Before I started my course I went to visit my mother who lives in Goa. It was really hot over there and I was told the heat would help me, it did. Amanda had told me to avoid breast stroke if I went swimming but back stroke would be OK; she was right. I swam every day while I was there. I did feel more of an ache after swimming from a lack of exercise but it felt great to swim again. My mum insisted that I see her massage therapist because he was amazing and he used Ayurvedic oils, so I agreed.

The first time he came over I explained that I was in a lot pain on a daily basis, pretty much my whole body except my forearms. I told him I hadn't received any kind of massage, only a tiny bit on my neck once from my work physiotherapist but it was literally five minutes. He told me not to worry and that I really needed to clear toxins from my system, they had probably been around from the accident. That confused me but I laid down and he started massaging me. He started very light at first. Then he started going deeper into my muscles exerting more pressure; it was horrible. It felt like my whole back was bruised, I groaned so loudly. The more he massaged the more it hurt and I pleaded with him to stop but he kept telling my mum that I needed it so she tried to calm me down. By the end of the session I was in tears, it was so painful. After he finished he told my mum that I should have had that treatment straight after my accident and was surprised that I'd had treatment in the UK but no massage.

He said I would need a few more sessions. I felt really sore the next day but I did feel a bit looser. By the end of the 10 days, although I felt very sore and bruised, I did feel some relief although I was in more pain for at least a week. I later realised my reaction was my body responding to the treatment. After the extra pain from the massage had subsided I felt like I had more range of motion. He was right, I should have had hands-on treatment after the trauma I had suffered over two years' prior.

When I returned home, I became a bit excited at the thought of learning about the body. I hadn't been excited about anything for so long, and I didn't realise how much focus I had lost in life. All my physical hobbies were my life. They were how I got my kicks like other people enjoy baking or fishing. In psychology, when your life focus is taken away, it's easy for your brain to lose self-worth, self-esteem and self-confidence. I had completely lost everything, hence the severe depression.

It was quite comical on my first day of the anatomy and physiology course. I was the oldest person there. The course was full of 20-somethings! The other thing I found very funny was trying to learn: the last time I had used my brain to study was in the mid 80's at school and I was clearly extremely rusty. Although I found it very hard to study, I enjoyed learning the actual subjects. I passed the test two weeks later and signed up for the next course.

During my next course, which was the physical side of personal training, we had to do a cardiovascular threshold test where you test aerobic (a steady jog) and anaerobic (a sprint) thresholds on a treadmill. I spoke to my tutor and told him that I could no longer run because of all my injuries. I had to sit that out as well as some other physical tests involving impact. It made me feel very frustrated and quite sad and I could feel my depression worsening. By the end of the day I had become very inert and didn't want to talk to anyone. The following day we were back in the gym doing weight training exercises and core work. The tutor went through a lot of core work and we all had to perform the exercises, one of which was the plank. This is where you lie on your tummy, rest your elbows (under your shoulders) on the floor, tuck your toes under your feet and lift your hips off the floor until your body is straight so the only thing touching the floor are your forearms and toes. More on these types of exercises later in the book.

The easy version of the plank is when you leave your knees on the floor and only lift your hips up. I thought great, at least there is one thing I can do really well today, I could hold the plank for ages. We started with the easy version on the knees and to my horror I couldn't even hold it for 5 seconds. WHAT? I really didn't understand; I had been doing these exercises for years in martial arts. I used to be able to hold the harder version of the plank for well over 4 minutes. I couldn't believe it so I tried again. It was even harder, 3 seconds felt like 5 minutes. I was horrified and confused. "How could I have lost that much strength?", thought. What a horrible time I was having with all the physical exercises, I thought "I couldn't run, I couldn't hold a half plank for more than 5 seconds, what was next?" I later learned this was typical of someone with back pain. The tutor saw how disheartened I was and came up to me at the end of the day and suggested I go and see the in-house physiotherapist, Mike, who taught the sports therapy course.

Mike seemed quite a cool guy. He asked me a lot of questions and got me on the treatment table and did a variety of tests for strength and range of motion. He mentioned that my range of motion was pretty poor considering my accident was two years ago. He didn't have much time so he did a very short treatment on my spine by moving each vertebra left and right and did a quick massage. Although it only lasted about 10 minutes, it was very painful but I kept my mouth shut because everyone had raved about him so I had a fair amount of trust in him. The following day my back pain was horrendous. I was in so much agony, "what had Mike done to me?", I thought. It was a Saturday and I wasn't due back on the course until the Monday so I had to suffer until then.

I finally caught up with Mike on the Wednesday of the following week. We sat in reception and I told him how much pain I had been in and that it had lasted for a few days. He said I shouldn't have been in that much pain that long after my accident and after such a short treatment; even he was confused. Mike asked me why hadn't I mentioned I was in pain while he was treating me and I told him I thought it was best to stay quiet. He explained that feedback is most important when you're treating someone as you never want to cause them or their tissues more stress. We had a long conversation and he then asked me if he could do a longer assessment. Of course I said yes so he arranged to fit me one day after the course.

This time Mike went through everything in fine detail and he asked me to be honest and if anything was tender that I must tell him. He explained again how important feedback is when it comes to treating injuries. After the assessment he told me it seemed like I had suffered multiple fractures in my mid back and neck and it was possible I had fractured my lower back too. He was horrified that I hadn't been sent for an X-ray for my whole spine. I told him he was the third therapist who had said exactly the same thing. He then became extremely concerned and actually apologised for putting me through more pain; he hadn't realised the extent of my spinal injuries because it wasn't normal after this length of time. I told him not to be silly, how could he know? He was very comforting, Mike was a very intelligent and caring physiotherapist and undoubtedly the best one I had come across to date. He had previously worked in professional football and had an extremely varied CV to be proud of. He told me to come back the following week for some more treatment. I felt very grateful.

I did just that. Mike was very concerned about the click I had in my mid back when I walked. When I had seen the physiotherapist at my workplace, he had taught me how to sit in a chair in a very upright position but too upright. I hadn't realised at the time that I was hyperextending (over-arching) my spine when I was sitting down which basically meant I was arching my back too much. Mike explained that two of the bones in my spine had almost become fused together as a result so I hardly had any blood flow in between those muscles in my back. Oh my goodness, I was horrified to think that a therapist had taught me to sit incorrectly which had given me even more issues. We spoke about the diversity with various types of therapists – it's just one of those things to be aware of. Mike told me we had caught it in time, if I had left it another year or two, I may have needed surgery to correct it. He told me I was going to fix it myself. I was confused. He got me into a position pretty much hugging myself and leaning forwards, then he told me to take a big breath and BANG he forced me into a position where my back clicked on its own. It was VERY loud. I immediately felt loose around the area where I had the click. We were both pleased!

That day I felt great, I was walking around feeling more loose, not pain free but I had more movement and the pain seemed to have eased off around that particular area of my spine. I was feeling better, wow what a great feeling! Then came the downside. Mike had mentioned that I might be a bit sore for a while. He was right. The next day I was in agony; it lasted for a week. I didn't manage to catch up with him until after the pain had subsided. He told me it was typical of a chronic issue and that if your muscle tissues have been stuck for that long, eventually they stop getting oxygen and fresh nutrients so when you loosen them, in turn they release toxins and then your brain has to re-adapt its connection to those muscles. He told me it was a reaction to the treatment, the consequence of which can be discomfort or pain for a few days but when it goes away you should feel better. The longer you've had the issue the longer the response, initially. It made sense. Part of that reaction is the brain has to re-adapt its relationship to each muscle, that's called proprioception and the process can usually take 24 hours but in some cases it can take up to four or five days. Either way, once the pain had subsided I felt better, not as good as the day he released me but I understood what Mike had said. He also mentioned that if I had received more hands-on treatment right after the accident I wouldn't have been anywhere near as bad as I was at that particular time. He told me that hands-on treatment is imperative in the first year of injury as well as rehab exercises to restore normal function back into your muscles and joints. I didn't know it at the time but he was so right. That said, you can still help restore function in muscles that have had long-term issues – it just takes longer.

I continued with my studies. I had more movement in my spine but the pain was the same, I still suffered numbness in my feet and legs but more so when I used a cross trainer. I still had pain in both knees, shoulders and feet as well as the stomach cramps and sharp electric pains. I still couldn't do a lot of exercises with weights but I had some kind of focus now with my courses; it was the only thing I got slightly excited about. I got through the courses one by one and eventually I passed everything but I still had the massage and sports therapy course to do. I had run out of time off work, so I would have to wait until the following year for those courses.

By October 2003 I had various qualifications under my belt including being a gym instructor which is a basic certificate to work on a gym floor. I was speaking to my friend Dave who worked at my local gym and he mentioned they needed a new gym instructor and personal trainer for the weekends and asked me if I was interested. I was speechless – I hadn't even thought about that.

He said I had all the qualifications and the gym would insure me so I could work part time on the weekends with set hours. I said I was very honoured to be offered a job but I asked if I could I do it voluntarily as I was only interested in learning and being around like-minded gym enthusiasts but mostly because it would give me focus. He said I couldn't work for free and that I had to be paid. It wasn't a lot of money, in fact it was just over the minimum wage so I accepted.

On my first day I was given a uniform and a tour around the staff rooms and was told how all the processes worked. I was given a list of members that I would be writing programmes for and demonstrating how to use the equipment. I was quite nervous about the job itself but once I got the flow of it, I was in my element. The next day, I was even better; it felt like I had developed confidence overnight, wow! It made me realise how much confidence I had lost since my accident especially given I had always been such a huge extrovert.

By the end of the weekend I was smiling, a lot. I came home and suddenly felt a wave of satisfaction. For the first time since my car crash I had experienced self-worth. I felt self-esteem flow through my body. WOW, life had meaning again. Every member I had written exercise programmes for were asking ME for advice, it made me feel wanted, like I had a purpose in life again, what an amazing feeling. Regardless of the pain I was still suffering I was on cloud nine. I only really wanted to learn, I hadn't thought about the fact that I was actually doing a job that whole weekend. I had achieved self-worth for the first time in two years since my accident. It felt great; I finally had focus again.

It's always difficult to explain this type of situation to people who have never suffered any type of pain or strife. It's not until you start feeling better that you realise just how much you've been through and more so how much your personality has changed. Sometimes when I meet new patients with back pain, its like déjà vu, they remind me of me and what I went through and a lot of them tell me how difficult it is to explain to friends and family about those feelings of insecurity, loss of self-worth and lack of desire and motivation. They tell me: it's like walking around with a rain cloud over your head – well, of course I know exactly what they mean.

I worked every weekend from then on and I didn't care if that meant working seven days a week because the gym instructor role didn't seem like work. Well it was on paper but it didn't seem like work, it was addictive because I was getting so much out of it from a psychological standpoint. The sense of satisfaction was so great that I started to look forward to the weekend to get my 'buzz' from feeling so important. I continued with my studies and passed my body massage course and moved onto sports massage. The teachers were awesome and I enjoyed the hands-on work, I felt like I was meant to do hands-on treatment; it felt good.

During the course I told the tutor that I had been receiving cranial osteopathy and but had only received sports massage once in Goa. I asked if I could pay him for regular treatment. He told me he wouldn't touch my back because I was guarding it so much. I didn't understand. Muscle guarding is when your body subconsciously knows you're injured and so will 'guard' and protect you from certain movements to avoid further injury or pain. This can happen with any injured area of your body. The problem is your body can guard you all day long meaning you gain even more tension 'just in case' you perform a certain movement that causes you pain; it's a protective mechanism.

Eventually I finished the sports massage course and started learning sports therapy, how to diagnose and resolve injuries. It goes without saying that when you have a large number of injuries, learning about their physiological intricacies and how to resolve them is very, very satisfying. I didn't know at the time that specific therapy course was only scratching the surface. The course was six weeks long and extremely intensive. It wasn't easy: you had to learn so much more anatomy and a lot of new words and phrases as well as a huge range of whole body orthopaedic muscle tests, range of motion tests, the list was endless. It was very complicated. Mike, the physiotherapist who taught the course, had re-written the course content so all the testing was based on physiotherapy. He said it was a year's diploma that he had condensed into six weeks of intensive learning.

The course was very fulfilling. I learnt so much about my injuries and it was extremely satisfying to get some form of understanding as to why I was still in so much pain. One of the most common forms of feedback I receive from my own patients is they love it when I explain why they have their injury. When you're in pain, it's extremely gratifying to understand the ins and outs.

Sports therapy was the most intense course of all and it was the last one. I passed with flying colours and got 98% in my exam, Mike joked with me about what had happened to the other 2%! For our graduation, they arranged for us to visit the Royal College of Surgeons. The basement contained lots of injured bones, tissues and cadavers (embalmed bodies for medical purposes). It was truly an amazing experience. Then we had a huge party – I was exhilarated albeit still in a whole lot of pain.

I was finally out of denial and fully accepted what was wrong with me. I had a different life now and the best thing I could do was try to be positive and do everything in my power to make myself better whilst focusing on what I could do rather than what I couldn't do. About four months after my sports therapy course I got into a situation at my workplace. It wasn't an overnight fix, but it only took four weeks. It was another life changing experience, except this time for the better.

7
The New Beginning

What happened next wasn't a pleasant experience at the time, but it was the best thing that ever happened to me with regards to my career. One of our departmental bosses saw me working at the gym, and she told Dave's boss. He called me into his office one day and asked me about my job at the gym. I explained that I didn't see it as a job but as something that had instilled focus back in my life after my accident. He didn't understand at all and questioned me more and he said my gym role was in direct conflict with my role in TV. I didn't understand, what I did on the weekends had no impact on my full time job in TV. I started panicking. I could feel my stress levels increasing by the second. My role at the gym was giving me enjoyment in my life for the first time in over two years. Moreover, I finally had self-worth again and it was helping with my depression; I couldn't stop it now. My heart started racing.

I got very flustered with all of his questions and tried my hardest to explain how hard life had been and that this gym position had given me back some self-esteem, confidence and security. It was my new hobby not a job, it was all I had, I was clinging to it. I went on to explain that I tried to do it voluntarily but for insurance purposes they couldn't let me; either way it was so poorly paid and I didn't care about money anyway.

He didn't get it, in fact he got quite angry that I didn't see his point of view. I got really upset, "How could he not understand?", I thought. I was explaining myself to the maximum. I could feel the tears rolling down my face, I was overwhelmed with frustration, I could feel myself starting to crack; everything had been going so well. Eventually, he said I could leave and I went back to my desk feeling dreadfully low and drained of emotion. My boss Dave was away on vacation so I couldn't speak to him.

When you suffer pain day after day, it changes you. Your normal character changes, you become a totally different person. A lot of my patients have told me they changed jobs or have had to give up their full time positions prior to seeing me because they were in so much pain. When things in your life become out of your control frustration sets in and when that increases eventually you become very sad and depressed. Over time it just feels like you walk round with a rain cloud over your head. For those who have never been through depression or have suffered an injury that has caused immense pain, it can be hard to empathise with others or ascertain what it feels like to lose control in life and lose every aspect of what made you happy.

Early in 2005, after seeing my mother over the Christmas period, I returned to London and decided it was time to go. Within four weeks after that horrible confrontational talk with Dave's boss, I left my job in television. That conversation had done me a huge favour; it made me realise that I was destined for another huge change, this time to enrich my life. It was about to take a whole new turn. I had spoken to the new manager at my gym and she told me that I could come on board as a full time personal trainer; there was a space just for me. How convenient – things were looking up.

I had to take a very big drop in salary but I didn't care. Amanda was right, I enjoyed working at the gym, weirdly it felt like I was home even though I had no spare finances to go out and enjoy myself. Soon after I had joined full time, I decided to continue my studies and I signed up for another course. It was two courses in one, a diploma in advanced personal training (APT) and a diploma in sports psychology. The APT course was an intensive week at the fitness centre learning about biomechanics, advanced physiology, corrective posture exercises, advanced therapies and advanced gym exercises. After that, I had to do a six-month case study using all the new tools; it was an excellent course for its time.

The sports psychology course was mostly reading and writing long essays. To this day it is the hardest course I have ever accomplished. It was a year-long course but I finished it in six months. I worked overtime to get it done, I had a real thirst for it probably because of the depression I had suffered. I still use all of the psychology tools, some of them are in this book. Sadly however, all the reading and writing made my back pain worse. I didn't realise how much sitting for long periods reading and typing could increase back pain. So I stretched regularly during my long periods of sitting and I started having weekly sports massages.

Amanda suggested I may need rehab exercises as my spine was in better shape so I probably didn't need to continue seeing her. She said I needed a fair amount of 're-education' (rehabilitation exercises – more on that later in the book). I told her I had already found a sports massage therapist and I was qualified to administer my own rehab exercises. I was very grateful for her treatment and support during our sessions.

My back was still so painful that I couldn't lie on my back or front but I could get through a day with patches of lower grade pain. I still had daily headaches and I still had pain and numbness in my feet but more so if I wore high heels. The numbness in my legs would also come on from using the bike or the cross trainer at the gym. I still had pain in my left knee more than my right one and the right side of my hip and neck ached all the time, I was still leaning to the right but it was better after having treatments over the previous year. I still had the continuous nerve/stabbing pains in my pelvis so my doctor was still sending me for more tests, they had no idea what the pains were or where they were coming from. Having spoken to my massage therapist and researching scientific research papers, we both came to the conclusion that the pelvic stabbing pain was down to a trapped nerve in my pelvis called the pudendal nerve. My GPs didn't agree, so I continued with their process of testing, they knew best.

Sports massage felt great; it hurt during the session but it felt better afterwards so I booked myself in twice a week. I was basically spending all of my salary on treatment but it was worth it. I started getting more personal training clients at work so my salary started to increase. I had also been treating friends, family and colleagues at home for free so I could gain experience with resolving injuries. I didn't feel justified charging anyone until I had at least six months' experience under my belt. By then I had finished my APT course and passed. I was extremely proud of myself, and I could feel my depression lifting.

After the horrific discovery during my first PT course doing a half plank I was very wary of doing any core exercises but I knew I had to start somewhere. I started on the half plank and worked up to the full plank. I noticed that the more core work I did, the less pain I was in. It then occurred to me that I still hadn't tried performing overhead exercises in the gym. It had been three years.

I tried doing an exercise called a lat pulldown (a bar is over your head, you pull it down to your chest and control it back up again) and to my surprise it didn't hurt. That said it was very difficult because I had lost all my strength but I could do it with a light weight – that was a start. I tried another machine, a shoulder press where you push a machine up to the ceiling and back down again. Success, I could do overhead exercises again, another achievement of self-efficacy. Although I was very weak, it felt great! My confidence was returning. I was starting to feel mentally stronger.

Self-efficacy is an extremely important factor in daily life as well as exercise and a must for recovering from any back issue. It is a necessity to help depression. Self-efficacy is a belief in your ability to accomplish a task or to achieve success in a particular situation. Once you have that belief, you can enjoy progressing with that particular task – in this case, for me it was overhead exercises. Most people don't like performing certain gym exercises because they can't physically do them, especially if they are in pain, but once they are able to perform them they start to enjoy that particular exercise. A lot of people who experience back pain are never sure which exercises they can perform and if there are exercises they should avoid. Chapter 19 is dedicated to this subject.

Life was a lot better, I had focus again, my pain had decreased and my strength was coming back. I had started experimenting with my own weaknesses and trying out new rehab exercises. Mike, the physiotherapist, had taught me that you can make up any rehab exercise as long as you know the muscle movement. He always used to say "just think like a five-year-old". What he meant was that the exercise should be simple enough for a five-year-old to do and he was right! My salary was increasing and I had started to charge for working with injured patients. I was content with life again, with the exception of still living in pain. I felt freedom for the first time in years.

In 2006 I went to a fitness conference at Loughborough University which is renowned for being one of the best in the UK for learning all aspects of health, fitness and sport. The conference consisted of multiple lectures, physical classes and a big exhibition of books and tools/equipment for the health and fitness industry. I knew it would be a lot of walking and even though I was still in a lot of pain I was a lot stronger, so I decided to go with my friends Emma and Chris who were personal trainers that I worked with.

One of the lectures we attended was with Charles Poliquin, a world-renowned strength coach who was based in the US. We had all read a lot about him about so were very excited to hear him speak. The conference room was packed out with people trying to squeeze in. Charles was awesome, his knowledge of the body, training methods and in-depth nutrition was unreal. I knew that he was very well known all over the world and that he had trained multiple professional athletes. He was as elite as you could get. I was so impressed with his presentation. We all signed up two of his courses.

The second course I attended was strength and conditioning level one, in Ireland. It was amazing. I learnt so much that I wanted to know more. I had developed a huge thirst for learning and I realised early on that being a therapist made me a better trainer and vice versa, they're very interlinked. Strength and conditioning is the next level up from being a personal trainer where you learn a lot of advanced physiology, science/theory and how to train athletes in various sports.

During the course, on a lunch break I watched Charles assess a man's whole body and then he started treating him with a technique called ART® (Active Release Techniques). I was speechless. Charles increased the man's range of motion in a squat position by about 7 or 8 inches, in 25 minutes. I was seriously impressed so I asked his assistant, Clarke, what on earth was this ART? He explained that it was a very advanced soft tissue technique which was based on releasing connective tissue, known as fascia, and it could free up other tissues in the body that no other modality could do.

I decided there and then that I needed to learn this amazing treatment. I found out that it was only taught in the United States. Charles told me to make sure that I would be taught by Dr Leahy, the founder of ART, who he knew very well. That same day I booked onto a course in San Jose for November that year, I was very excited.

I had found the strength and conditioning course with Charles amazing but quite hard. I never knew there was so much science involved in training people. He also talked about how to train people returning from injuries and injury prevention. I learnt so much. It was a lot of information and I was in my element. I couldn't wait to get home and put everything into practice with my clients.

By November I was physically stronger but I still had all the same symptoms. I didn't really understand: how could I be getting stronger, especially doing heavy squats and deadlifts, and still have lower back pain? I went to San Jose to attend my first ART course, the upper extremity. I found it quite hard to learn, as the anatomy was EXTREMELY in-depth. Plus, you can learn a fair amount from the learning manuals and DVD but ultimately you have to attend the courses to learn the hands-on skills, it's all about the touch. More on this later in the 'skills and services' chapter.

The course was run by a lady called Dr Faye Jones. She was so knowledgeable and very organised; there must have been over 70 people. I met some amazing therapists and I was mesmerised with some of the instructors, their hands-on skills were incredible. I was very inspired and wanted to be as good as them. On my last day I met Dr Leahy – he joked that he thought my accent didn't sound very local! He was awesome; his hands are as big as spades and his knowledge is unbelievable. I thought, "he's like the therapy version of Charles Poliquin, how lucky am I to have been introduced to this elite world?"

I passed my exam and I attended another course the following year. I was super lucky because Dr Leahy was teaching for the whole duration. I asked him if I could pay him for some private sessions as I really wanted him to look at my lower back but he told me he wouldn't accept payment, he was delighted to treat me.

After the course on the first day Dr Leahy got me on the treatment table. I still had a long list of issues but I concentrated on the main ones as I thought 10 were enough to start with. He treated all 10 areas in less than 20 minutes, I was shocked at his proficiency. Dr Leahy assessed the stabbing pain I had around my anus area. He said it was my pudendal nerve, I had been correct all those years ago. In fact he said I had two entrapments i.e. it was trapped on both sides of my pelvis. He went on to say it was trapped so badly that he changed the ART manual after treating me because it was trapped in a different place to the norm. My sciatic nerve, which had caused the travelling pains and numbness in my bum and legs, was also trapped really badly. He said I also had two entrapments of the sciatic nerve, one on each side of my pelvis. This is very common with people who suffer lower back pain.

Dr Leahy explained that various parts of my lower back and pelvis including the nerves were stuck and once he released them I would feel very different. After he finished treating me, I stood up and almost fell over. I felt really weird because I felt so GOOD! Oh my goodness, what a massive relief!

WOW! I couldn't believe it, I felt seriously amazing, my lower back pain had eased SO MUCH. I was still amazed that Dr Leahy had released so many structures in such a short period of time. It was nuts! I had suffered that stabbing nerve pain in my anus and vagina 30-40 times a day for SIX years. After that one treatment it decreased to about five times a month, just like that; it was a miracle. I needed more work on the nerves but I honestly couldn't believe the difference after one session.

As you can imagine I was enticed to attend the ART Nerve Entrapment course, especially to learn more about the sciatic nerve as it can be a major cause of lower back issues. The symptoms can appear as a dull ache, swelling, stabbing, electric or travelling pains. When I first had my sciatic nerve released, I hadn't realised how stuck it was until afterwards. I walked differently after that, I had more control of both legs and after four weeks of training in the gym I gained even more strength and muscle. Nerves take longer to heal than muscle so sometimes you may notice more of a difference a week or two after treatment. Regardless, having a nerve released means your muscles can communicate more efficiently with your brain so it's very common for you to gain more muscle and strength following ART treatments.

My life changed a lot after that. My success rate with resolving injuries and restoring patients back to full function went through the roof. Every course I attended was helping to decrease my back pain and increase strength, so I was gaining way more than just the course content. I started applying my new-found knowledge with my patients and personal training clients, noticing crossovers in certain areas especially those with back pain. More importantly I was experimenting with treatments and rehab exercises on myself. This was paramount in helping my own patients recover even quicker and more efficiently. It was very rewarding. I learnt so much from Charles Poliquin and Dr Leahy that I felt empowered and inspired to continue learning more and more so I could get my patients back on their feet even quicker. I owe them both a lot.

During my third course with Charles Poliquin I was taught how to squat properly. Soon after that course, I noticed that my left knee pain was getting better and within three weeks, for the first time in seven years, my left knee pain had totally disappeared. It was very distinct and it never came back. It taught me that what my knee needed was strength but at full range, probably because I had suffered so much atrophy (muscle wastage) on that whole leg after the accident. The treatment helped the communication with my brain and muscles and the weight training helped to re-build strength back in those muscles.

I had completely cleared my depression and I was learning at 100mph but I still couldn't understand why I still had lower back pain and why my legs were weaker than my upper body. So, I started experimenting with even more exercises and stretches and noticing patterns with my lower back patients and personal training clients. I observed that some back exercises would work and some wouldn't. Charles had taught me a lot about strength and how the body needs to be balanced as a whole. This included strengthening the smaller stabiliser muscles and if one area is weak other areas can overcompensate; that notion has always stayed at the back of my mind. I wanted to know why back pain could still exist regardless of having whole body strength in the gym and stamina during sporting activities.

After a decade of experimenting with my own injuries, I came up with exercises that do work for everyone and a specific system to diagnose, treat and rehabilitate lower back pain, entirely created from my own experiences while using the most advanced and efficient soft tissue methods. I also learnt that rehabilitation strength is totally different to strength from exercising in the gym. I'll explain this in more detail later on. I realised that to heal most types of back pain and make sure it doesn't come back, you need the rehabilitation exercises as well as the soft tissue work. I became back pain free.

I now have a very efficient, progressive table of exercises and stretches that can enable you to build a strong and capable back along with a maintenance programme. Remember that once you're pain free you want to keep it that way. In my experience ART is the king of soft tissue or 'gold standard' as we call it and there is no way I could resolve back issues without it. I have come across other efficient techniques that are very useful for various parts of the body related to back pain, like IASTM tools, reflexology and acupuncture. They have very useful properties like organ release or improving bowel movement which can become impaired when you suffer stress and pain. More on these subjects in the next few chapters.

Emotions are also a huge part of the healing process when you're in pain. On that note there many other subjects involved with healing back pain and there are a lot of things you can do to help recover as quickly and efficiently as possible.

That brings this part of the book to a close and duly onto the next section of how one resolves back pain without re-occurrence. The following chapters explain all the ingredients you need!

8

It's Nothing To Do With Age!

If you're reading this book because you have back pain, you may wonder how and why it started. It's a question I get asked all the time. There is always a reason. One day if you wake up and feel a twinge, it isn't a sudden thing; it's probably an issue that has been building up for some time.

When it comes to back pain I hear "I'm getting old" ALL the time. This is simply NOT true! It's nothing to do with age! Don't get me wrong, age can sometimes dictate whether your muscles and joints are healthy but so can bad choices in nutrition, lack of sleep, a negative mindset and a whole load of other factors.

Why do you get back pain?

A lot of back issues typically stem from two types of injuries, extrinsic or intrinsic. Extrinsic basically means your issue has derived from an outside source such as a clash during an event like a car accident or a sporting event like rugby or football, falling off a horse, a fall down the stairs or even a drunken night out. You'd be amazed at how many patients experience those! Intrinsic injuries are classified as an internal source which can develop over a long period of time. They are typically caused by bad posture or a repetitive factor in your environment such as bending over a lot like a tradesman (p1) (plumber, builder), sitting at a desk all day (p2), travelling in cars, trains and planes a lot or playing a sport like tennis or golf. I'll talk about other causes later on.

1

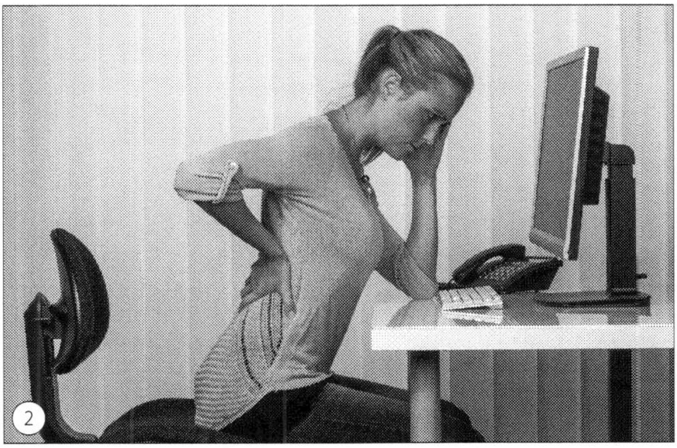
2

Muscles work in pairs, like a see-saw. Each muscle on the front of your body has a 'paired' muscle on the back of your body; an example of this would be your hip flexors (p3) (muscles at the front of your hip) and your glutes (p4) (bum muscles). When we sit down for long periods, certain muscles around your spine and hips become shortened like your hip flexors and others can become overstretched like your glutes. Over time this causes weaknesses in some muscles and overcompensation (overworked) in others, which can eventually lead to dysfunction.

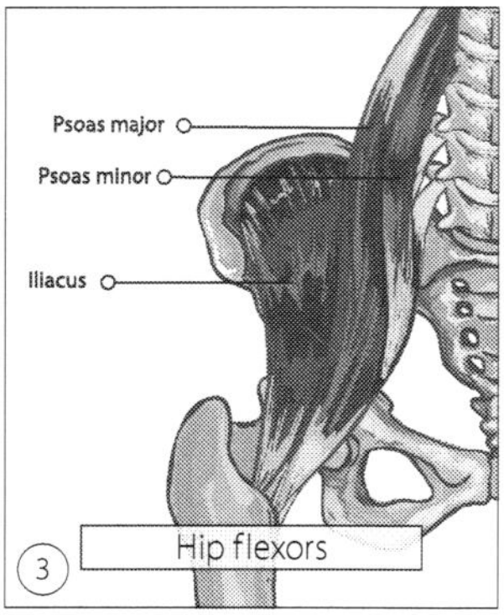

3 Hip flexors

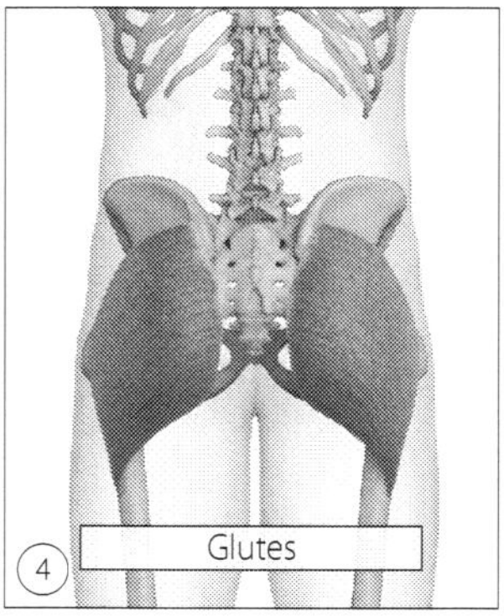
4 Glutes

This means that dysfunctional 'paired' muscles can instigate an imbalance of your hip complex and ultimately lead to pain. This could take up to six months to five years to develop or longer. I've seen some patients who have had back pain on and off for 20 years, sometimes 30 years.

Your hips comprise of your lower back, muscles on the front and side of your hips and muscles the front and back of your thighs, they are often referred to as the hip complex as they are three-dimensional. As time goes on, imbalances get worse leading to stiffness, aches and pain which can leave you vulnerable to further injury such as a disc bulge, more on this later.

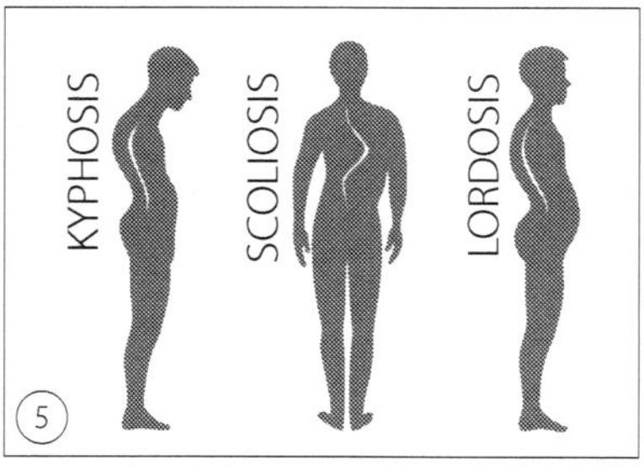

5

A lot of people I treat that have hip imbalances have what I call 'duck bum' otherwise known as lordosis (p5). It's where their pelvis has tilted forward and the curve in their lower back has increased so much that their bum sticks out like a duck. This happened to me.

Another type of imbalance in the spine is called kyphsosis (p5) which you see a lot in people that sit a lot. This is where your head and shoulders start to move forward. This type of condition can affect the curve in your lower back. Your neck curve affects your lower back and vice versa. Having this condition can also partially shut down your diaphragm too. If one side of your hip becomes weaker and the other becomes too dominant it can cause a spinal issue called scoliosis (p5) where your spine forms an S shape. Most people who have scoliosis usually have back pain on one side of their lower back and hips.

Causes of lower back pain aren't just about hip imbalances and accidents. Sometimes having an epidural in your lower back can cause a build up of scar tissue around the insertion of the epidural needle which can affect surrounding muscles and fascia/connective tissue. This follows suit for lumbar punctures, hip replacement surgery, lower back surgery, spondylosis (bone degeneration), types of arthritis (bone/joint disorders) and broken bones. These issues can have a huge effect on surrounding muscles and can cause imbalances of their own.

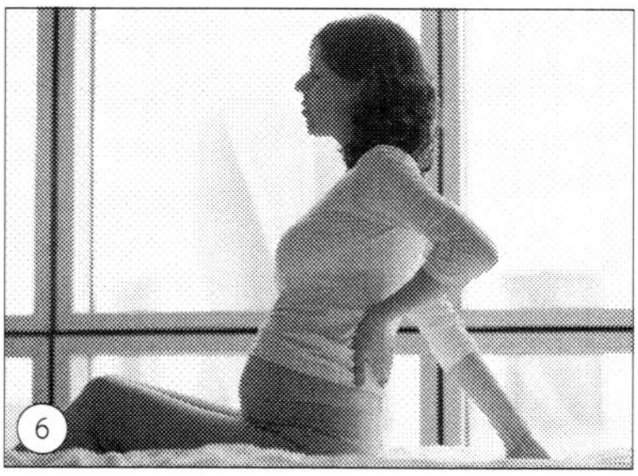
6

One of the most common causes of back pain that I've seen in women is from giving birth. It appears to happen during pregnancy (p6) and straight after a child is born but symptoms may not develop until many years later. Carrying a baby can put a huge strain on your lower back due to the weight of the baby bump pulling you forward. For some mothers this causes an imbalance of their hips which can seriously weaken their core and glute muscles and lead to horrific back pain.

The real cause

Over the years experimenting with my own injuries and observing injured patients with back issues, I realised that three groups of muscles were involved with resolving lower back pain: your glutes, your lower back and your core muscles (muscles around your trunk, stomach and pelvis). When I say "resolving", it's a mix of releasing some muscles and rehabilitating (strengthening) others.

With those three groups in mind, by far the most common muscles to become weak are your glutes. They are huge muscles that support your lower back and if they become weak, their 'paired' muscles, your hip flexors, become too dominant and start to pull your pelvis forward or as I like to call it, duck bum. Your hip flexors attach to the bones in your lower back so if they overwork and get tighter, your lower back curve increases in size (the curve gets bigger) to form the lordosis position. Your lower back muscles then have to over compensate for their new position which can cause pain, stiffness and instability. The main reason for this is usually overcompensation because one or both sets of glutes cannot support your lower back any more. Furthermore, the curve in your lower back is the most vulnerable part of your spine because of its small size. If your curve gets bigger and lessens in height, your lower back becomes even more vulnerable and can leave you susceptible to disc issues and ligament tears. Every single person I have ever treated with lower back pain has had weak glutes on either one or both sides of their hips.

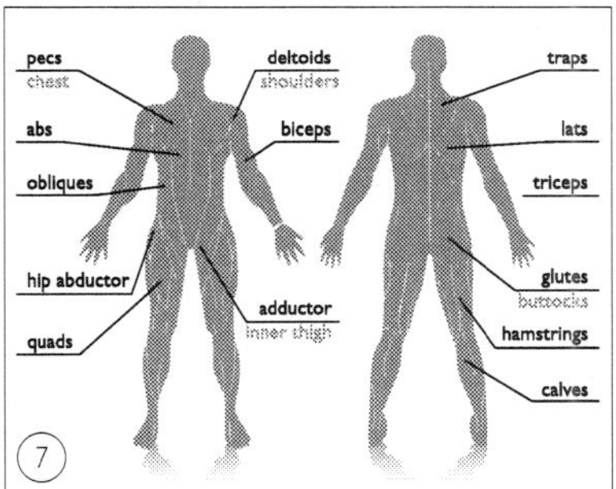

7

Often when you get a duck bum and your glutes become weak, your hamstrings (p7) (muscles at the back of the legs) can elongate a bit too much. One of the most common symptoms of this is sitting can become very uncomfortable or even painful at the base of your bum. Actually it's not your bum, it's your hamstrings and what you're feeling is where they attach to your pelvis, right at the base of your bum.

When this symptom gets really painful, it can hurt to sit down, full stop. For some people this may hurt on one side of their hamstrings, for others it's both. I had this symptom for many years on both of my hamstrings, I couldn't sit on a wooden chair for years and I could never sit still because of the pain.

In-between the bones of your spine (vertebrae) you have spongey intervertebral discs which act as shock absorbers for your spine. They help with movement of your spine and help protect the nerves that run down the middle of your spine. When your hip becomes imbalanced, over time it can lead to one or more of your intervertebral discs shifting out of their normal shape and bulging or compressing on nearby spinal nerves. Every patient I have treated for a disc bulge or disc herniation has had one or both weak sets of glutes.

The consequence of glute weakness could also lead to a trapped nerve in your glutes themselves. This is called sciatica: it's a term for sciatic nerve entrapment. Your sciatic nerve runs from your lower back down to your toes. So when you sit, stand or walk, you might feel a pain travelling from your glutes, through your hamstrings, your calves (p7) and down to your toes. It's a NASTY sensation and very painful. In most cases after your nerve is released your glutes will need to be rehabilitated.

A lot of patients I treat for lower back issues have very weak core muscles. If you remember from my story, after my accident I went from doing a plank exercise for 4 minutes down to 5 seconds of an easy half plank. There are lots of muscles that make up your 'core' but for this explanation I will stick to the deep spinal muscles and abdominal (stomach) muscles only.

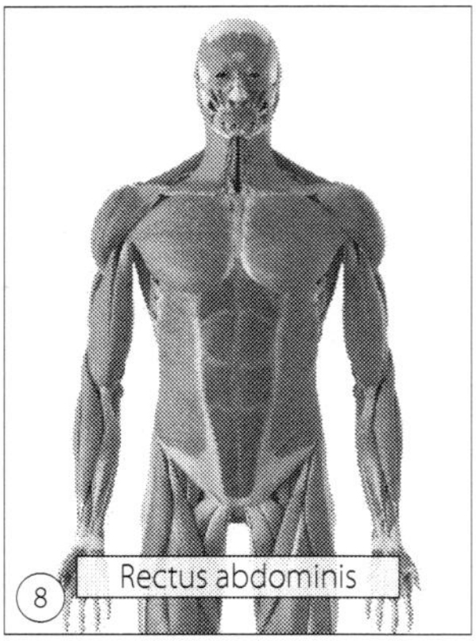

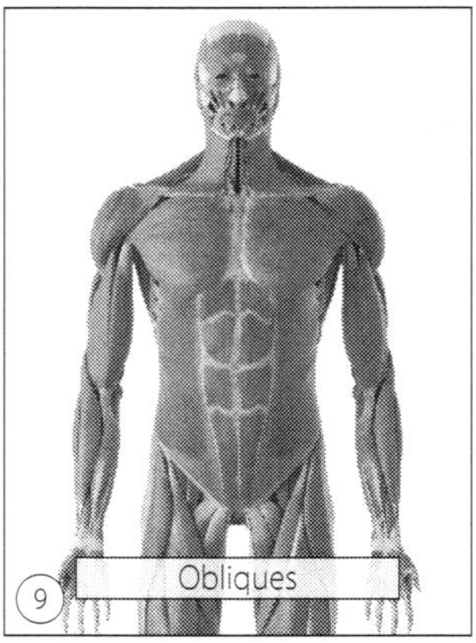

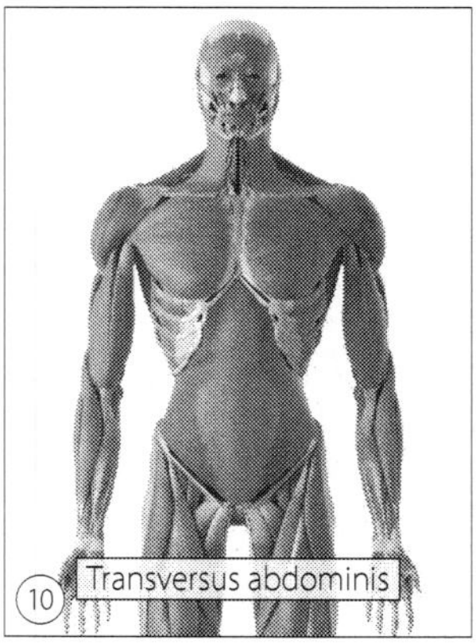

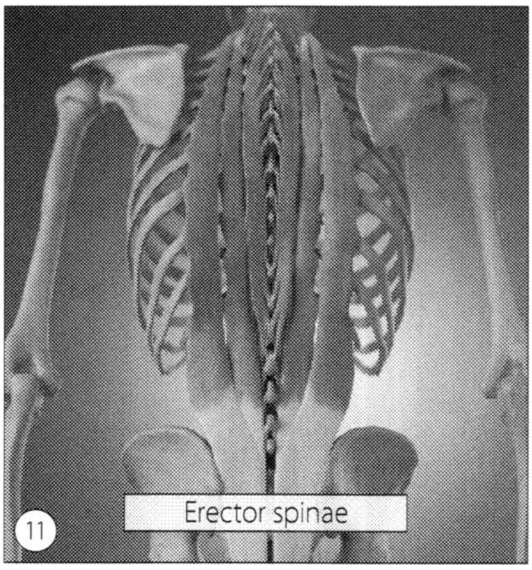

While discussing your abdominals I'm not just talking about a six-pack although they are part of your 'core'. The 'six-pack' is called the rectus abdominis (p8) and the muscles on the side of your stomach are called the obliques; there is a superficial layer (p9) (external obliques) and a deep layer (p9) (internal obliques). Sometimes when one glute is weak it's harder to perform oblique exercises on that particular side of weakness. I describe these later in the book.

You also have a very deep layer of abdominal muscles called the transversus abdominis (p10) (TVA). I call this 'the corset' because of the way it almost wraps around your whole torso. The TVA works together with some of your back muscles (p11) (erector spinae, multifidus). All of these muscles help to stabilise your spine and are interlinked. Your core muscles are more complex than that but the exercises I prescribe for core work are for your back muscles and all of your abdominal muscles so that they work in conjunction with each other.

Not everyone that I treat needs core work. A lot of my patients have attended Pilates classes before coming to see me. I am a huge advocate of Pilates whether it's a class or a one-on-one session. They really help to strengthen your core and lower back muscles.

Foundation strength

A lot of people get confused about strength. When I was trying to gain strength after my accident I realised there were exercises I could no longer perform. I couldn't even think about advanced exercises but I found that I couldn't even a perform a medium hard exercise so I had to go back to basic exercises – actually exercises I had never performed because they were so basic. This taught me that when it comes to rehabilitation exercises it's always best to start at the beginning, regardless if the exercises appear easy and then progress up through the levels as you accomplish each target. Most of all, it taught me that rehab strength is totally different to gym strength.

They both communicate via different nerve pathways brain from your to your muscles, tendons, fascia and ligaments. The way I explain the difference between gym and rehab strength is to think of a house and the foundations underneath it (p12). If the foundation under the right side of the house has crumbled, the right side of the house will always be in need of re-building. So, no matter how many times you re-build it, it will continue to fall apart and stay vulnerable because the foundation underneath it is weak and unstable. The house is gym strength and the foundation underneath is rehab strength.

When the foundation has been restored to full strength, that part of the house should never need to be re-built because it is finally stable. However, foundations need to be maintained. So if you rehabilitate your glutes, lower back and core, your lower back should stay strong and stable as long as you continue to maintain your new-found strength and full function. Some people want a quick fix and will go straight to the top of the rehab table and miss out half of the basic exercises. Unfortunately, in this case, the pain usually comes back so it's always best to cover every base.

Rehabilitation simply means 'to re-educate the brain'. Think of it like your brain has forgotten about certain muscles in your body and you have to reacquaint them, then strengthen their relationship. The brain works on repetition so, as you'll see when you get to the rehabilitation chapters, most of the exercises comprise of a LOT of repetitions.

The length of time it takes to restore function in your lower back, core and glutes can depend on a multitude of elements, it's not just about performing exercises and stretches. It can depend on how long you've had your injury, how old you are, if you've had previous related injuries, how healthy you are, how well you sleep, your state of mind (are you positive or negative?) and how much you avoid aggravation (anything that makes you worse).

I will explain all of these other factors in great detail in the following chapters. Remember, everyone is individual so if you're patient and disciplined you should see great results.

9

Skills & Services; It's All About Hands On

When it comes to treatments it's really important for you to find the right therapist to help restore function in your lower back and any other muscles that may be involved. Trust is a big factor with therapy. I believe the more trust and belief you have in your therapist, the quicker you recover.

There are many types of therapies around such as sports therapy, physiotherapy, chiropractic, osteopathy and they all come with specific diagnostic skills and a combination of treatments. My preferred methods of treatments to resolve lower back pain are purely from my own experiences.

Every therapist should be insured for their services and should have the relevant certifications for each technique. I always try to resolve issues as quickly as possible so I am wary of therapists who suggest you need to buy a block of 10 sessions, when in fact they could resolve your issue in two to five sessions. It goes without saying that some people need more, others may need less treatment but therapists selling blocks is not a great sign in my experience.

As a general rule I always suggest to ask a friend, family member or colleague for a recommendation. Good therapists are always talked about, that's how I found all of mine!

Active Release Techniques® (ART)

Active Release Techniques solves the unsolvable! In my opinion ART treatment is by far the best soft tissue release in the world. It is an exceptionally quick and efficient method to release muscles and structures in your body and it lives up to its name of being 'The Gold Standard in Soft Tissue Healthcare™.' It is a very hands-on technique that's based on releasing fascia, otherwise known as connective tissue, which is primarily made up of collagen. In short, fascia is like lots and lots of stringy cotton wool that connects and stabilizes all kinds of structures in your body like organs, muscles, tendons and nerves. There are multiple layers of fascia that intertwine in and around muscles, nerves and organs; fascia is literally everywhere in your body.

I've seen some crazy, amazing results using this technique such as resolving vertigo, Osgood-Schlatter disease (a painful knee condition), surgical scars, Bell's palsy (paralysis of facial muscles) and brain injuries – yes brain injuries. I was originally taught there was nothing you could do for all of these conditions until I started using ART protocols. The results are truly remarkable.

In 2011, I felt honoured when my favourite ART Lead instructor, Pali Cooper, asked me to become an instructor. It is a great privilege to teach such an awesome technique. Since then I have taught a variety of health professionals; sports therapists, physiotherapists, personal trainers, chiropractors, osteopaths, strength coaches and sports massage therapists including those in the Premier League of English football and various other elite sports. A lot of therapists and trainers like to combine their modalities. I think it is great to have a selection of effective techniques in one package and ART should be at the top for soft tissue release.

People always ask me, "But why is ART treatment better than massage?" It's not that it's better – they each have different uses. Although ART is described as a soft tissue system that is based on massage, as a technique massage is used for relaxation and facilitating flexibilty/pliability in your muscles via your circulation and lymphatic system whereas the ART method is about releasing fascia where it gets 'bunched up' preventing muscles, nerves, tendons, ligaments and other structures from sliding and working properly.

The beauty of this modality is that it releases tissues that are 'stuck'; think of it like ironing out lots of bumps and creases in a shirt, some small, some big and some super thick that need more work to iron out. When muscles become very tight or very weak for a long period of time they create a lot of dysfunction, especially with long-term back issues. ART treatment can help with releasing those tissues to restore oxygen and function back into those tissues, quickly and efficiently. Rehabilitating muscles is much easier after an ART treatment because of the instant changes to your brain that occur following treatment.

Every ART session is a combination of examination as well as treatment. The basic concept is a therapist shortens your joint, applies pressure on a particular muscle or structure with their thumb or fingers and then lengthens your joint (p13). The reason it is such an advanced technique is because the depth of tension, direction of tension and movement of your joints are all extremely precise. Therapists have to learn in-depth anatomy in order to know every movement for each muscle or structure. Elite professionals in sport that I teach say that every therapist (physiotherapist, osteopath etc.) should take an ART course just because the anatomy is so in-depth.

13

ART treatment is a finesse, it's not just about grabbing a muscle and moving a joint in your body, it is ALL about touch. The magic happens under the therapist's fingers and thumbs. The more a therapist performs ART the better they get at administering it. What I really love about this modality is that Dr Leahy (founder of ART) constantly evolves it, so I learn new things every year!

There are specific protocols that help release muscles where a nerve runs through it but there are other meticulous protocols that release all the peripheral nerves (a network of nerves that connect your brain to your muscles), directly from your spine. If you have been diagnosed with a trapped sciatic nerve in your lower back (sharp pains, throbbing pain, constant ache, swelling, travelling pains down your leg) or glutes this is an excellent method to help you. ART nerve releases are genius.

In the case of scars around your hips and lower back, ART protocols are very efficient at working the scar itself as well as the surrounding tissues to get oxygen back into the area. I've treated quite a few patients who have undergone back surgery with huge scars to prove it. Once you free up the scar and the muscle tissue around it, the muscles in your back can move freely again. I've seen some patients who have had scars that were 10-15 years old and been successful with getting them pain free.

If you have a chronic (long-term) back issue it's highly likely that your pelvic ligaments have shortened. Very often during a first session for a lower back issue, an ART therapist will work your hip flexors, hamstrings and pelvic ligaments and won't touch your back, yet you'll get off the table feeling loose, and with less or no pain. There are over 500 protocols (moves) that are unique to ART and that is just Level 1 protocols. Dr Leahy has taken ART treatment to a new level by creating a Level 2 of super advanced protocols.

I still have regular ART treatments to keep my muscles healthy as a preventative method. For more information or to find your nearest therapist go to the main website www.activerelease.com

Cranial osteopathy

I had cranial osteopathy for almost two years after my car accident. I must admit I thought it was a really weird treatment; it seemed like my therapist wasn't even doing anything! However, I noticed a lot of warm sensations during the treatments, felt super relaxed and less stiffness in my spine after every treatment, sometimes days later.

The technique is very holistic and views your body as a whole rather than just one injury. The emotional aspect is very important too so case history is key. A cranial osteopath usually treats what they find i.e. however your body is functioning on that day. They aren't very different to osteopaths but they do focus more on your spine and cranium (skull), hence the name cranial.

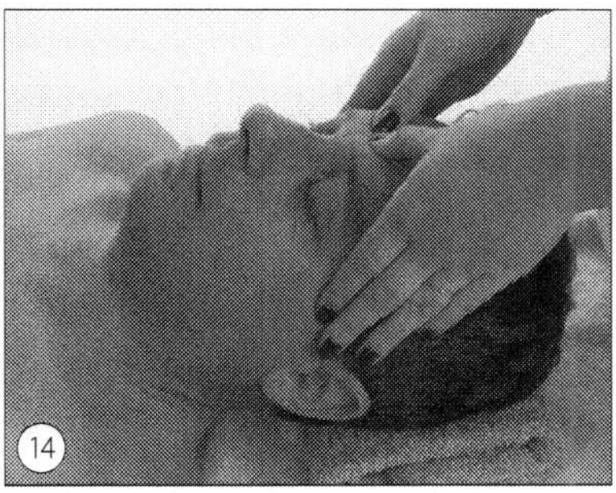

14

It's a very subtle and gentle treatment (p14). The therapist places their fingers on different areas of your spine and head and gently moves them when they need to. It's weird you hardly feel much going on but the effects are noticeable. It's a very relaxing technique especially for those who are in a lot of pain and have a lot of stiffness in their spine. Sessions normally last for about 30 minutes. It is a very unique and effective therapy for back pain especially when combined with rehab exercises, soft tissue work and other modalities such as the ones I've listed in this chapter.

I regularly refer my own patients to cranial osteopaths if I feel their spine is too stiff for me to work on. Sometimes this can be an emotional aspect but regardless, a good therapist should know when to refer to another specialised therapist; more on this in chapter 20.

To find out more information or for your nearest cranial osteopath go to the craniosacral therapy association website www.craniosacral.co.uk

Massage

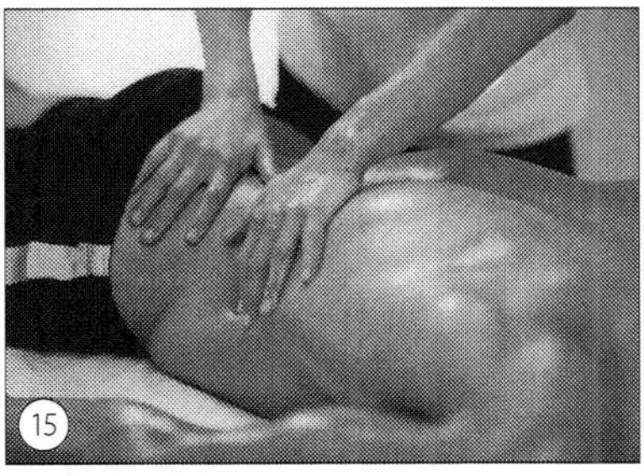

15

I'd say most people have experienced a massage of some kind in their life. It certainly has its place with easing back pain. In my experience, it helps with releasing muscular tension and helps with restoring flexibility and pliability in muscles especially for those people who exercise or sit down for long periods of time. Massage is a hands-on technique that uses a combination of broad and specific stroking movements, some light and some deep, to work with your circulation and lymphatic systems to help relieve muscular tension and pain (p15).

Massage is thought to elicit homeostasis. Without going into too much detail this basically means achieving the balance of all bodily functions. When we are closer to homeostasis we are generally happier and more relaxed. Most people report they feel de-stressed and calm afterwards.

I always get asked what are the differences are between Swedish massage, body massage, holistic massage and aromatherapy massage. They're all the same! Well, apart from aromatherapy massage which focuses on using specific plant scented oils during a massage that are believed to help heal pain. A body massage can be very helpful to relieve the stress of pain and give you a 'feel good factor'.

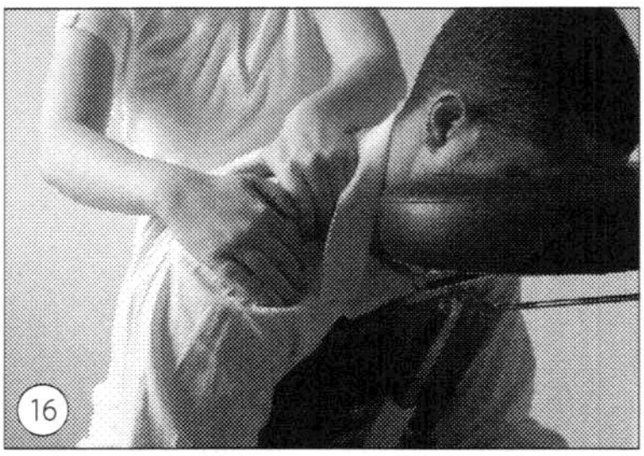

16

17

One form of massage is called Thai massage which is typically a combination of pressure in certain areas of your body and pulling your joints into end ranges of movements. I do not recommend this for anyone with any type of back injury.

Shiatsu massage is very much a 'trigger point' type technique. Shiatsu means 'finger pressure' so a therapist applies pressure to certain areas of your body and you are often fully clothed (p16). You will usually be seated on your front, slightly leaning forward in a chair designed for shaitsu massage.

Hot stone massage is where a therapist uses hot stones with warm oil to heat up muscles to promote relaxation and improve circulation in a particular area of your body (p17). It is a very calming technique and an excellent way of de-stressing.

Sports massage and deep tissue massage are the same thing. This is a much deeper massage so the therapist will exert way more tension than a body massage after warming up your muscles first. I advise my patients that although I am a huge fan of sports massage, which I occasionally administer myself, sometimes deep tissue massage is best avoided in the initial stage of trying to resolve a back injury especially if your issue is long-term.

Some patients with lower back pain can often feel worse after a sports massage but this hugely depends on several factors: what your injury is, whether it is short or long term, what stage of healing you are at and, mostly, how weak your muscles are.

When I first experienced massage it was about a year after my accident and boy did it hurt, mostly because it was so long after an extremely traumatic event but also because I had become so weak. The longer a muscle has had a shortage of oxygen the more bruised it feels to touch. After my third massage the bruised feeling got easier. My range of movement was better and I felt lighter. Although the pain was still there I felt more relaxed. To this day, I still have a sports massage once every four weeks on my whole spine, it's great to use as a preventative method.

To find your local massage therapist go to website for the Association for Soft Tissue Therapists www.thesma.wildapricot.org

IASTM tools

I wish I had known about these tools earlier in my quest for resolving back pain. IASTM means instrument assisted soft tissue mobilisation. Basically they are extremely efficient tools for releasing fascia, especially where there has been a build-up of connective tissue.

I'm really lucky that my good friend, Mark Warren, created his own line of tools called K-tools. He even got some of them made 30% smaller to fit my small hands! On first glance they may look a bit dangerous so please don't be put off. I get a lot of comments from patients walking into my treatment room asking if they are for patients who don't do their rehab exercises!

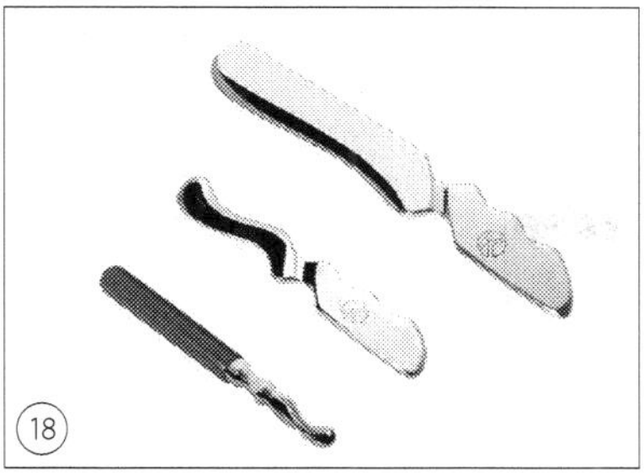

18

There are incredibly useful in certain areas of the body to promote healing. I find they're great to use around your hip bone, IT band (iliotibial band – a long, thick band of fascia on the side of each leg) and around your abdominals to help with back pain. Your abdominals can be hugely affected with back issues and I find using tools on these muscles can alleviate a lot of pressure on your lower back (p18).

They are specifically designed so that the therapist can feel what's going on underneath the tool so they feel what you feel and each tool has a different design with a variety of edges. They are particularly efficient at releasing thickened tissue (multiple layers of connective tissue) and where scars have become very condensed. Each practitioner uses a variety of stroking methods and as always patient feedback is a necessity. They are a great addition combined with using ART treatment.

To find your local IASTM practitioner go to their main website www.kiastm.com

Dry needling

Dry needling, often called trigger-point dry needling, is a technique that has become more popular over the last few years. Although you may not like needles it is worth getting over your fear!

It is a very efficient technique when used in combination with other methods to help with back pain, especially around your hip capsule. It is also very efficient at helping relieve tightness in muscles that tend to overwork such as your quadriceps (quads) and hamstrings muscles. A few needles are inserted gently into an area of your body in order to release a tight band of fascia, to stimulate relaxation and increase more movement in that particular muscle or structure (p19).

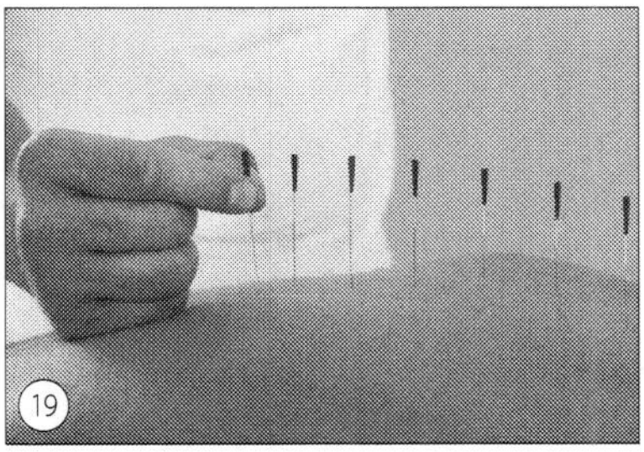

19

A lot of people ask what's the difference between acupuncture and dry needling. Well, they both use needles but dry needling is generally used for pain and injuries whereas acupuncture can be used for an extremely wide variety of medical issues such as asthma, thyroid issues, fertility as well as injuries and pain. I have found that most therapists who perform dry needling technique usually practice multiple disciplines in their clinic.

To find your nearest dry needling therapist go to the Dry Needling Association website www.dryneedlingassociation.com

Reflexology

If you don't like your feet being touched, reflexology is not for you! This technique is very hands-on and is based on reflex areas of your hands and feet that replicate every area of your body. For instance, the arch of your foot reflects your spine and underneath your foot in the middle reflects your kidneys.

It's a technique that is a bit 'out there' for some people to grasp. A therapist uses their fingers or a small implement that looks like a pencil (the flat end) to apply pressure in specific areas of your foot and toes. It's quite amazing how they know where you have areas of pain in your body by using pressure on your feet (p20).

Reflexology is very holistic. It's extremely relaxing and a great way to help relieve tension in your spine. A huge bonus with reflexology is that it often stimulates various other systems in your body that are connected to back pain such as digestion, or ovary issues for women. So you may come out of a treatment and find your toilet routine becomes more regular!

To find your nearest reflexologist go to the Association of Reflexologists website www.aor.org.uk

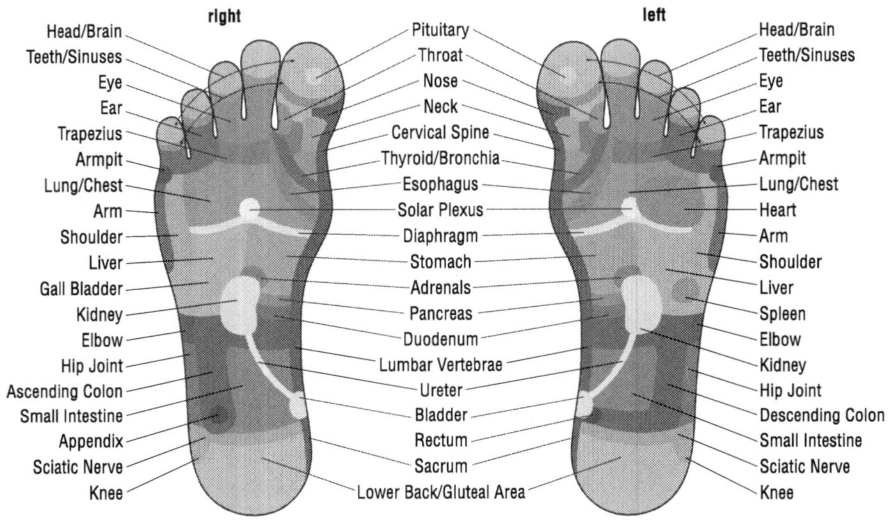

20

10

Should You? Or Should You Not?

There are many things I can tell you about healing back pain that you cannot know or learn unless you've been there, courses can't teach you everything. Avoiding aggravation is one of them. A major aspect of healing back pain is 'doing things right' – in short, being sensible. Here are some useful tips to help you and some that I would suggest you should avoid or at least be mindful of while you're recovering. If you are a gym goer there are a few tips in this chapter on that specific subject but I discuss that in great detail in 'the gym' chapter (19).

Should you? Yes!

Stay hydrated

I cannot tell you how many patients I have helped lessen their back pain by asking them to drink water! It started with my friend Warren Baker. I treated him once for back pain and although he felt better he still wasn't completely pain free. He couldn't get over to me for another treatment so we talked on the phone instead. When I asked him how much water he drank he went quiet! We laughed about his reaction and I suggested he increase his water intake by a glass a week until he was drinking 8 glasses of water a day. Within 10 days his back pain had totally disappeared.

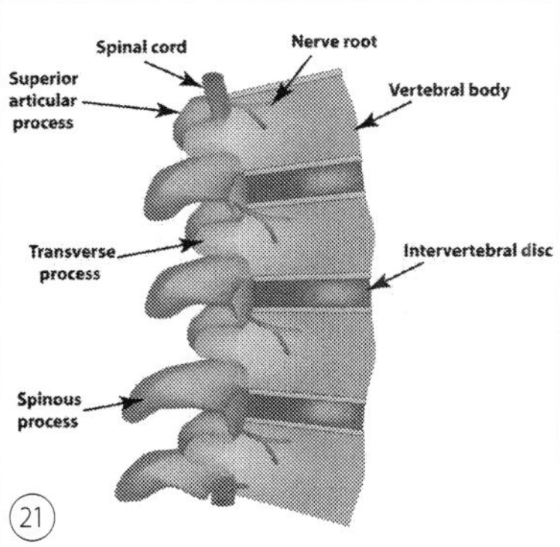

21

Your intervertebral discs (shock absorbers for your spine) are composed of around 80% water (p21). By the end of the day your discs dehydrate and gradually decrease in size so they need watering or 'pumping up' again first thing in the morning and through the day. If you are dehydrated, over time your discs can decrease in size and eventually cause pain. Think of it like a tyre that needs pumping up first thing in the morning, and by the end of the day it is half the size.

Hydration is very important for most injuries especially back pain. The average water intake for an adult is two litres a day (approximately eight glasses). This changes depending on your height and weight. A lot of people ask me if this includes tea and coffee. No, water intake means water only not hot drinks or squashes.

If you're not used to drinking a lot of water I would recommend to start with two glasses a day then add a glass every week until you reach eight glasses a day. Increasing your intake by a glass of water per week allows your body to get used to it and then maintain it. When you're not used to drinking water it's easy to forget to drink it so I would suggest buy yourself a BPA free (non-toxic) water bottle in your favourite colour. That way if you have it on your desk or in your kitchen (somewhere where you will see it regularly), you are more likely to refill it and drink from it. You may go to the toilet more often but you can take advantage of this by stretching your quads every time you make a toilet visit! There is a full list of stretches in chapter 18.

Avoid aggravation

This may sound like it's self-explanatory but it still amazes me how many patients, friends and colleagues continue to aggravate their back pain! People who exercise are by far the worst; they find it extremely hard to taper down their training sessions when they are injured. Personally I think exercise is a healthy addiction but it can really get in the way of recovery.

When I say aggravation, I'm talking about doing basic, daily tasks that could be avoided such as lifting heavy objects, painting or any form of DIY, driving for hours on end, gardening, working for long hours especially if you have a standing job or if you sit at a desk for long periods of time, teaching multiple fitness classes, lifting your children up and down numerous times. Being sensible is as important as doing all your exercises and stretches.

Avoid heavy bags for groceries

Carrying heavy bags can really aggravate your back pain. My suggestions are: put your grocery shopping in smaller separate bags, use a shopping trolley when possible or better still, shop online until you are in a position where carrying bags does not affect you.

Listen to classical music or binaural beats

Even if you're not a fan of classical music I would try listening to it. Science has shown classical music can lower stress and even help post-traumatic stress disorder. Studies have shown that this type of music can tap into a lower frequency of brain waves, known to lower your stress and calm you down. I use classical music as quiet background noise in my treatment room; I like to think it works sub-consciously to help my patients feel calm during treatment. Binaural beats is another type of music designed to tap into your brain waves to help you heal, lower stress and reduce mental fatigue (Zampi, 2016).

Use heat

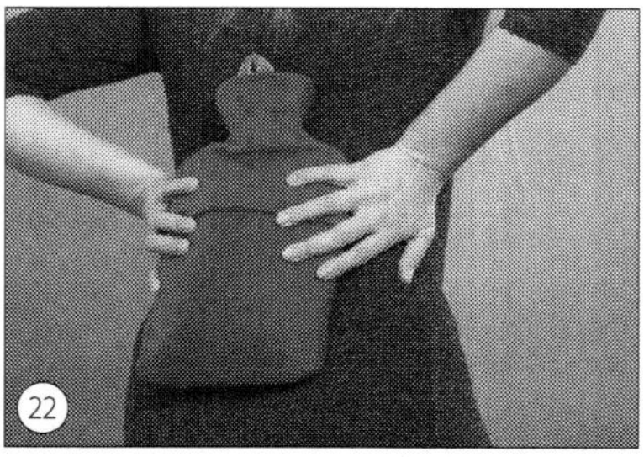

22

I'm sure some of you, or maybe even most of you, have tried using a hot water bottle (p22) and having hot baths/showers to help relieve your pain. The reason for this is when heat is applied to muscles, your blood vessels expand so blood can flow more easily which relieves tightness, soreness and pain. You could try using a hot/wheat pack which is like a scarf filled with little balls of wheat (typically scented with lavender) that you put in a microwave for two minutes, it stays hot for 15-20 minutes. In the winter months I use a hot pack every night especially if I've worked a long day or if I've been working at a football match and my body is tense from standing for hours in the cold – it's a great preventative.

In general, you can use a hot water bottle or hot pack and leave it on your lower back for 10-20 minutes. It is advisable to use a little bit of cold water in your hot water bottle, to avoid burning yourself. If you travel a lot I would suggest to pack your hot water bottle or buy a mini hot water bottle (half the size of a normal hot water bottle) because they don't take up much space in your suitcase and they're very easy to travel with.

Otherwise, a hot bath is great to help with back pain. Epsom salts are an excellent addition to help with recovery. The salts are very good for hydrating tired muscles and they contain magnesium, which helps decrease inflammation and helps to promote a good night's sleep. Therefore, I would recommend you have these baths at night, 10-20 minutes is long enough for a soak. Just be careful getting out of the bath. I would make sure you have an efficient, non-slip bath mat for inside your bath as you want to avoid slipping whilst getting in and out of the bath.

Portable heat patches are my last suggestion for heat. They heat up and stick to your skin so they're convenient if you're on the go. You can get some that contain NSAIDs (non-steroidal anti-inflammatory drugs) and other opioids but I'm not a huge fan of these because of the chemicals that can leech into your body and cause gut issues. More on this in chapter 13. Nevertheless, if you are in dire need and you're on the go, they can provide a simple solution.

Do hot and cold treatment

This easy and cheap method of treatment is the closest you can get to a self-massage. Use a hot water bottle or hot pack on your back for 3-4 minutes then use frozen peas or an ice pack for 3-4 minutes then put the hot water bottle/hot pack back on again for 3-4 minutes. It needs to be done in that exact order so it should take 9-12 minutes. The heat expands your blood vessels, the ice constricts them and the heat expands them again so you get a pump of fresh blood propelled into your muscles. Fresh blood in tired, painful muscles brings with it fresh oxygen and nutrients to help heal your muscles and relieve pain. You can use hot and cold treatment up to five times a day as long you wait at least an hour in between each treatment.

You can also do a version of this in the shower. Stick to the same order of hot, cold, hot but this time you only need 1-2 minutes of each temperature. Be careful with extreme temperatures, you don't want to burn yourself. So go as cold/cool and warm/hot as you can comfortably handle.

Use heated seats

When I got my first car that had heated seats, I had the biggest smile on my face! When you have back pain driving can be a huge aggravation so having heated seats makes the world of difference. If you haven't got heated seats in your car you can buy a heated seat cover that fits over your seat and is powered by the cigarette lighter. You can also use heated seats indoors on a chair. I had two of these for many years after my accident, they really helped with my journey to and from work and sitting at home in my armchair at night. These are a great preventative once you are pain free.

Get a mattress and pillow just for you

Buying a new mattress can be such an expensive task. One of my patients bought four mattresses over a period of two years until he found the best one for him. We are all very individual so annoyingly there is no one size that fits all. Thankfully there are now lots of companies that have a money-back return so if you buy their mattress and you don't like it you can send it back free of charge within a set period of time.

I've personally been through six mattresses over the last two years and I'm finally happy with what I had originally, a Sealy posturepedic. There are so many choices these days between memory foam, latex, gel etc. Then what firmness do you choose, soft, medium or hard? It really is whatever suits you. I'm a huge fan of the Sealy posturepedic range and the Simmons suite range but that's just my preference for my spine.

My recommendations to find a mattress to suit you is to first try companies that offer a money-back guarantee. It's a hassle arranging delivery and collection but you don't lose any money in the process. If that doesn't work, I would ask your friends and family members if you can sleep on their bed for a night to see if their mattress suits you. That way at least you could rule out certain makes and models during your search. Also, if you ever stay the night in a hotel and sleep well, make a note of the mattress then search the internet to see if you can find one to buy, that's how I found out about the Simmons suite mattresses!

Pillows are as important as mattresses and again, everyone is different. The same as mattresses: I would ask your friends and family members if you can try theirs out for a night. Otherwise, I would definitely suggest trying out a camping pillow. My sister introduced me to these amazing self-inflatable lightweight pillows. You can put as much air in as you want, so you can experiment with the height and feel of it every night. The one she uses is called EXPED but they are easily available to buy at camping shops or via the internet. I was amazed at how well I slept, plus the bonus is you can take it travelling with you!

One thing to note is when you buy a new mattress it can take a few days to get used to it so bear with it for at least a week. If it makes your pain worse after seven days, it most definitely is not for you.

Do Pilates

I refer a vast majority of my patients for Pilates classes. Pilates is an awesome technique for strengthening your core and lower back. Regardless whether you are in classes or a one-to-one session you can go at your own pace so it usually doesn't matter what stage of healing you are. You will usually perform a lot of core work which is great to maintain a strong spine.

Swim with care

Swimming is great if you initially stick to back stroke. I can say from personal experience that back stroke is usually the safest stroke when you have back pain. Front crawl is a possibility depending on what level of healing you're at but breast stroke is a total no-no. A therapist once told me I could swim while on holiday so I did breast stroke for three mornings in a row. I wondered why I was in more pain every day – as soon as I stopped swimming my pain decreased. It is best to wait until your back pain reduces and you become more stable, before trialling breast stroke. When you are ready to test it, see how you feel during your swim, straight after and the following day. If your pain doesn't increase, then you're good to go.

23

Do wall angels

Wall angels is an awesome rehab strength exercise which has been around for many years (p23). Although it focuses on your mid back, upper back and neck, it is fantastic for your spine in general, especially for people who have kyphosis. When we're stressed we tend to slouch forward so this is great for anyone with back issues. I describe this exercise in full in chapter 16.

Do basic yoga

Yoga is like doing an hour of stretching combined with body weight strength work. I would advise sticking to a basic class to begin with. Whatever you do, don't attend an hour's bikram yoga class if you've just been diagnosed with a herniated disc. For anyone newly diagnosed with any disc issue, yoga is best avoided in the early stages of recovery. My friend Marcia is an excellent yoga teacher and understands the body very well. If you go to a class just tell the teacher that you're recovering from a back issue and they should help you stick to poses that won't aggravate you. However, like swimming, yoga is one of those types of exercises to be trialled; a basic class or home DVD is usually OK but if you are in a really bad way, you may want to avoid it until you're in less pain and feeling more stable.

Stretch

Gentle stretching is advisable for anyone with back pain, regardless of what your issue is. The most important thing to remember is: ALWAYS stretch to tension, NEVER to pain. Typically, stretches are best held for 15 seconds. Stretching is a great when combined with deep breathing, more on that later. There are some stretches to avoid with particular back issues but I explain all the necessary stretches you need for back pain in chapter 18.

24

25

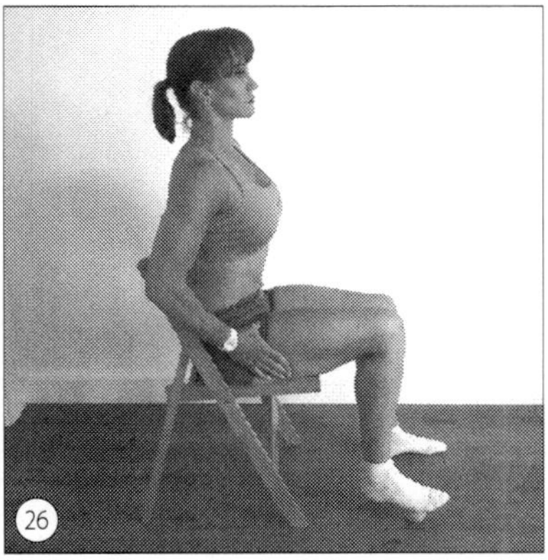
26

Maintain good posture at your desk

Sitting down all day aggravates back pain, a LOT. Just being aware of having good posture at your desk can help massively (p24). The more you self-correct, the better (p25). I have a great tip for posture at your desk in chapter 20. Some companies provide ergonomic help for sitting at your desk. If you work from home or if your job doesn't provide this service check your desk height. Ideally your hips, knees, elbows and feet should be bent around 90-100 degrees. If your feet are dangling around then you may need a stool for under your feet.

Ride a bicycle

Gently riding a bicycle (in a gym is very safe) can really help in various ways. Firstly, you increase blood flow which helps to relieve pain. Secondly, you get a release of endorphins (feel good hormones) from exercise. I would recommend doing your glute exercises first, cycle on an upright bike, do some core work then have a gentle stretch afterwards. If you have access to a steam room or sauna, either one is a great way to finish off after your cycle and stretch. You will feel great for doing something constructive to help your back pain.

Tennis ball roll

A lot of people who suffer back pain also suffer pain, soreness and/or stiffness in their feet. For some people this may turn into a condition called plantar fasciitis (foot and heel pain). If this gets really bad you will need treatment on your feet; ART, IASTM tools and reflexology are great for this. For others, your feet may just feel tight and sore so a tennis ball roll would really help. There is a full description of how to do the tennis ball roll (p26) in the rehabilitation stretches chapter (18).

The other bonus with tennis ball rolling is that it elongates a long line of fascia from your feet all the way up to your lower back, which releases your hamstrings without even touching them!

Take magnesium at night

Sleep is such an important aspect of healing, so many processes occur when we sleep including growth and repair for injuries. Magnesium is not only a natural aid for sleep but it's also a natural anti-inflammatory so it can help reduce pain and inflammation. I explain this in detail in the next chapter, which is solely about sleep.

Counselling

This is one of the best psychological aids while suffering back pain. When you're in pain you may not always want to talk to your partner, friends or family members because you feel like a burden. Talking to a neutral person one-to-one or in a group with people suffering the same thing allows you to expel negativity out of your system. In my experience, negativity really hinders recovery whereas positivity is one of the main aspects of healing so being able to vent is a big deal. If you feel you can talk to your friends, family and colleagues then great. If not, seek a counsellor – it'll be worth it. More on this, later in the book.

Should you not? No!

Be wary driving a manual car

Driving a manual car can really aggravate lower back pain. This is because changing gears with your arm and leg affects your spine and not in a good way. Obviously it's not cheap to change your car but if you can borrow a friend or family member's car who has an automatic, it may be worth it until you are in less pain and feel more stable. If this is not possible, it is a good idea to try and cut down on the amount you drive until you feel better.

Avoid long drives

I've treated quite a few patients in their 20's, who have developed back pain within eight to twelve weeks after starting new jobs that required long hours of driving. This happened to my friend James Guiney who is a loyal patient of mine and has always used treatment as a preventative with his busy work and training schedule. His job installing and maintaining high-end weight training equipment became very intense when he started driving for extremely long hours followed by installing very heavy equipment. He ended up in tremendous pain with horrid stiffness. Now he stays overnight in a hotel or with friends to avoid extremely long hours behind the wheel. He also bought a bigger car that suits his back for longer drives. I am happy to report that he is pain free and back to having treatment as maintenance, not out of necessity!

Long drives can massively aggravate you and are also dangerous especially if you are on pain medication. You may feel ok but all it takes is a split second to have an accident. So I would suggest if possible, share the driving with your partner, friend or colleague, have regular breaks and make sure you have a good stretch when you get out at the other end.

Avoid horse riding

Within a few months of my car accident, I was advised that I could go back to horse riding. I cannot tell you how bad that advice was. I was in absolute agony for nearly 10 days afterwards. Horse riding is a wonderful hobby which uses muscles in your whole body especially your spine. If you have weak muscles and an unstable spine, horse riding can aggravate you so I would wait until you're closer to being pain free before you even think about getting back on a horse. When you are ready to trial horse riding it may be worth getting a horse-riding protector to keep you stable. For more information check out the body protectors under safety equipment at the British Equestrian Trade Association website at www.beta-uk.org

Avoid soft sofas

Like driving a manual car, changing your sofa/couch is no cheap or easy feat. I have many patients who complain that their pain is worse when they sit on their sofa every night. The minute they are able to change their sofa to a sturdier one, their pain gets better. If you can't afford to change your couch, maybe get yourself a big cushion to sit on so you have more stability when you sit and your spine will be more upright.

Alternate sitting and standing

Standing still and sitting for long periods of time can seriously aggravate back pain. This is usually a sign of weak muscles so I would suggest that you get up and walk around as often as you can and stretch your quads for 15 seconds through the day. As I mentioned previously, try and train your brain to stretch your quads every time you go to the toilet so it becomes a routine. You will find variations of quad stretches in chapter 18.

Standing desks are a great alternative at home or where you work. It means you can alternate standing and sitting through the day which may bring you a lot of relief. Plus, while you're standing you can perform your glute tenses, a rehab strength exercise! Glute rehab exercises can be found in chapter 15.

Avoid bad gym machines

27

28

After having back pain for many years I can honestly say the worst machine I've ever used is the seated recumbent bike, the one where you lean back (p27). Back then I was told that it was made for people who were suffering with back pain. Well I can tell you from personal experience, it can GIVE you back pain. It is without doubt the worst machine ever made for a bad back! It's so poorly designed that healthy people I know have experienced back pain after using it. Even when you're pain free I would always suggest to stick to an upright bike, the one where you lean forward (p28).

Avoid long walks

Occasionally one of my patients attends a treatment session and states that they are feeling worse. The first thing I ask them is have they done something to aggravate their pain. Often enough they say no, all they did was go on a long walk. If your glutes are weak and not supporting your lower back walking can make you 10 times worse especially if you have a weak core. Follow the rehabilitation programme (end of chapter 17) for two to three weeks then try a small walk and build yourself up from there.

Your injury will not fix itself

A large number of people continue to live in pain without seeking help for so long that by the time they seek help their issue takes longer to resolve. If you've had back pain on and off for many years and it is NOT going away, I would suggest get it looked at asap so it doesn't become more of a long-term issue. Everything you need to know is in this book!

Get off the NSAIDs

I DO NOT advocate taking three times the dose of NSAIDs or painkillers especially while drinking alcohol. I certainly DO NOT suggest using alcohol as a painkiller. Medication should NEVER exceed the maximum dose. If you are in extreme pain, you may not have a choice to take pain medication but as your pain lessens try to wean yourself off NSAIDs and painkillers/opioids as quickly as possible.

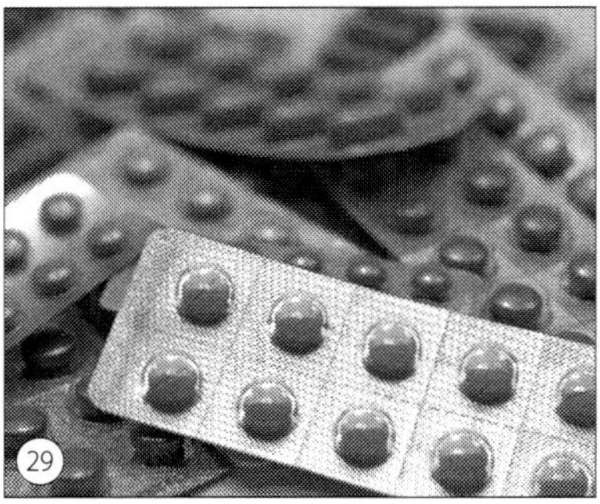
29

NSAIDS can often have the opposite effect to what they are intended (p29). I've seen patients of mine stop using them (when they feel able to) and their pain and inflammation has reduced within days.

Please note that NSAIDs and painkillers can hinder your gut function – a lot. So many important processes happen in your gut for healing purposes. I ended up getting a stomach ulcer because I was taking a large amount of prescribed painkillers and NSAIDs daily for three years. This is a huge subject and I explain this is in detail later in the book.

Instead of using NSAIDs, fish oil and magnesium (described in chapter 11) would be good alternatives. Magnesium is a natural anti-inflammatory and fish oil helps to reduce your inflammatory response (described in chapter 13), they can both lead to a reduction in pain, particularly in your joints. Fish oil is not a direct painkiller like others on the market; however it is a very powerful anti-inflammatory. Taking 3g of fish oil a day can also aid depression although that is over long-term use of around three months for it to have that specific effect. Regardless, I personally recommend 3g of fish oil a day for a reduction in joint pain, arthritis and joint stiffness. I take Omega 3 Plus Finest Fish Oil (orange flavoured capsules or liquid) from Aliment Nutrition (www.alimentnutrition.co.uk); they are the highest potency fish oil in the world and totally contaminant (heavy metals/mercury) free. Fish oil should always be free of heavy metals.

Don't give up!

A year after my car accident I was told by a physiotherapist that 'time would heal me'. On a scale of 0-10 if 0 is nothing and 10 is agony I was a 30 out of 10 in pain even though I was taking a serious amount of very strong prescribed NSAIDs and painkillers. I will never forget how badly my stomach flipped when I was told 'time will heal you' and I thought: this is my life now, my life is all about pain, I was devastated and instantly wanted to give up. I NEVER EVER want anyone to be in that situation, which is the whole reason for writing this book. You have a problem and I have a solution.

I would urge you to NEVER give up (p30). There is ALWAYS a way to feel better. I've come across countless numbers of patients who were told they would never play their sport again; they would never jog or swim again – but they all do. Positivity is one of life's cheapest, easiest therapies, it costs nothing but time and effort and it can help so much when you think your life is nothing else but pain. Keep your thumbs turned up not down!

I discuss many tools for positivity in the next few chapters. After my crash, I lost every ounce of hope

and faith that I would ever become back pain free. I didn't believe it at first but when I did, I started seeing progress. It was a really long journey for me but I want it to be a really quick one for you!

*NB: Please remember these are my suggestions purely based on my personal experiences and from what I've learnt through my education. Please ALWAYS check with your doctor or functional medicine/health practitioner before taking any natural health supplements, especially if you have a medical condition.

11

To Sleep Or Not To Sleep?

Have you ever wondered why being in pain makes you feel so exhausted at the end of each day? I must admit I did think about it a lot but I didn't understand it back then. Pain is physically exhausting and mentally draining. You may not realise how important a good night's sleep is for healing injuries – I certainly didn't.

Why is sleep so important for recovery?

When you are injured your body has to work much, much harder, so you need good quality sleep to help with your recovery. Having back pain tends to lead to a lot of muscular dysfunction which makes you walk incorrectly, so essentially your body has to use your muscles in a way that you're not accustomed to. Using muscles this way exerts far more energy, so walking or moving in general becomes an actual workout. As if that isn't stressful enough, if you have a trauma associated with it (such as a fall or accident), your body has to deal with that too.

Another thing that happens when you're in pain is your body tends to tense more often as a protection mechanism. This is called muscle guarding and your brain does this subconsciously so that you don't hurt yourself any more than you need to. Consequently, you stay in 'alert mode' which affects your sympathetic nervous system (I explain this in the 'stressed and depressed' chapter). Having to stay alert all the time uses even more brain power and thus more energy. Hence, sleep is one of the key aspects of recovery. By night-time you just want to flake out, the problem is pain doesn't always let you.

When you sleep, a lot of repair takes place while your body and your brain can rest, so more energy can be spent on repairing your muscles through the production of hormones which stimulate growth and repair. Also, during your sleep cycle less blood flow is needed to get to your brain as it rests, so more blood can be supplied to your muscles for recovery. When you get stressed from pain, sleep can be affected in a big way, growth and repair can become limited and subsequently slow down your recovery.

On average we should sleep around eight hours a night, straight through the night. A lot of people tell me they wake up in the middle of the night to go to the toilet because they drink too much water before they go to bed. Water should not make any difference to your ability to sleep through the night. We weren't designed that way; if your body works properly you should sleep straight through the night regardless. Sometimes you might wake up but not go to the toilet – this could be for various reasons such as stress, fatigue, anxiety, alcohol, hormonal issues, deficiency in protein and/or vitamins and minerals. Over time sleep deprivation can cause weight gain as well as depression.

Trying to sleep when you're in pain can be very stressful. I was an insomniac (someone who is unable to sleep) at the time of my car crash because of a trauma I went through as a teenager. Regardless, suffering so much pain after my accident made my troubled sleep 10 times worse.

It can be hard to get comfortable in the first place. You find yourself shifting around in bed (or trying to) so much that it makes you more stressed so you either get up, cry or just stay awake and feel even worse. An increase in stress can lead to a decrease in sleep. On that note, I have listed some suggestions to help improve your sleep.

20 tips to help you sleep

1 Use heat on your back where you feel pain 30 minutes before you to go to bed. You can use a hot water bottle or hot/wheat pack (you heat this in a microwave for 2 minutes) on your back. When you apply heat to your body blood flow increases which helps alleviate pain and soreness. Subsequently, this puts you in a calm and peaceful state of mind, which can help you to fall asleep. It is a good idea to use a small amount of cold water in your hot water bottle so it doesn't burn your skin; padded/furry water bottle covers are good for that too. If you wake up in the middle of the night, you could use heat again to help calm you down. As you start to feel sleepy, take the hot water bottle/pack off and put it on your bedside table or on the floor.

2 Try to avoid sleeping on your front. This puts your neck into a really twisted position which can play havoc with your back pain. It can be painful to lie on your back too so lying on your side is usually the best option. However, if you can lie on your back you may be more comfortable with a pillow under your knees. If you have a prolapsed or herniated disc injury you may find your pain free side easier to lie on until you gain strength on your injured side. For some of you it may be more comfortable to lie on your side with a pillow in-between your legs. I did this for a few years. This usually means you have weakness on one or both sides of your glutes. Turning in bed can be a real challenge so it's best to bend both knees first, then turn slowly using your hands to support you. As you get stronger your sleep symptoms should change – this is a great marker for you to know that you are recovering and getting stronger.

3 There are various natural health supplements that can help you sleep such as valerian root, phosphatidyl serine, inositol and melatonin (Xie et al., 2017). Taking valerian root extract* is great for lowering stress and anxiety levels. A good valerian root supplement should always be very smelly! Phosphatidyl serine is very good for depression, improving your memory and helps you sleep through the night. Inositol* is known as vitamin B8 and is used to help insomnia, depression and anxiety by trying to re-balance your brain chemicals (neurotransmitters) especially when you're stressed. It helps regulate your nervous system and it can act as an anti-depressant. If you're really stressed the recommended dose could have the opposite effect and keep you awake half the night. I was advised to always start with a small dose and increase it slowly. Melatonin is a hormone released from the pineal gland in your brain which makes you sleepy and helps control your sleep/wake cycle (internal body clock). It also helps your brain to detoxify waste products. Recommended dosages are 400mg valerian root extract*, 100-300mg phosphatidyl serine*, 500mg inositol* (start with a small dose and build up to 500mg), 1-3g melatonin*, all to be taken 30-60 minutes before bedtime. If your sleep is really bad you could increase melatonin by 1mg per night until you find what works for you. Please bear in mind that some people feel groggy after taking melatonin, remember everyone is different so this may not be for you. Most people take an average of 3-5mg. I would suggest only taking ONE of these supplements, not all of them, and it's always best to start with a lower dose first.

4 There are many herbs that can help with anxiety and depression and help your body to deal with stress. For those of you that have suffered long-term stress then schisandra berry*,

ashwagandha* or rhodiola rosea* may be able to help you (Chan, 2012), (Pratte et al., 2014). I tried taking rhodiola rosea at a recommended dose of 300mg but it kept me awake so I cut it down to 100mg and that worked really well. Rhodiola should be taken earlier in the day to avoid interfering with sleep. Schisandra berry and ashwagandha are adaptogens so they can stimulate energy or give you a sedating effect depending on what you need. The recommended dosages are; rhodiola rosea 100-300mg after breakfast, schisandra 1000mg-1500mg (1g-1.5g) 30-60 minutes before bed and ashwagandha is 500-1000mg after breakfast and/or after dinner. I started taking ashwagandha at night but my sleep wasn't as good so I found it worked better for me taking it after breakfast, everyone is different. I have tried all of these herbs at different stages but always one at a time and they've all worked very well. Taking ONE of these supplements daily with magnesium (listed below) is a great combination. When you're stressed these herbs really help to support your adrenal glands especially if you've been suffering long-term pain. Your adrenal glands have many functions but one of the most important is controlling your reaction to stress whether it be from injury, disease or otherwise. Supporting your adrenal glands with these types of herbs helps to balance your response to stress which is very difficult when you're in pain and can't sleep.

5 Magnesium is a powerful, natural health supplement for sleep but it has many other benefits that help with back pain. You could use Epsom salt (magnesium citrate) baths as I mentioned previously but if you find it really hard to fall asleep, try taking 300-500mg magnesium* after your dinner. Magnesium has many different uses; it has anti-inflammatory properties, it induces relaxation, calms your nervous system and helps to inhibit muscle cramps. There are many forms of magnesium but for anyone suffering back pain I recommend magnesium taurate or magnesium glycinate. Taurine is a great supplement to take at night because it increases your neurotransmitter GABA which helps your brain to calm and switch off for sleep. When taurate is combined with magnesium as magnesium taurate you get two for the price of one! Glycine alone helps to combat inflammation and acts as a precursor to boost levels of glutathione (your body's most powerful anti-oxidant) which can help increase your energy levels, it's also great as a sleep aid. It is fairly common for glutathione levels to deplete when you are stressed. Magnesium combined with glycine as magnesium glycinate is a very efficient, natural supplement to help you sleep and give you energy. Magnesium can also improve your gut health by helping to break down food for easier absorption when you eat. This process slows down when you are stressed. Gut health is very important when you're in pain – I explain this is in great detail in the next chapter.

6 Try having some herbal teas during the daytime to help lower your stress and inflammation levels – ginger, licorice root, schisandra and turmeric are great.

7 Try to go to sleep and wake up at a similar time every day, it helps your circadian rhythm. This is your internal body clock that monitors your natural sleep/wake cycle. In an ideal world we are meant to wake up around 6am-7am and go to sleep around 10pm-11pm. For people who work night shifts or have newborn babies, this can get extremely tricky. Working through the night and waking up constantly in pain or to feed your baby upsets your circadian rhythm. This is where supplements and other sleep aids can help.

8 Use dark, lined curtains or blackout blinds, and you'll be surprised at the difference in the quality of your sleep with no light coming through from street lights or car headlights. This helps you to produce more melatonin.

9 Try using an eye mask while you sleep to help block out light if you don't have blackout curtains. This also helps you to produce more melatonin.

10 If you have trouble falling asleep try doing a grateful log before bed. It's a well-known strategy to calm your brain. When you are stressed and in pain, you can keep yourself awake with negative thoughts so the grateful log is a very powerful way to combat this. You can write it or say it; I prefer to speak it. Either write or say 20 things that you are grateful for such as your loved one, your job, your house and other things in your life that make you happy... like being around your family or having great friends. The more you think about things you're grateful for, the more positive you'll feel. The reason for this is that positive thinking instills an instant positive physiological response which in turn calms your brain and helps you to 'switch off' and sleep well.

11 Turn off your mobile phone, laptop or iPad if you leave them in your bedroom or if you live in a studio apartment. Better still, leave them in another room on silent (with vibration turned off) or turned off, well away from where you sleep. This allows your brain to rest from the neurological activity of computerised equipment. Your brain works through various waves of electrical frequencies from the most active to the least active and if there is any electrical signal close by, even if it is a lower frequency, it can keep your brain alert and prevent you from being able to switch off properly. Even if you have your phone on silent next to your bed it can still keep your brain awake.

12 Turn off every electrical socket in your bedroom before you sleep to allow your brain to rest and de-stress.

13 Avoid using a laptop for at least an hour before bed. This allows your brain to stop thinking about work or personal issues so you can wind down and get into sleep mode. My personal laptop and tablet curfew is two hours before bed. If your sleep is very bad, I would suggest having a curfew three hours before bed so you can focus on pure relaxation to sleep well.

14 Use a battery-powered alarm clock to help you wake up rather than your mobile/cell phone. This type of alarm clock uses batteries so it doesn't keep your brain awake. They are very cheap and the batteries usually last for ages. If you travel a lot, it may be worth investing in a small alarm clock that doesn't take up much room in your suitcase.

15 Try reading a fictional book or a magazine that is non-work related before sleep, it can take your mind away from pain, work and personal issues and allows your brain to get into sleep mode. I like to watch a programme on TV that is either comedy based or a dating programme like 'First Dates', one that will give me a happy feeling. These types of programmes promote positivity that help calm your brain to wind down.

16 This may sound weird but regulating your body temperature through your feet can help you sleep. If it's extremely cold weather you may want to keep your socks on all night but if the weather is hot you may fall asleep easier by taking them off; it depends on your individual body heat. Body temperature is important to fall asleep and to stay asleep.

17 Eat your last meal/snack two hours before you sleep, to allow your digestion system to rest. Your body needs time to digest food after you eat which can keep you awake.

18 Try using breathing techniques before bed. I think it is one of the best ways to help you fall asleep along with the use of heat. There are many different types of breathing techniques which can help you to de-stress very quickly. I'll talk more about this subject in the following chapter.

19 Try to limit your coffee intake and avoid having it late in the day. Coffee contains a lot of caffeine which is a stimulant and can keep your brain awake at night. This is because the stimulating effects of coffee can take up to eight hours to wear off. Some black teas also contain caffeine. Everyone has a different reaction to coffee which can depend a lot on your genetics. Some people can drink coffee in the evening and it won't affect their sleep. For most people, coffee is best taken earlier in the day and not after 4pm, for some people their cut off is 2pm. It is also recommended to have no more than 4 cups a day because of the stimulating effect that caffeine has on your brain. Having too much tea and coffee and drinking them too late in the day can interfere with your sleep. I can't have caffeine because I have a brain injury but even as a decaf drinker I still avoid drinking tea and decaf coffee after 4pm because it has hindered my sleep when I've had it in the evening.

20 Avoid drinking too much alcohol. It is a well-known fact that alcohol dehydrates you so it can interrupt your sleep if taken in larger amounts. A lot of patients tell me if they have a few drinks they usually wake up at 3-4am super thirsty and have to visit the toilet so the next day they feel very de-hydrated and their pain is worse. Everyone needs an emotional release but if large amounts of alcohol are clearly affecting your sleep it may be a good idea to cut down until you feel better. Remember, hydration is important for your intervertebral discs.

*NB: Please remember these are my suggestions purely based on my personal experiences and from what I've learnt through my education. Please ALWAYS check with your doctor or functional medicine/health practitioner before taking any natural health supplements, especially if you have a medical condition.

Lack of sleep and high stress levels can lead to weight gain so when they are combined, your weight can escalate and give you another reason to feel low. I put on 2 stone (12 kg) in weight after my car accident and it made me feel so much worse on top of the pain and inhibitions. Regardless sleep is very important for healing and should be a top priority for your recovery.

That is a long list of tips so I would suggest experimenting with them bit by bit. Two more things to factor in with sleep aids are nutrition and gut health. They are both very important for a good quality sleep and to help with your ability to deal with the stress of daily pain. Being deficient in various proteins, vitamins and antioxidants can prevent you sleeping through the night too. More on this in chapter 13.

12
Stressed & Depressed

Invisibility & inhibitions

Have you ever got to the stage where you feel you're in so much pain, you will never experience normality ever again and you will be in pain for the rest of your life? Do you ever think nothing can help you so you will have to pretend to enjoy life forever? Do you even remember what is was like to live pain free? Those are horribly sad thoughts. Nobody should EVER have to suffer in pain and most definitely NEVER have to suffer in silence.

In my experience, there are two things almost worse than the pain itself; the first is, pain is invisible and the other is, the crazy amount of life inhibitions. I don't know what's worse, suffering pain, suffering pain in silence or not being able to do a long list of simple daily tasks and activities. Whether it's with family, friends or colleagues, you know there are activities you simply cannot do any more so life then becomes difficult to plan anything. If a friend says let's go to the cinema, your first thought is "Will the seat be comfortable?" or "Will I be close to the exit so I can get up and walk around?" In that case you'll miss part of the movie but you know that's the only way you can join in with the activity. If a family member says "Hey, let's go for a walk in the park and have a picnic," your first thought is "I can't walk too far because my back will hurt even more, my nephew and my niece will want me to swing them around and it will make my pain worse".

This type of thinking becomes the norm and the inhibitions can really get you down. What do people say if you are honest with them and express how much pain you are in? "Well, you look alright!" That is the most frustrating and annoying sentence to hear for someone who is suffering in pain. People mean well but it is hard not to take comments like that personally. You cannot see pain and most people who are suffering know very, very well how to disguise it; they just deal with it.

It's interesting how many of the patients I treat don't talk to anyone and go through very similar days as described above. Some people who are referred to me by their colleagues say they had no idea their work-friend was in pain. This is a very typical scenario.

Onset of depression

Does this day sound familiar...? You're travelling to work on a tube/train and you desperately want a seat but of course nobody will give it up because they cannot see your anguish. The jerking from being on a bus, coach or train makes you wince but there's nothing you can do, you just have to suffer in silence. Then you get to work and you don't bother telling your colleagues because you don't want your pain interfering with your job. Then again, you might mention your pain to colleagues once or twice but then decide you don't want to burden anyone with your problems.

So you suffer the pain, in silence, and by the end of the day your pain is unbearable so you leave your workplace faking a smile to your boss and colleagues and go home feeling worse than when you arrived, in agony. The journey home is worse than on your way to work because you are now more fatigued. When you get home you moan to your partner about how bad you feel but then you start feeling like a burden again so eventually you just keep it to yourself – it's easier that way.

Or... If you're a mum or dad at home, you suffer in silence because your child or children cannot comprehend why mummy or daddy is looking upset or even crying, because they are too young to understand. You cook, clean, wash, do all the daily chores that are required, in pain, and say nothing to anyone because you are alone. You consider talking to a friend about your agony, if they are willing to listen but eventually you don't want to feel like a burden so you just stay silent. If you have a partner, they come home and at first you feel like you can have a good moan about how bad you feel but then you start feeling like a burden again, so you just keep it to yourself and suffer in silence. After all pain is invisible, it's hard to gain sympathy when nobody can see your physiological distress.

Eventually you just stop talking to anyone except maybe to your physical therapist, psychologist, or your doctor – or nobody. It's often the case that people prefer to talk to someone who isn't close to them because they feel less of a burden. Alongside suffering in silence, pain causes you to stop socialising so you become a bit of a hermit outside of work and eventually you realise that you're in a deep depression. For some of you this may not be a typical scenario but for some of you, you may go through this EVERY day – I did and it was soul destroying.

Depression is HORRID, there are no other words for it. It is a typical, nasty, horrible consequence of pain. When depression sets in, it's amazing how you learn to 'fake it' every day. You are able to go through a whole day without anybody realising what you are going through. I've found that men are usually worse than women with regard to opening up to talk about how they feel. That said, I've come across some females where you literally have to pull it out of them. Either way depression is a huge topic to discuss if you're suffering with back pain.

The consequences of depression can change your personality. Some people can continue faking it for a very long time whereas others simply get to a point where they literally have had enough. These consequences can have serious implications to the point of suicide. I have tears in my eyes writing this because of people I know who have been so severely depressed due to pain that they have taken their own lives. I came very close myself, more than once after my car crash. This is a typical scenario if you've suffered head trauma. It is also typical of thousands of people who suffer pain regardless of the cause. In layman's terms, over time your brain chemicals start to imbalance from the stress that affects your gut (I explain this in the next chapter) and poor gut health which also affects your ability to produce 'calming' feel-good brain chemicals. Eventually your brain chemicals become so imbalanced that you can end up crying daily and wanting the ground to open and swallow you up.

On a side note if you are suffering back pain because you had an accident that involved head trauma, you may have been diagnosed with a traumatic brain injury (TBI). In this type of situation your hormones imbalance instantly - the severity of the imbalance is very individual. It is typical to suffer a head injury and instantly gain weight and become depressed soon after the event. The first time I interned with Dr Serrano (a genius specialist medical doctor in the US) one of the first things we talked about was head trauma. He said, "I bet you put on weight and got depressed after your accident?" I was shocked and thought he was a psychic until he made me research the subject. TBI's have a massive knock-on effect with your gut health which leads to a decline in your immune system so repairing your gut should be high on your list of priorities. I will explain the relationship between your brain and your gut health and why it affects pain in the next chapter.

Motivation

Motivation is the act of behaviour in a certain way. More so, I explain it as having a desire or need to do something and that desire has different levels. High levels of motivation can mean you have a very strong desire to walk up a set of stairs knowing you may not be strong enough, nothing can stop you and you don't need any help from anyone, you pretty much feel like superman. Whereas low motivation could mean you have no desire to even brush your hair or teeth even though you know you need to. I remember letting my laundry build up for weeks because I had no motivation to do any washing (or anything for that matter), such a simple task.

Motivation can often be driven by incentives. Knowing you will feel better after doing an exercise may increase your motivation to perform it. However, asking a depressed person to motivate themselves, just get over it, stop being useless and do something is no easy task. It's not because they don't want to, it's because they have no choice. You may as well ask your dog to tell you what it wants for dinner.

Depression has many causes and is very typical of someone coping with daily pain and the stresses that come with it. Pain is stressful, faking a smile every day is stressful, walking differently is stressful and coping with stress is stressful. They all have a serious effect on your bodily functions; your immune system, your gut, your hormones and your brain chemistry (chemicals that affect your mood and bodily functions). All of the aforementioned can disrupt your sleep which only exacerbates the situation. The less you sleep, the less you recover, the worse your gut health is and the more your brain chemicals can imbalance. This can leave you feeling alone, sad and desperate, with little or no self-worth. You end up feeling soulless.

When you are in total despair it may seem like you are in a hopeless situation but there is a way out of that dark, grim, dingy, ugly hole. I call it 'baby steps of control'. Coping with daily pain and stress usually means there are lots things that are out of your control which leads to frustration. Using baby steps to take back even just a little bit of control can give you a sense of self-efficacy – your personal belief in your ability to accomplish a task, however simple it may be.

Small steps of self-efficacy can help you to regain control of your life which in turn leads to self-confidence and an increase in your motivation. Baby steps of control means being realistic, asking yourself to do 10 lots of laundry is too much, start with one, that's enough. That way it's not too much of an overwhelming thought but one you know you could achieve more easily. It's also VERY important to pat yourself on the back after you have achieved a task too. For instance, performing just one exercise a day deserves a smile and a 'congratulations you did it' comment, even if it's you saying it to yourself. This may sound silly but regardless of how small it may be, achieving small 'baby' tasks in this way is progress and progress means EVERYTHING. Rewarding yourself with progress is self-motivating. Then you know you are on your way to recovery. One baby step at a time.

Support network

Mental health is a serious issue. When pain gets too much and your motivation drops really low you NEED help. One of the ways you can help increase motivation is via counselling. If you are a man or woman with so much pride you think that you don't need help like I did, I would urge you to think again. You would be amazed at how much a counselling session would help you, talking to someone neutral who doesn't know you or have feelings for you and is trained to listen can be very beneficial. It can be a huge relief and this is what I believe is one of the benefits of removing negative, built up emotions from being in pain all day. The relief can instigate an amazing amount of motivation to adhere to your rehab programme but most of all leave you feeling satisfied and in more of a positive state of mind.

It's very satisfying to remove negative feelings and load them onto someone else, preferably someone who is qualified to deal with people who live with pain. I guarantee you that your shoulders will feel like they've dropped a couple of inches after a counselling session. It's good to talk to somebody neutral because they don't know you and have no emotions for you so you don't feel like a burden, at all. More importantly, you don't feel anything for them, which can make you feel very comfortable. For a mental health professional, it is their job to listen to you and advise you without judgement. Some people have issues talking to strangers and prefer to talk to friends and family. However, sometimes friends and family may not be very empathetic or they may not know what to say to you even though they fully sympathise. In that case I would suggest it may be worth talking on the phone to a helpline which might be more comfortable if you don't like the idea of talking to a stranger face to face.

I can only speak for the UK: we have a Samaritans helpline, whereby you can call any time of the day, any day of the week. You can discuss whatever you need to talk about without judgement, mental health is taken very seriously on this helpline and in this country. I don't know how this works in other countries around the world but if you don't have a helpline I would consider talking to your local doctor about counselling. Medical doctors should have contact details of a local clinic you could visit.

Aside from face to face or talking over the phone, without doubt, you need support from family and friends, work colleagues too. Even if you don't feel comfortable talking to family members or close friends, just having their support can help so much. I'm lucky to have some very good friends to support me. When I would go out to socialise, as soon as I walked in the door of a busy bar my friend Marcia would always find me a chair, even if it meant asking a stranger to give up their chair for me. My friend Emma would always ask me how I felt every single time she saw me, we worked together so I saw her 6 days a week. My friend Sharma would always encourage me to talk to her even if it was just to tell silly jokes and make me laugh. If it wasn't for my friend Jasmine I may not have even considered that I was depressed and sought counselling to help deal with it which helped me to talk about depression to my friend Monique. This was a huge weight off my shoulders and made me realise the importance of talking to someone. That kind of support was very much appreciated. I didn't realise how much I needed it at the time.

I would ask you to be brave and talk to your family members, tell them how you really feel, even ask them to read this book so they have some kind of understanding of what kind of agony you go through on a daily basis. It can be difficult for your non-injured partner, family and friends to deal with someone who is in constant pain and suffering because they may feel frustrated by not knowing how they can help you. Now they may get some satisfaction knowing there IS a way to help you by encouraging you to do your exercises and stretches, cook healthy food and take your supplements. Just by asking you "how are you feeling today?" can give you a huge feeling of satisfaction knowing your friend/family member has acknowledged what you are going through. Tell them that. It's a simple question that can provide a huge amount of relief and contentment.

If you can be honest and upfront with your family, friends and colleagues I think you'll be amazed at what reaction you'll get back. It's most satisfying to have your friends say, "I'm here for you, whatever you need", "how are you doing today?" or something along those lines. I consider myself the luckiest person on earth to have friends and family who have stuck by me, always asking if I need help and if there's anything they can do for me or if I just need company. Try it.

There are a lot of other methods that can help you combat depression such as good nutrition, healing your gut and taking specific supplements. I discuss all of these in the following chapter. Of course there are lots of other ways to help cope with depression and help you relax which I can honestly say, they all work.

Relaxation techniques: visualisation

Visualisation was created by yogi's, the people that created yoga. The meaning of yoga is 'reversing the outward flow of consciousness within, to a powerful state of quiet, joy and peace'. Imagine that, feeling joy and peace with no pain? Visualisation, otherwise known as imagery, relaxes your brain and muscles by focusing on a positive situation which can help you recover at record speed.

Find a quiet place, close your eyes and visualise your recovery – or should I say, visualise yourself already being pain free. It is better to imagine a typical scenario of your end outcome rather than the process of you achieving it. To get the most benefit from this process you need to see the images in real time and use all the brain's senses: tasting, smelling, touching, hearing and seeing.

An example of this would be... you're sitting at your desk, you can smell the flowers next to your computer, you answer your phone and feel the warmth of the handset, you feel happy, it's near the end of the day and you are sitting comfortably with no pain or stiffness. You finish an email to your boss and read it again to check there are no mistakes. You can hear your colleague on the phone beside you. You take a sip of your water and taste the tanginess of the fresh lime in your drink. You feel on top of the world, you've had a great day and now you're off to have a fabulous evening at your dance class.

Another example: you hear your baby girl crying, you pick her up and you can smell an odour that tells you she needs her nappy changed. You can feel the warmth of your baby as you pick her up. As you kiss her on her forehead you feel the love you have for her. You feel super capable in this process, you feel strong and happy.

A last example: you see yourself doing a particular exercise, a squat for example... You can hear the clang of weights around you, you can see yourself in the mirror and you feel the weight and temperature of the barbell across your shoulders. You can smell the odour of the gym and you can still taste the sweetness of your intra-workout drink; you feel strong and powerful. You see and feel yourself squat down with the weight of the bar on your shoulders and slowly raise your body back up again. You feel the exhilaration of being able to squat with this amount of weight, with perfect technique and capability. You feel amazing!

Ideally you need to do this daily, it may only take you five minutes but it can decrease your stress and anxiety levels very quickly. It's also a great distraction away from your pain. Regardless, it can enhance your confidence to KNOW that you are healing.

Relaxation techniques: breathing

I suffered daily headaches for three years following my accident. They went away but then came back intermittently four years later and in November 2013 the headaches became one constant pain in my head that I still have now. In 2016, I found out that I had suffered a rather bad, traumatic brain injury (TBI) from my car accident which is the reason for the permanent pain. I'd been suffering brain dysfunction for over 10 years but had put that down to mercury toxicity, that's a big subject for another time. At the time of writing this book (2018) I am still in pain 24 hours a day but it has decreased with the help of my amazing, genius US brain doctor, Dr Peter Jaillet, and regular ART treatment. However, one thing that really helps me to stay calm when my pain gets really bad is using breathing techniques, I wish I had known about these techniques when I had severe back pain because they really do help you to relax and stay calm when you're in a bad place.

Breathing techniques are an awesome way to help depression and put yourself in a state of serenity when you're in pain. They have become more well-known in the fitness industry but they are still fairly uncommon in the therapy realm. These techniques are an immense aid for stress. A lot of people know that we carry stress in our shoulders and neck. What a lot of people don't know is that we ALL carry stress in our diaphragm. When I treat a patient with back pain they usually have a very tight and sore diaphragm particularly on the side of their weak glutes.

Breathing techniques offer a calming effect on your diaphragm and help to promote more oxygen into your body which can aid stress in order to speed up your healing process. These techniques also help: to slow down your heart rate (helps with anxiety), stimulate your lymphatic system (helps get rid of the waste products and helps your immune system), stabilise your torso and spine (this is essential for lower back strength), improve your digestive system (multiple processes happen in the gut that affects stress and depression), balance your endocrine system (explained below) and relax your hip flexors (they are connected to your diaphragm and lower back, healthy hip flexors are essential for a healthy and stable lower back) which have a major impact on back pain and recovery.

Your autonomic nervous system (ANS) is the part of your nervous system responsible for the regulation of various bodily functions such as breathing, heart rate and digestion. The ANS has two divisions, the para-sympathetic nervous system (PSNS) and the sympathetic nervous system (SNS) but "What has this got to do with back pain?" I hear you ask!

Well, the SNS is your 'alert' mode and always ready for action, especially when you get stressed. More importantly when you suffer prolonged periods of stress, like being in pain, you become accustomed to always being in 'alert' mode as I mentioned previously. When your SNS becomes dominant it pushes blood away from your internal organs and flushes it into your muscles so you are always ready for action. That mode can hinder your ability to digest food properly, repair muscles and can suppress your immune system. This can lead to anxiety, constipation, depression, muscle tension and poor quality sleep. This is the exact opposite of your PSNS which helps promote relaxation and assists your body with rest and digestion amongst various other functions. So having a balance between both divides of the ANS can help your recovery in many ways. Specific breathing techniques can help tap into your PSNS 'calming' system in order to help promote serenity, digestion and in turn lower your stress levels.

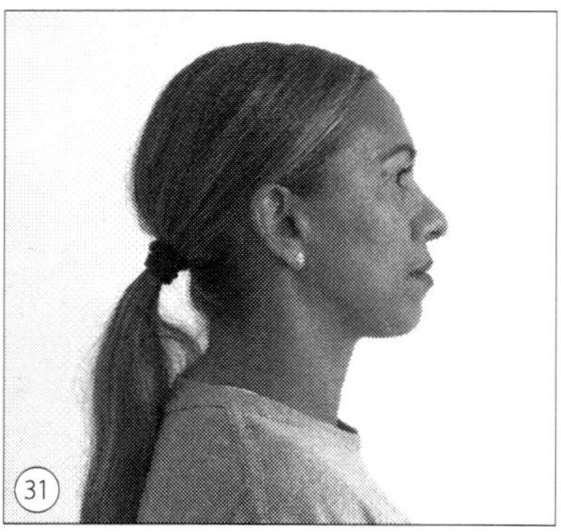

31

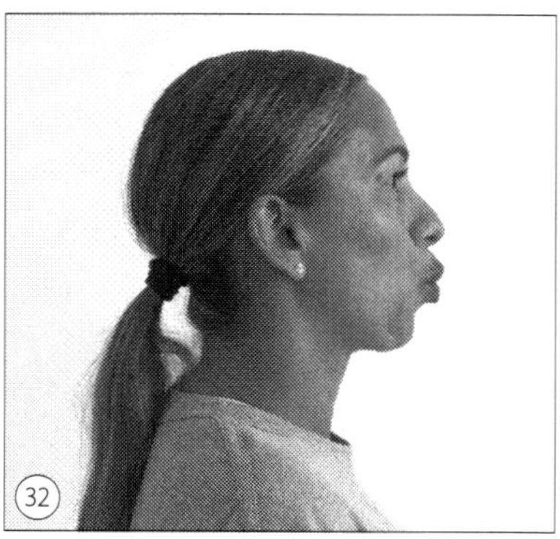

32

By triggering your PSNS it means breathing techniques can induce instant relaxation. This may sound weird while we're talking about back pain but after you've performed your glute, core and lower back exercises, and put a hot water bottle on your back, performing breathing techniques makes for a fabulous package of relaxation and de-stressing for pain.

There are so many styles of breathing techniques, such as Wimhoff, Buteyko, Papworth, 478, and 628. By far, my favourite method is called measured counts which I was taught by Luke Webb, former professional football player (Arsenal FC) turned very successful Director of Football at Bradfield College. He is an ace with psychology tools and is featured a lot in my next book, Back Pain Free for Athletes. Measured counts is a very simple deep breathing exercise to help when you need a quick fix to help you stay balanced, positive and calm. For this type of breathing technique, you count the seconds that you inhale, hold your breath and then exhale. Perform the breaths up to 5 seconds and back down again like a pyramid. You can go higher but I wouldn't recommended higher than 7 seconds.

Close your mouth (p31), inhale through your nose for 1 second (with your mouth closed), hold your breath for 1 second then exhale through your mouth only, with pursed lips, for 1 second (p32). Then inhale for 2 seconds, hold for 2 seconds and exhale for 2 seconds. Continue with this process up to 5 seconds then back down to 4,3,2 and 1 second.

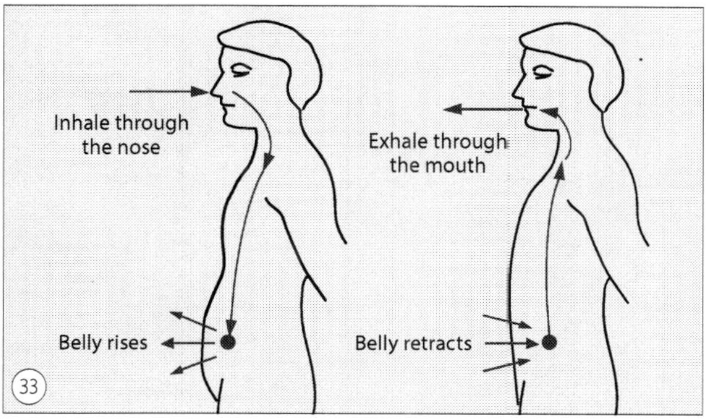

It is important to deep breathe correctly when you perform these techniques. When you inhale, breathe in through your nose, both your chest and your belly should expand and then when you exhale, breathe out through your mouth (with pursed lips) they should both relax (p33).

You can use breathing techniques at any time of the day and they are also great when used as part of a meditation or at night to aid sleep. I've also found deep breathing holds are great when combined with stretching. I explain how to do this in chapter 18.

Relaxation techniques: meditation

Meditation has become very popular in recent years to help people with stress. I am a huge fan of meditation to aid with the recovery of injuries.

I ask almost every patient whether they meditate. For those who are in extreme pain, I suggest meditation as part of their homework. Meditation helps your body to de-stress. If you are worrying about your pain and if you will ever get better, your body will be very stressed from the worry itself. Meditation can help to combat your concerns. It is a way to focus your mind on something whether it be something specific like a candle or a mantra (statement) or listening to someone talk, asking you to think about specific things When it comes to pain relief, meditation is a great way of focusing your attention on something other than your pain, so it is also a great distraction.

Why is meditation so powerful? It regulates your response to stress which can also help to keep your gut healthy. When your brain has perceived emotions about pain or injury, it will have an emotional stress response about those initial emotions. This may sound a bit confusing. In short, we have primary emotions of initial pain from an injury. After a while, your brain then has a secondary emotional reaction to your primary emotions of pain and suffering. Your secondary emotions can be way more intense and last for a very, very long time and eventually turn into agony. This can lead to immense rumination i.e. thoughts of de-stress, I call them the "what if..." thoughts. "What if I am going to be in pain forever?", "What if I can never run again?", "What if I become bedridden?" This is often a subconscious process which can increase the intensity and frequency of your pain. This negative cycle can go on for years.

Meditation can help you tap into those sub-conscious secondary thoughts and make your brain conscious of them pain to give you the chance to do something about it. If you can tap into these secondary thoughts, you can decrease the intensity of your pain enough to distract your brain and allow it to focus on healing.

It is a very powerful way of rising above your pain. There are literally dozens and dozens of types of meditation such as focused attention, mantras, visualisation, zen to name just a few. Science has shown that meditation can help you reduce stress, anxiety and depression and increase your ability to deal with stress (Jerath, Barnes & Crawford, 2014). The only way to experience the benefits of meditation is to try it.

Focused meditation is where you look at an object such as a candle, close your eyes and keep thinking about the object/candle for the duration of time you want to meditate for. If your mind starts wandering, open your eyes to look at the object again, then close your eyes and try to focus only on the object. This may sound quite boring but it can be rather difficult when you first try it, it's a real challenge!

Guided meditation is probably one of the more common types of meditation around. It's a verbal guide where someone tells you what to think of while your eyes are closed, and there is normally calming music in the background. This takes the focus off you so you can listen to someone telling you what to do and, before you know it, you're totally focused on the voice and comforting music, relaxing you and distracting you from your pain. There are lots of guided meditations available on the internet.

Mantra statements are one of my favourite types of meditation which I suggest to a lot of my patients, athletes and anyone I know in pain. For this type of meditation, you pick one to five specific positive statements and keep repeating them and that is all you focus on. I always suggest using the words 'I am'. From my own research and experience, I have found that 'I am' are two of the most powerful words in the universe. Whether you are a believer in that or not those two words are a done deal, a given statement that says something has already happened. So you could say "I am perfectly healthy" or "I am playing football" or "I am swimming with my children". These statements also bring about positive thoughts and memories, which promote a positive physiological response, one of the principal players in the healing game. If you can change negative to positive, then you are winning!

Positive visualisation is another one of my favourites that I practise daily. As described previously visualisation can also be used as a meditation. Remember to use all the senses of the brain and imagine the situation in real time. You could also add a few mantra statements in your visualisation to make it even more powerful - that's what I do!

Breathing techniques can be used as a meditation by way of focusing on how you are breathing. Focus on every breath and how you feel with each breath inhaling through your nose and exhaling through your mouth. Counting your breaths is helpful too. This is a great way of eliminating distraction and calming your mind and body.

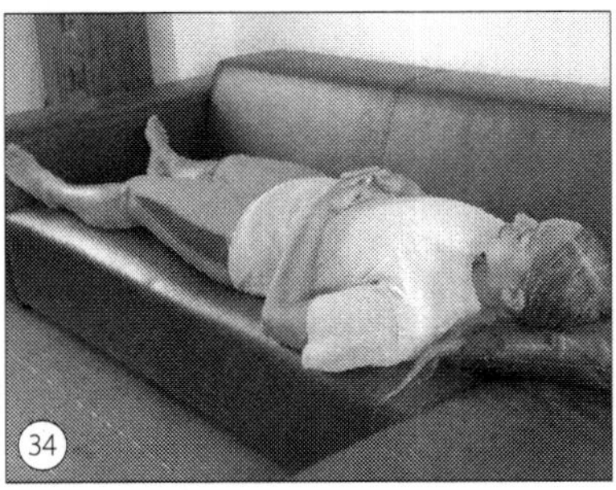
34

The best way to meditate is to find a quiet place, sit or lie down, close your eyes and away you go (p34). If you are focusing on an object, make sure you can see it easily if you need to keep opening your eyes. I would avoid crossing your legs if you're seated on a chair; this is not advisable for someone with back pain. If you're at home, then you could lie down on your sofa or on your bed first thing in the morning, after work or last thing at night when you have free time. It really doesn't matter what time of day you do it. Adopting a hand position is optional; common ones are a prayer position (p35) (enhances balance and energy), touching your thumb and first finger together (p36) (heightens calmness) or interlaying your fingers together (p37) (generates loving energy).

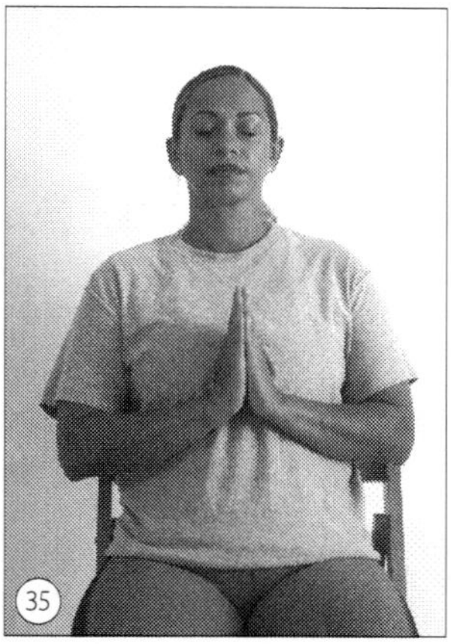
35

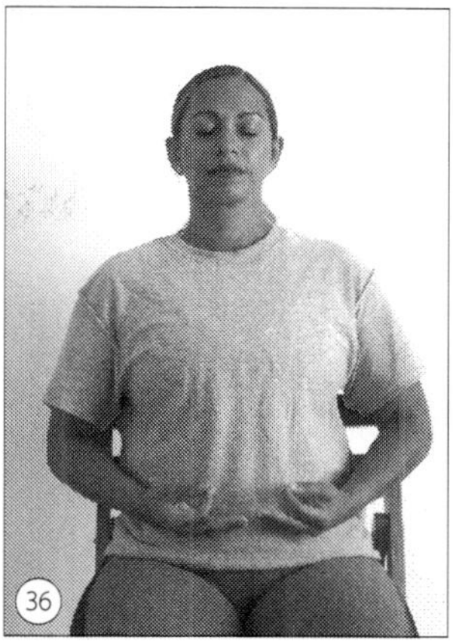
36

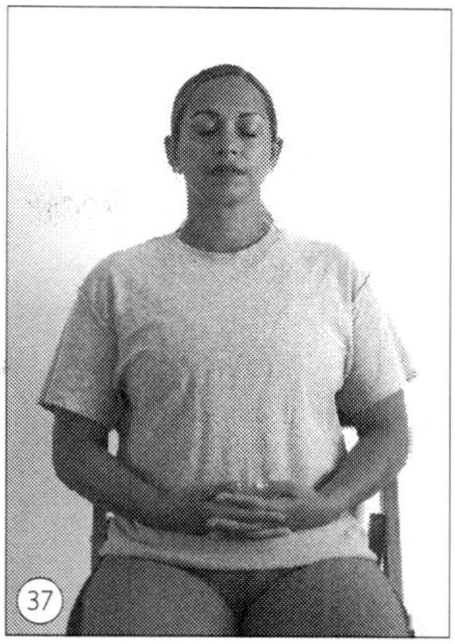
37

I would advise to start with just a few minutes and slowly build up to 10 minutes. Ultimately you can meditate for as long as you want. The average is 10-20 minutes but even a few minutes, once a day, can make a huge difference to your pain and positivity.

Relaxation techniques: progressive muscle relaxation

This technique has been around for decades. It is a way of relaxing your mind and muscles together and can be used as a form of meditation too. It is a very simple concept whereby you move your joints to squeeze or clench a particular group of muscles for a few seconds then release them. It can be performed any time of the day seated or lying down. Typically, you start at one end of your body (head or feet) and work your way to the other end.

Close your eyes and squeeze your toes for a few seconds then release. Then lift your toes up towards the ceiling for a few seconds then release. Then move your foot upwards to feel the muscles on the front of your shin, hold for a few seconds then release. Then point your toes and feet to feel your calf muscles, hold for a few seconds then release. Continue moving your joints up and down/into the floor or up to the ceiling to squeeze as many muscles and you can. Work your way up to your head. They are gentle squeezes/clenches; it should feel like tension then a release.

Positivity tools

Negative thoughts create a negative physiological response in your body while positive thoughts promote a positive physiological response in your body. Promoting positivity on a regular basis not only helps you to stay more positive but also helps to accelerate the healing process. I am witness to this with my patients with lower back pain and also from personal experience. The are many tools to help promote positivity.

Word association

This is a process where you associate a word with something that makes you feel happy, calm, serene and peaceful. The best way to do this is to sit and close your eyes in a quiet room and think of a word you want to use, let's say sand. Then think about everything that makes you happy, peaceful, joyful and loving while thinking of the word sand such as feeling the sun on your face, fresh air, calmness of the waves. Ideally you need to practise this daily for a few minutes a day so that when you think of this word in any given situation you instantly feel calm and peaceful. You can use this at any time of the day.

Positive self-talk

Self-talk is where you encourage yourself to think positively by literally talking to yourself in a positive way. Imagine you have a friend who is in pain, what would you say to them? Things like, "You can do this" or "You can stand up on your own" or "You are doing really well". Instead, you say these statements to yourself and use 'I' instead of 'you'. Positive affirmations can help you conquer fear of not being able to do something like walk up a set of stairs or turn over in bed and encourage you to keep going with your rehabilitation exercises and positively reassure yourself that you're progressing and doing really well and to be proud of yourself. It's not easy to stay positive when you're suffering so these tools can really help.

Goal setting

One of the most powerful psychological techniques for achieving success with anything is goal setting, I use this with my personal training clients and athletes from a non-injury stand point. It's a way of achieving a particular goal by setting tasks and different methods to reach that goal with a specific and realistic time limit. It is usually written out in a formal document that details your goal, sub goals and a given, realistic deadline.

I DO NOT like using goal setting with injured patients because it can be psychologically detrimental. Everyone heals at difference speeds so if you put a time limit on your healing process and you do not achieve a certain level or strength or recovery by that given time period you can get depressed and regress; this is not good.

However, you could use a different type of form, more like a symptoms chart. I use this in my treatment notes every day to use as a motivational tool but some of my patients have adopted this on their own. I always encourage people to avoid dwelling on the past but in this instance, you can use your symptoms, past and present, as a motivational tool.

Write down every symptom you have, then give each symptom a number out of 10 for how you feel at that time (10 is absolute agony and 0 is nothing). It is better to do this weekly rather than daily to see how much you've progressed. Once you've written your number down try not to look at your chart again until the following week. Some symptoms reduce quicker than others. Regardless, it is a great way to see how much you are progressing and look at how far you have come in order to motivate yourself to continue with your regime and also to reward yourself as you see your numbers coming down. Rewards are very important with psychology, they give you a sense of achievement which motivates you to keep progressing.

Symptoms chart	**Wk1**	**Wk2**	**Wk3**	**Wk4**	**Wk5**	**Wk6**	**Wk7**	**Wk8**
Pain turning over in bed	8	7	5	3				
Discomfort tying up shoelaces	5	5	4	2				
Pain getting out of bed 1st thing	9	8	6	4				
Pain sitting for long periods	6	6	4	3				
Discomfort getting out of the car	5	4	4	1				

Thought stoppage

This is slightly different to positive self-talk. Whenever you have a negative thought you stop it and instantly change it for a positive one. An example would be, you might have a thought like, "I'm so weak today" but you stop and change it to "I will do my rehab today". Both positive self-talk and thought stoppage techniques promote a physiological response in your mind and body.

Negative thoughts	Positive thoughts
I can't do this exercise it's too hard	I will do what I can and stop when I fatigue
I am in so much pain	Breathing will help me focus on relaxing
I am better but still in pain	Look how far I have come, I am progressing
What if my pain comes back?	I am proud of myself for doing my maintenance work

---

That's a lot of tips! I would suggest you try these bit by bit and see what works for you. The only thing I would advise is to keep an open mind. I've had a lot of patients who feel a bit silly doing things like visualisations or meditation but have had a lot of success so please don't knock it until you've tried it!

13

The Good, The Bad & The Downright Awful

A healthy food regime is often overlooked when you think about injuries. Feeling stressed because of pain can cause bad choices in food – unfortunately this can play havoc with your recovery. A lot of my patients tell me they just want to eat chocolate when they are in pain. They claim that sweet products are a good way to feel better. Whatever works right? We are all different. The problem is that 'stress eating' can mess up your body even more and slow down your recovery in the process.

When your body is injured and you are stressed your brain sees it as being under threat so it undergoes an inflammation response. Your brain sends out a message to fight off the invaders which leads to inflammation in your body. This is part of your immune responding to healing and your body's attempt at self-protection towards anything harmful. The problem is when this process becomes prolonged from injury your immune system goes into overdrive. This can lead to a huge regression in recovery and cause even more inflammation. On top of that pain medication causes yet more inflammation. Eating foods that cause inflammation when you are already in overdrive just adds fuel to the fire and makes this whole situation worse.

The good

Good food choices can really help your when you're recovering from an injury. I always suggest having a bit of everything is a good thing but I'm not talking about eating chocolate, crisps, chips and sweets! When I say having a bit of everything I mean eating sensibly is the way forward. Foods contain various nutrients such as proteins, fats sugars, vitamins and minerals so if you have a good balance of all of them it can help you to heal, sleep and combat the stress of pain.

Foods rich in anti-oxidants (substances that help prevent cell damage) like fruits and vegetables help to combat inflammation and stress. So it is good to have a healthy balance of proteins (meat, fish, eggs, pulses), vegetables and good fats (avocados, olive oil, nuts) and cut down on foods such as refined sugars (doughnuts, sweets, high sugar snack bars, soda/fizzy drinks), dairy (milk, cheeses), artificial sweeteners (low-calorie diet drinks), processed foods, refined flour (breads, pizza, breakfast cereals, pasta), fast foods, processed meats and foods that are high in saturated fats.

For more information on this subject you can visit the back pain free website and check out the nutrition article page at www.backpainfree.me/nutrition

The bad

I find that a lot of people eat too much refined sugar and carbohydrates such as sweets, chocolates, fast foods, crisps, chips and doughnuts (p38) and seem to lack protein, good fats and vegetables.

When you're injured and stressed from being in pain reducing inflammation is a major key to your healing process. Choosing the right foods and avoiding others until you are out of pain can help you recover so much quicker (p39). Variety helps too so you don't get bored!

38

39

40

Good fats help to reduce inflammation. Examples of good fats are avocado oil, flax seeds, olive oil, nuts, olives, sardines, salmon, coconut oil, avocados, nut butters and chia seeds (p40). These are a mix of omega 3's and omega 6 good fats. Having a variety of these daily is a good thing although a lot of people tend to stick to omega 3's and not consume enough omega 6's. You also need good fats to help nerve communication between your muscles and your brain via a protective covering called the myelin sheath. These sheaths protect and insulate nerves, and around 70% of the sheaths are made from good fats.

Protein helps to keep your immune system healthy, repair muscle and minimize muscle loss especially if you're an active person and can't exercise because of your pain. We need certain enzymes to break down protein into smaller particles called amino acids. Being deficient in protein, vegetables and good fats is a key factor that can slow down your healing process and affect your ability to sleep through the night. If you are deficient in protein your body can actually steal protein from itself to retain adequate levels, which can drastically slow down your recovery. Protein is also an abundant source of collagen which makes up fascia/connective tissue and is essential for healing injuries and healthy muscle tissue.

For more information on this you subject you can visit the back pain free website and check out the nutrition article page at www.backpainfree.me/nutrition

The downright awful

After my accident I had stomach pain, cramps, acid reflux (p41) (where your food travels back up your throat) and nausea for six years. I also suffered constant constipation for well over two years and then intermittent constipation for well over a decade. After a three-year duration of having all kinds of stomach tests after my accident I was finally told that my stomach was badly inflamed because I had an ulcer. I was told this was due to taking so much medication – particularly the NSAIDs (non-steroidal anti-inflammatory drugs) for three years. The gastrointestinal doctor told me this was extremely common. In fact, he was quite apathetic about it. I was then given anti-acid tablets because I had too much stomach acid, or so the doctor told me. The anti-acid tablets made my nausea a tad better but they didn't have any impact on my reflux or stomach cramps and pains.

During my very first course with Charles Poliquin, I was taught that my stomach symptoms probably weren't due to having too much stomach acid but that I didn't have enough. Charles said I needed to take hydrochloric acid (HCL) and digestive enzymes (they both help your digestion process) because I probably wasn't digesting my food properly. He was right; more on this later.

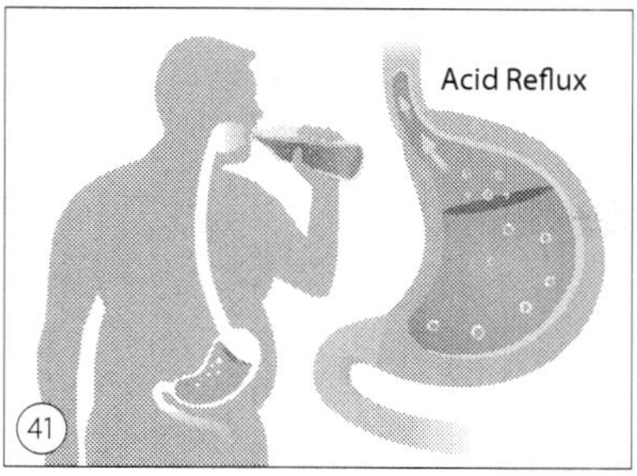

When I told my cranial osteopath about my ulcer, she told me it was due to the NSAIDs and opioids/painkillers. She said it so matter-of-factly. I was a bit shocked. She said it was very typical after years of taking pain medication. Some of these symptoms are written as side effects but you don't realise how much damage they can cause you, as well as more pain.

An awful consequence of suffering back pain is the amount of medication you need to take for pain relief and the inflammation caused as a result. Don't get me wrong: if you're in absolute agony it's hard not to take medication, you need to function somehow. The problem with pain medication is that it can actually hinder your healing process if you take it for a long period of time even though it can help decrease the pain itself. It doesn't matter whether you take NSAIDs, strong or mild painkillers or anti-acids, they can all damage your gut also known as your gastrointestinal (GI) tract (Sigthorsson et al., 1998). By damaging your GI tract and the bacteria in it, medication and anti-acids can also hinder your sleep and make you susceptible to emotional disorders like depression and anxiety because of the very close relationship between your gut and your brain. NSAIDs are also connected with kidney issues and I have seen many cases where they appear to reverse the effects of their intended use.

Gut health is so important for so many reasons when you are in injured. In layman's terms pain medication can cause a fair amount of dysfunction in your gut. This can eventually lead to an increase in bad bacteria as well as leaky gut. This is where particles of undigested food can 'leak' through your gut into your blood stream because your gut lining becomes more and more permeable. It's more complicated than that but it means all the good stuff you eat doesn't get through your gut to do its job. If your gut health deteriorates, so does your immune system. On top of that, long-term fatigue from being in pain suppresses your immune system even more, especially when you're in constant 'alert mode as explained in the previous chapter.

Gut dysfunction can also stop you producing enough stomach acid. You need stomach acid to help break food down, activate enzymes to help digest food, kill harmful bacteria that may be ingested with food and for the absorption of various minerals important for health and healing. This may not be the case for everyone but in my experience, taking anti-acids didn't help the real problem for me at all, if anything my acid reflux got worse. Many of my patients have had similar experiences. Not only do they suffer back pain with an array of symptoms and restrictions, but then they start having even more symptoms like stomach cramps, acid reflux (p41), constipation or diarrhoea. If you have suffered any type of infection while suffering back pain and were given antibiotics this can add to your gut demise. Antibiotics are renowned for destroying your friendly gut bacteria that can lead to a decrease in your immune system as a result.

Bad gut health doesn't stop there. In your brain you produce certain chemicals called neuro-transmitters that send messages around your body and affect functions such as appetite, mood, fear and heart rate. One of them is called serotonin. It helps regulate your moods, digestion, sleep and also has an effect on sexual desire and anxiety. Around 90% of it is made in your GI tract. So if your gut is compromised from years of pain medication and stress it can hinder the amount of serotonin you can produce to help you keep calm and deal with stress. Hence, it's no wonder there is usually an emotional factor with back pain especially if you're taking various forms of medication.

Think of your gut as your second brain; the two are very closely linked. This connection is called the gut-brain axis (p42). They are connected via cells and various pathways including your vagus nerve - a cranial nerve that has a link from your brain to your gut so they feed back to one another (it's

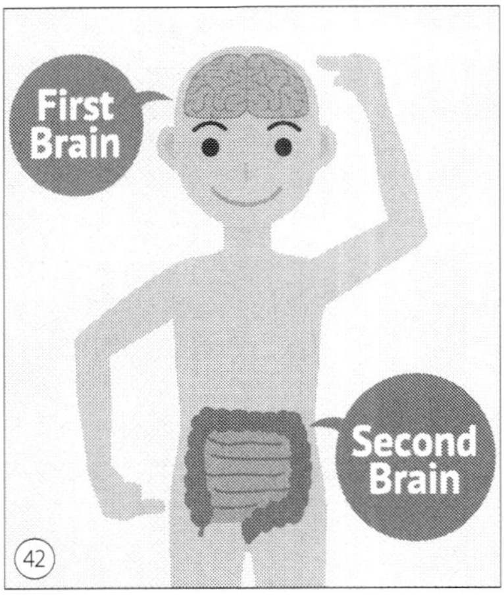

a lot more complex than that). Have you ever heard the expressions: trust your gut instinct, gut reaction, do you have guts, my gut feeling is...? I could go on; the list is endless. Those expressions are typical of the relationship between your brain and your gut!

They communicate constantly back and forth and healing one helps the other. If your gut is unhealthy, your response to stress is seriously affected. If your gut is compromised, you can't produce specific brain chemicals (neurotransmitters) to stay calm and cope with stress. If your calming neurotransmitters become deficient and imbalanced this can leave you vulnerable to depression, anxiety and other neurological disorders on top of your pain. It is a vicious circle. So how can you improve this situation? You re-build your gut.

How to re-build your gut

I am lucky to have interned with Dr Eric Serrano (as mentioned earlier), an esteemed medical doctor who lives in Columbus, Ohio. He specialises in hormones and nutrition and he understands the gut like nobody else I know. Dr Serrano taught me a lot about the gut and a simple way to remember how to heal it. It is called the 4 R's: remove, replace, repair, re-inoculate. It's basically a process to re-build your gut after it has suffered a lot of damage.

First you **remove** whatever is causing your inflammation and damage to your gut i.e. pain medication/anti-acids. Then you **repair** the damage with specific supplements like L-glutamine (an amino acid that helps heal your gut) and healthy foods, then you **replace** the relevant nutrients to help with digestion like digestive enzymes and HCL and lastly you **re-inoculate** with good bacteria by taking probiotics.

The recommended dose for L-glutamine powder is 5-10g* per day mixed in a small glass of water. Take one digestive enzyme* with every meal and start off on a low dose of HCL 300mg* in the middle of your food with every protein meal for the first 1-2 weeks. Then gradually increase to 2 x HCL 600-650mg* capsules with every protein meal. Some people react to HCL at first (nausea, diarrhoea, headaches) so you may need longer than 2 weeks to increase your HCL so see how you feel. Probiotics are different for everyone but an average is a 5-10 billion* capsule 1-2 times a day after food is recommended. You might need to take more than that if you're suffering with stomach issues*.

If you're in a lot of pain, the first part of the 4 R's (stopping pain medication) will be very difficult. That's where supplements like magnesium and the use of heat can help instead of taking medication. However, this process should help decrease your pain as you rebuild your gut. Plus, your pain should start to decrease with soft tissue treatment and as you increase strength with the rehab exercises.

After Charles Poliquin taught me about HCL and digestive enzymes, I came off the anti-acid tablets immediately and decided to apply my new knowledge. Within three weeks of taking the two natural health supplements along with a multi vitamin, my reflux reduced by about 60% and my nausea and stomach cramps disappeared altogether. Within three months my reflux had totally gone. I'd had those symptoms for six years. Charles was right. What a huge relief. A few months later I noticed something else, my sleep had improved, I realised was sleeping through the night for the first time in many years and I'd lost a stone (6kg) in weight as a result – what a bonus!

Bone broth

In my experience by far the most amazing way to help heal or as I like to say 'seal' your gut is with a home-made remedy called bone broth, where you literally boil bones to make a broth! I learnt about this amazing remedy many years ago but completely dismissed it. Bone broth has been around for hundreds of years all over the world. When you boil meat or fish bones on a low heat for a very long time they release many powerful nutrients like vitamins, minerals, amino acids (proteins), good fats and collagen (p43). Theses nutrients help to reduce inflammation, improve your immune system and help to heal your gut and its functions. Bone broth is also great for your connective tissue health.

Bone broth is typically cooked with bones, herbs and vegetables for 12-36 hours depending on whether you are using meat, chicken or fish bones – fish bones need less time to cook (Normal Stock vs. Bone Broth, n.d.). Ideally organic bones are best which you can buy from your local butcher or via a farm or website online. I use Coombe Farm Organic bones (www.coombefarmorganic.co.uk) to make mine – it tastes delicious!

43

When I first tried bone broth I had severe constipation and my head pain increased. If you take bone broth and you suffer any type of gastric distress like constipation or diarrhoea and headaches, it's likely that your stomach is in pretty bad shape and probably very 'leaky'. If this is the case then you're probably really sensitive to bone broth and your brain may be too. In that instance you're better off making stock, a softer version of bone broth, until you can make the switch to bone broth.

Stock

The only difference with stock is the time you take to boil it which is typically 2-4 hours, again depending on whether you're using meat, chicken or fish bones. You can cook it on your stove or in a slow cooker, which I find far easier. With stock it is recommended to use meat on the bone so it's gentler on your gut. I tried this first for three weeks and then switched to just boiling bones to make the stock. After about eight weeks my bowels got back to normal for the first time in years. After six months I switched to bone broth. This is a long time but you might have to play around with it as for some people even two weeks may be long enough before switching. I usually suggest its' best to go by your symptoms. Once you've made the broth or stock you can have it as a soup with other meat, fish or vegetables. I prefer to have mine as a hot drink twice a day and flavoured with lots of Himalayan salt and black pepper.

For more information on bone broth and stock recipes check out the back pain free website and go to www.backpainfree/bonebroth

Organic castor oil packs

If your gut is very unhealthy it may be distended like mine was. I found that castor oil packs helped a lot with this. Castor oil contains properties that can speed up healing in many ways by reducing tension and pain, detoxifying toxins in your body, reducing inflammation, stimulating your immune system, improving your digestion and reducing painful joints. It is a natural healer for sure!

There are a few different ways to make castor oil packs. My preferred method is very quick and easy. Lie down on your back, gently rub organic castor oil all over your stomach then cover it with a hot flannel cloth (run it under a hot tap and wring the water out, be careful not to burn yourself). Cover the flannel cloth with half a towel then place a hot pack or a hot water bottle on top. Then cover your hot water bottle with the rest of the towel. You may need to re-heat your hot pack/hot water bottle half way through. Leave the castor oil pack on for 45-60 minutes and when you're finished, wash the oil off your skin with a tablespoon of baking soda in water. It's best to wash your flannel cloth and towel separately as they can make your clothes smell. Originally I used castor oil packs for four successive days of every week for eight weeks then I cut down to once a week for two months. You can use castor oil packs weekly (four days a week is plenty) for up to three months and you should see a difference.

For more information on castor oil packs go to www.backpainfree/castoroilpacks

*NB: Please remember these are my suggestions purely based on my personal experiences and from what I've learnt through my education. Please ALWAYS check with your doctor or functional medicine/health practitioner before taking any natural health supplements, especially if you have a medical condition.

If I could go back in time I would have started using bone broth as soon as I started taking HCL and digestive enzymes. I have seen so much success with bone stock with myself and my patients that I literally suggest it to everybody I meet that has experienced pain, stress, sleep deprivation and gut issues. Although it's very inexpensive to make yourself, making and taking bone broth/stock is a lot of effort as are the castor oil packs but the pro's definitely outweigh the cons.

There are a lot of other health supplements that can help you while rebuild your gut like vitamin C (helps boost your immune system), colostrum (helps repair your GI tract), ox bile (helps digestion and absorption of fats), garlic (helps to feed healthy gut bacteria) and many more, but the ones I have mentioned are my favourites.

14

The Pearson Method

When I have a new patient who has lower back pain I need to know three things: do they have weakness in one or both sets of their glutes and weakness in their lower back or core muscles. Then I need to find out what muscles have overcompensated (they will need releasing) and also determine which muscles need strengthening. As I explained previously muscles work in pairs so if one group of muscles are underworking, their 'paired' muscles will usually be overworking. Over time, the body recruits other muscles to take up the slack of the weak ones so within a couple of years it's common that two to seven groups of muscles may be overworking.

Often new patients who come to see me are told they didn't need soft tissue treatment by a doctor and pain killers would be enough or that exercises in the gym would help them. I can tell you from personal experience as well as a therapist if you have back pain you will need both treatment and rehab strength and then maintenance exercises to stay pain free. As I mentioned previously there is a huge difference between rehab and gym strength - gym exercises can often make you worse, more on that in Chapter 19. Sometimes you may only need one or two treatments but if you are in chronic pain and you have a lot of muscular dysfunction you may need more. Regardless, most people need way more strength work than treatment. Plus once you are pain free, rehab strength is the major player if you don't want it to come back.

Through experimenting with my own injuries and observing patients with back pain over a ten year span, I created a successful process to diagnose, resolve (with treatment and rehabilitation strength exercises) and maintain these issues. I call it the Pearson Method.

Your core

Most new patients that I treat either don't do any or do some core work in a Pilates class or with their personal trainer. There are many ways to self-test your core. I find the easiest way to do this is try to perform a full plank (p44). To do this, lie on your tummy, raise your upper body and place your elbows (facing forwards) directly underneath your shoulders. Tuck your toes under your feet and raise your hips and knees off the floor until your body is straight (without arching or pushing your hips up to the ceiling) from your shoulders to your feet.

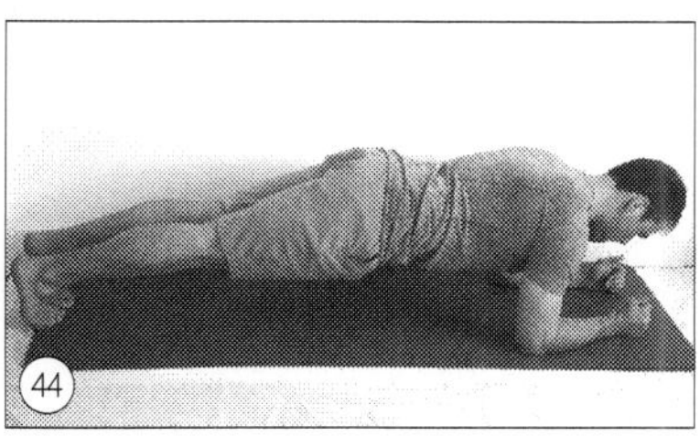
44

If you can only do this for five seconds or less it's likely that you have a weak core so you would need to start with the easier half plank along with other beginner core exercises and work your way up to the plank. I explain all of the rehab exercises in the following few chapters.

When I first started working in a gym I was asked to teach a Swiss ball class, the first of its kind. It catered specifically for strengthening the core but it was pretty basic and the majority of attendees were mothers. Within a few weeks I had half of them coming up to me at the end of the class telling me how much their back pain had eased for the first time in months; for some of them it had been years. I was astounded. It was my first insight into how much core strength mothers can lose after giving birth. Not only did I help the mothers with their pain but I realised how much the classes were helping my own back pain, it was a win-win!

Your lower back

Most people who have lower back pain need treatment as well as rehabilitation strengthening exercises. Releasing the muscles at the front of your body (hip flexors) can instantly ease your back pain and releasing your lower back muscles gets oxygen back into those tissues again – leading to more flexibility and a decrease in pain. However, I've found that lower back muscles themselves still need to be strengthened and that's where rehab exercises come into play. Rehab exercises not only strengthen your lower back but they prevent pain and dysfunction from returning and that for me is the icing on the cake. I love the saying "prevention is better than cure!" It is a testament to my own rehab prevention – so far, my back pain has not returned!

Your lower back is not so easy to test for weakness, mostly because if you have pain, your muscles are likely to be overworking (overcompensating) and thus vulnerable. I'm not a fan of testing them when they are in that state especially because your symptoms should dictate if you have weakness. Symptoms like not being able to sit or stand for even 10 minutes, turning over in bed and getting out of bed with discomfort are typical signs of weakness in your lower back as well as your glutes.

I returned to training in the gym a few years after my accident but I realised my back wasn't healing so I had to go back to the drawing board. I experimented for years with various exercises and treatments and found that a combination of soft tissue releases particularly ART treatments and specific rehabilitation strength exercises for the core, glutes and lower back worked really well as a cure as well as a preventative method.

Your glutes

Your glutes are by far the main culprits of lower back pain. I have never, ever seen a patient with lower back pain who didn't have one or both sets of weak glute muscles. This is regardless of whatever back issue you are dealing with. This isn't necessarily the case for those who have had bone fusion surgery (bones fused together), stenosis (narrowing of disc spaces within your spine) or spondylosis or spondylolisthesis (bone issues of the spine). However, rehab exercises for the core, lower back and glutes can most definitely help people with those types of back issues.

How do you know if your glutes are firing?

A lot of people ask me why their glutes don't seem to be firing (activating) properly yet they perform lots of leg exercises and glute work particularly in the gym. If any muscle is not firing properly it doesn't matter what exercises you do, they will make NO difference. In that case you will have to get treatment first to get those muscles fired up. Start with the rehab exercises and only when you've gained rehab strength, will those same leg and glute exercises start to make a difference.

When I ask if your glutes are firing it is a term used to determine whether you have a good connection from your brain to your muscles; it is called the motor sensory feedback loop. Sometimes this feedback loop loses its signal and becomes very distant. This is where rehabilitation strength helps you. These exercises help to strengthen the feedback loop but first you need to get those muscles fired up to 're-connect' your brain to that group of muscles. Think of it like a car that won't start even though the engine is turning over. Only after you push the car down the road to give it a jump start will the engine finally start. Once your muscles are firing the rehab strength exercises will get you to the finish line, steadily and progressively.

There are quite a few typical symptoms to determine if one or both sets of your glutes are weak. The first one is having back pain; that's a given and typical of someone who has suffered a disc herniation or disc bulge as well as a hip imbalance. Others include:

1 Sitting down is painful and feels like you're sitting on concrete. Wooden chairs are the worst. It feels like the pain is at the base of your bum but it's where your hamstring muscles attach to your pelvic bone. You might feel pain on one or both sides and this means your hamstrings are overworking. If this has been chronic, your sciatic nerve might be slightly trapped too. I see this a lot. I had this for many years on both legs; it can be very painful to even sit on a soft sofa if you are really inflamed.

2 Standing from being in a seated position is painful whether you've been sitting for 5-15 minutes, 30 minutes or longer and you may feel a twinge or pain at the front of your hips (hip flexors) as well as your lower back as you try to stand.

3 Short, painful twinges that last for 1-2 seconds in your groin/inner thigh, hip flexors, quads, hamstrings, calves or under your feet. You might have these twinges in more than one of these muscles. For some, like I had, you might have painful twinges in all of those muscles as well as your lower back. This usually means your issue is long-term and your glutes probably haven't worked properly for at least one to two years or longer.

4 For gym goers, when you perform squats you only feel a muscle ache the next day in your quads, hamstrings and lower back but never or hardly ever feel it in your glutes. You might feel muscle ache in one set of your glutes but never the other side. This is the same with deadlifts: you may feel muscle ache in your lower back and hamstrings but never in your glutes. Also, during deadlifts you may only feel a contraction (muscle tension) in your lower back which limits the amount of weight you can lift. More on this in 'The Gym' chapter (19).

5 Knee pain with back pain. Almost every patient I treat who has knee pain has weak glutes, either one or both sides.

6 Plantar fasciitis with back pain. Every patient I have treated for foot/heel pain known as plantar fasciitis has tested positive for weak glutes, either one or both sides. With plantar fasciitis the pain might be under or on top of your foot. In that case you will need your foot muscles and ligaments released with ART treatment as well as glute strength.

7 Pain at the back of your heel, this is known as achilles tendonitis. Every patient I have treated for calf/achilles pain has had weak glutes, either one or both sides. Pain can be in your calf or on your achilles tendon closer to your heel bone.

8 Aesthetics. A lot of the time you might see a visible difference in the size of your glutes. Lie down on your tummy or stand sideways and ask a friend or family member to see if one side of your bum is bigger than the other.

9 Pain lying down on one or both sides of your hip usually indicates your glute muscles are severely tight and weak and have probably atrophied (muscle wastage) so will they need soft tissue treatment and rehab strength.

10 One leg seems to drag when you walk or it may seem slower to move than the other leg. In this instance your sciatic nerve may be trapped and you will most likely need rehab strength after releasing the nerve. I had this for many years and it affected my inability to walk long distances and run without getting numbness in both legs.

Your glute muscles have many functions but the two main movements are external rotation and hip extension. External rotation is where your leg rotates outwards and backwards and hip extension is where you extend your leg backwards, with a straight or bent knee. For the first part of the Pearson Method I created two tests for both of these movements as a guide to see if your glutes are firing properly.

Pearson clam test

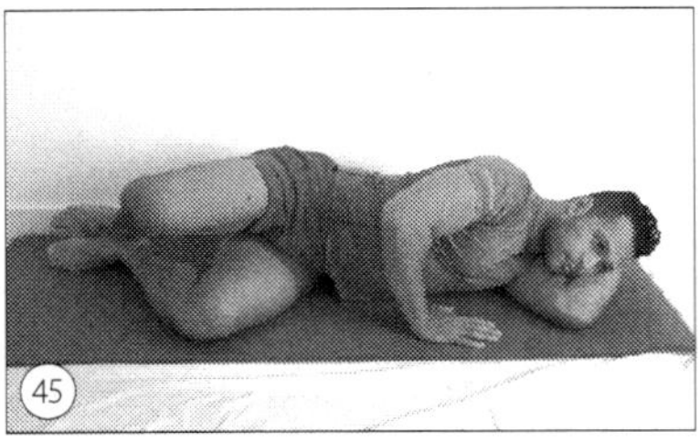

The clam exercise is a well-known Pilates and rehab exercise. However, I have evolved the clam to use as a diagnostic test in a very specific way to determine what muscles are overworking and to see if your glutes are firing properly in this particular range of movement (p45). To perform the test, lie on the floor or a flat surface on your left side with your knees bent around 90 degrees, keeping your feet in line with your hips and shoulders. Put your right hand flat in front of you to support you. Now roll your hips and torso forward as much as you can then tilt your bum out like a duck, as previously mentioned I call this "duck bum". Without rolling your hips backwards and keeping your feet together, lift your right knee as high as it can go, keeping your duck bum and hips rolled forward. It is a fairly small movement.

If you feel pain or discomfort in your lower back when you do the duck bum, you may be tilting your pelvis too much. In that case ease off the duck bum a bit.

Try to hold that position for a minute and monitor where you feel a contraction/tension (like a healthy muscle ache). If you feel a lot of tension in your right glutes and it's difficult to hold that position for longer than 10 seconds, it means your glutes are firing but they are weak.

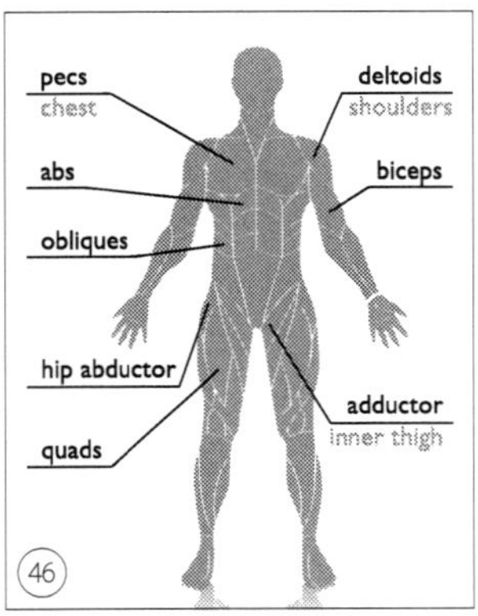

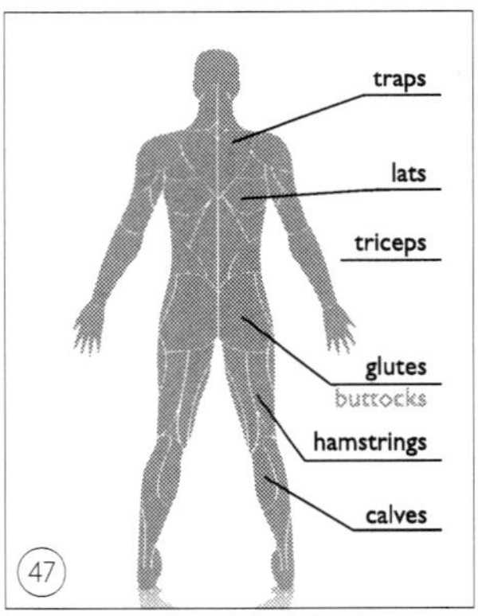

If you feel tension in your left glutes or somewhere else on your left leg, then press your right hand into the floor, this takes the pressure off your left leg. Then see if you start to feel something in your right glutes. If you do, then it just means your right side is extremely weak. If you don't feel anything in your right glutes but you feel tension in other places like your hamstrings, lower back, calves, quads or inner thigh and/or the other leg, this means you are overcompensating in those muscles and your glutes on your right side are not firing (p46/47). If you feel a small contraction (tension) in your right glutes but you also feel tension in one or more muscles in your right leg this means your right glutes are firing a little bit but you are still overcompensating in other muscles.

Make a note of the muscles you felt tension in during the test as they will need releasing first. You could try stretching each of those overworked muscles for 15 seconds and see if that makes a difference then re-test. If it does and you feel a contraction, albeit a small one in your glutes, then great; if it doesn't then you will need treatment first. All the stretches are described in chapter 18.

If you felt tension in your glutes for the whole minute and it feels easy, that side of your glutes are probably healthy. However, they may still need releasing at least once, more on this in the last chapter. Even if your glutes are firing but they feel weak, ART treatment can still help to accelerate your rehab strength which will speed up your recovery.

All glute rehab exercises and levels of progression are described in full in the following chapters.

Pearson glute tension test

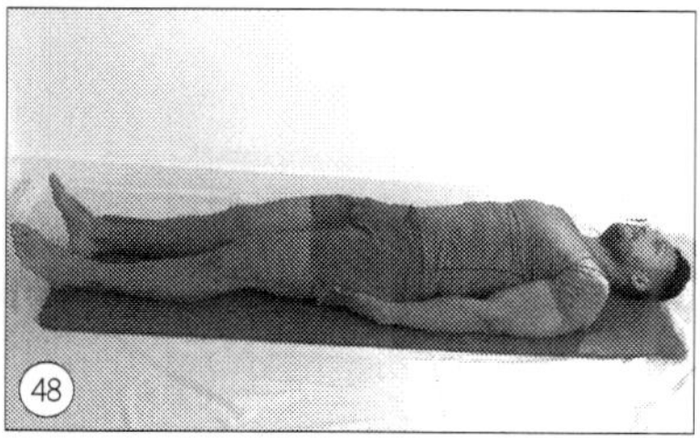

48

Lie on your back and try to squeeze your left glutes only (p48). Monitor if your right glutes tense at the same time or if you feel your left quads or hamstrings tense at the same time. Then do the test on the other side. Often you'll find that one set of glutes has a stronger contraction (tension) than the other side. Some people don't feel anything at all on one side. This can be quite a shock but it will give you an indication if your glutes are firing in hip extension. Please don't be alarmed, it's very common and can be resolved! Try performing the exercises in the rehab programme first. If you still can't feel anything on that side or both of your glutes after seven days you definitely need treatment on your glutes to re-connect your brain to your muscles in that particular movement.

If you feel pain during either of these tests, STOP and seek help from your doctor or health professional/therapist. Sometimes patients confuse a VERY strong ache for pain. If you feel a very strong ache this is most likely due to SEVERE weakness which is very common.

Both of these tests are a simple guide to see what's happening with your glutes. If you feel tension in the right place, fantastic, if you don't and you decide to try the rehabilitation exercises before having treatment just remember if you perform any of the glute rehab exercises in this book and you feel twinges or tension in areas OTHER than your glutes, you will make matters worse.

The second half of the Pearson Method is the rehab strength. There are specific exercises which have levels for progression. The next few chapters describe all of the exercises in great detail and I explain how to progress through each level. For simple viewing I have designed a rehab programme with all of the exercises and their progressive levels at the end of chapter 17.

If you perform the exercises for a few days and do not see a change so you decide to give up OR you skip some exercises and choose not to follow the levels of progression, you will not gain strength this way. Think of it like stepping stones from one to ten where ten is pain free. If you only step on one stone and stop then you're nowhere near the top. If you only do one, three and ten, the likelihood is you'll fall by the time you reach the top and will have to start again. Pain comes back if you don't progress the correct way, trust me, I've been there.

Soft tissue release is quick but strength takes time to gain. If you're having problems adhering to the exercises and stretches, ask a friend or family member to help and remember you have a LOT of positivity and motivation tools to help you stay on course. If you have children, get them to do your exercises with you, make it fun. Before you know it they will be pestering you to do the exercises because they will probably make it a routine more than you will, that happens a lot!

After you're pain free please follow the maintenance rehab programme (end of chapter 17) to make sure you stay pain free. It's very simple and easy to follow. Now on to the secrets of gaining strength in your spine and how to get you there!

15

Rehabilitation Part 1: Strengthening Your Glutes

Do you remember the house analogy? Think of rehabilitation exercises like re-building the foundations under your house. You wouldn't want to skip big chunks of concrete whilst re-building your foundation or else it would still be unstable. Hence, you always want to go through every step of the process. Rehabilitation in terms of injury simply means to re-educate. You are re-educating your brain to increase the signal between it and your muscles as I talked about in the last chapter. Once the connection is there the exercises will increase it. Your brain operates on repetition so you'll notice most of the exercises are high repetitions of 15. Your brain needs structure to understand what you're asking it to do.

The first rule of rehabilitation is called an isometric hold. This is where you contract (clench) a muscle by moving a joint into a certain position and then hold. The next stage is movements and the final stage is adding weight, very light weight. This doesn't always hold true for every muscle and exercise but I have experimented with these exercises for many years to make them as simple, but efficient, as possible in a feasible order to progress.

When you start performing the rehabilitation exercises it is important to only do as much as you feel comfortable with. Rehab exercises should NEVER be painful*. It is imperative that you STOP WHEN YOU FATIGUE when performing these exercises. I've seen some patients with low-grade back pain struggle with the basic level 1 exercises. They may be basic but if your muscles are weak they can seem very difficult and remember strength takes time to build so please go at your own pace.

Please remember that a target means a build-up i.e. you do not have to perform the target instantly; you build up to it. Rehab exercises are gentle so every day you try to do a little bit more and a little bit more. If you force exercises when you are weak and your muscles cannot cope you may risk straining them and sending yourself backwards; that's happened to a few of my patients. Please bear in mind some days you may not progress much if you are feeling more fatigued or stressed. This is normal so please try not to feel de-motivated. When you reach your target comfortably then go on to the next level. This is the safest way to progress and should give you a feeling of achievement and confidence. Some levels take longer to reach than others so please be patient.

* Rehabilitation exercises are gentle so please remember that if you feel pain during any exercise STOP AND SEEK ADVICE from your doctor or health professional/therapist.

1. The Clam

The clam is a great exercise for strengthening your glutes in external rotation and it is a well-known Pilates exercise. Various coaches and therapists use this too. However, I perform it in a very specific way and with specific timings. This is the same as the Pearson clam test (described in the last chapter), except this time you're going to hold for set periods of time and perform repetitions. Remember your target means you perform as much as you can until you fatigue. Every time you perform the exercise you should hold for longer. For level 1 of the clam, you should be able to perform a longer hold within a week even if it is 10 seconds longer, this is progress! Regardless, the key is to progress steadily and safely making sure you don't push through fatigue.

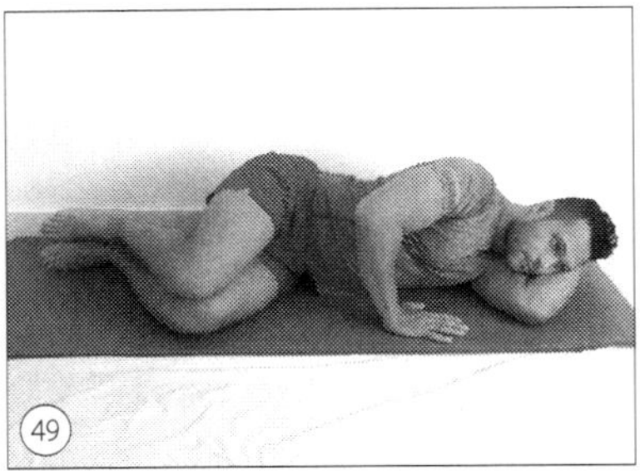

49

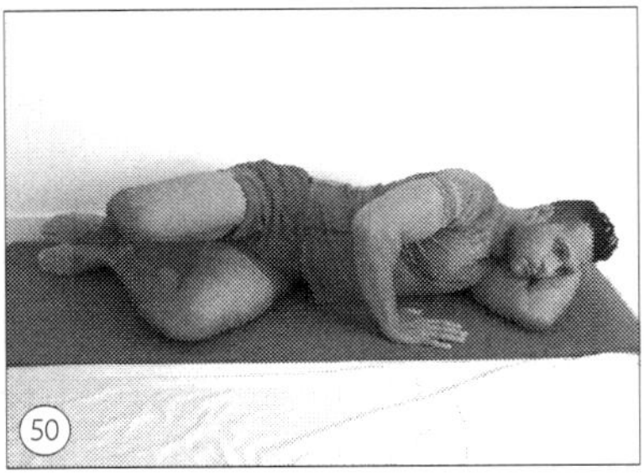

50

Level 1 (p49/50) – Lie on your left side, bend your knees around 90 degrees so that your feet line up with your hips and shoulders. Place your right hand on the floor to support you. Roll forwards as far as you can go then tilt your bum out, like a duck (duck bum). While relaxing your feet but keeping them together, lift your right knee to the ceiling, without rolling your hips backwards – make sure you stay rolled forwards with a duck bum. Hold that position for as long as you can up to a minute. Rest for 20-30 seconds then repeat two more times.

Your target is 3 x 1-minute hold, then 15 repetitions. This exercise should be performed 1-2 times a day but no more than twice a day or you can risk straining muscles. Each time you hold for one minute make sure you're in the right position and hold until you feel a strong fatigue, about 7-8/10 (if 10 is really fatigued) then STOP. Do not push through an 8/10 in fatigue.

To perform the repetitions, start in the same position except this time lift your knee, hold for 1 second at the top, then lower your knee for a count of three slow seconds, like '"1 mississippi, 2 mississippi...". It's easy to count too fast so make sure you count slow enough. When you reach an 8/10 in fatigue, STOP!

Every time you lift your knee try to relax your feet and avoid moving them. If you move your foot (of the knee that you're lifting) it changes the exercise so you won't achieve the benefit of gravity assisting you. If you feel your left leg or glutes start tensing push your right hand into the floor which should take the pressure off your left leg. As you get stronger you shouldn't have to keep doing this. If you feel an ache or discomfort in your lower back, ease off the duck bum. Try to only focus on rolling forward and lifting your knee, avoid trying to squeeze your glutes during any part of this exercise. It should be a natural occurrence.

Perform everything on one side then perform everything on the other side. When you reach the full target go to level 2.

Level 2 – Get into exactly the same position and hold for 1 minute then perform three sets of 15 repetitions. Each time you perform a repetition make sure you're in the correct position.

Your target is 1-minute hold then 3 x 15 repetitions. This exercise should be performed once a day. Rest for 10-20 seconds in-between sets. Do as many repetitions as you can until you feel a strong fatigue, about 7 to 8/10 (if 10 is really fatigued) then STOP. Do not push through 8/10 in fatigue.

It's easy to let your hips roll back during the repetitions so make sure you're always rolled forwards with a duck bum. As this is level 2 you may want to have less rest in between each of the sets to make it harder, this will increase the intensity on your glutes for added strength. When you reach the level 2 target move on to the single leg glute bridge.

2. The Ballet Step

I call this the ballet step because it is exactly that. This exercise utilizes both hip extension and external rotation of your hip. It is very simple and all you need is a wall!

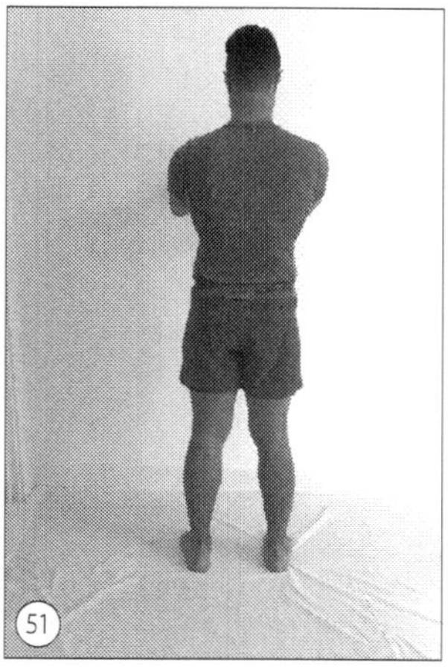

51

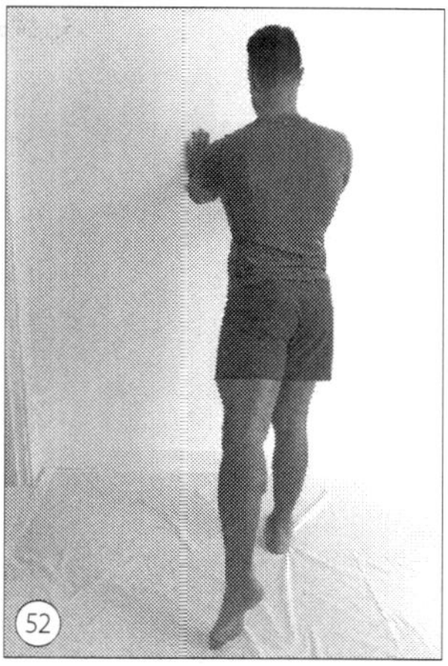

52

Level 1 (p51/52) – Stand up straight, facing a wall and with your hands resting on the wall. Extend your left leg backwards as far as you can while standing up straight, try not to lean forwards. As you extend your left leg back, keep your knee slightly bent and turn your toes outwards away from your body so that your left heel moves inwards towards your right leg. You should almost be pointing your toes. As you do this, you should feel a 'bunching' of your left glutes. Squeeze your glutes at that end range then bring your leg back to the standing position and repeat on the other leg. Continue alternating each leg for 15 repetitions. Rest for 20-30 seconds then repeat.

Your target is 2 x 15 repetitions on each leg and should be performed 2-3 times a day. If you haven't reached 15 repetitions but you feel a strong fatigue, about 7-8/10 (if 10 is really fatigued) then STOP. Do not push through an 8/10 in fatigue. This exercise should be performed alongside the clam level 1. You might be able to perform these straight away so I usually suggest performing this exercise for two weeks and then move on to level 2 but it's fine if you want to stay with level 1 for a while longer. Only progress to level 2 when you feel ready.

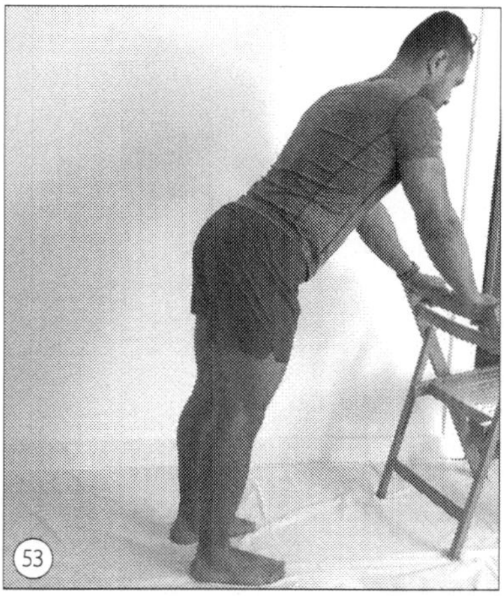

53

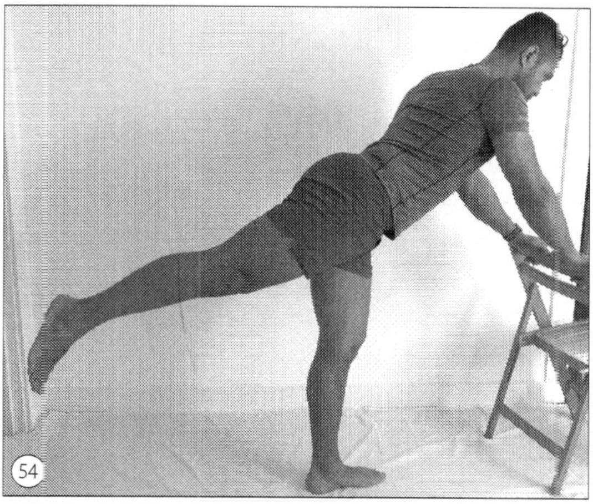

54

Level 2 (p53/54) – To perform the advanced ballet step lean forwards and place both hands on a chair or table about hip height. Keeping your spine in neutral (try not to hunch or arch your back) lift your right leg backwards, keeping your right knee slightly bent. Move your right toes outwards facing away from your body so that your heel is facing your left leg – this will increase the contraction (squeeze) on your glutes. Try not to twist your body too much, just enough to feel your glutes contract. Extend your leg back as high as you can without arching your lower back. Lower your right leg slowly for a count of three seconds then repeat on the other leg. Continue alternating each leg for 15 repetitions. Rest for 10-20 seconds then repeat.

Your target is 2 x 15 repetitions on each leg and should be performed 1-2 times a day. If you haven't reached 15 repetitions but you feel a strong fatigue, about 7-8/10 (if 10 is really fatigued) then STOP. Do not push through an 8/10 in fatigue. This exercise should be performed alongside the clam level 2.

It's very important to keep your back in a neutral position and avoid hunching or hyperextending (overarching) through the whole exercise.

3. Doggies

This exercise is an alternative to the ballet step and utilises both hip extension and external rotation of your glute muscles.

Level 1 (55/56) – Get onto your hands and knees. Keeping your spine in neutral and your knees bent, lift your right knee backwards and out to the side (like a dog going for a pee!). Turning your knee towards the ceiling will increase the contraction (squeeze) on your glutes. Lower your knee slowly for a count of three seconds then repeat on the other leg and continue alternating both legs for 15 repetitions. Rest for 20-30 seconds then repeat.

Your target is 2 x 15 repetitions on each leg and should be performed 2-3 times a day. If you haven't reached 15 repetitions but you feel a strong fatigue, about 7-8/10 (if 10 is really fatigued) then STOP. Do not push through an 8/10 in fatigue.

It's very important to maintain a neutral spine and avoid hyperextending (overarching) through the whole exercise. You can alternate this exercise with the ballet step i.e. one day you perform the ballet step and the next day you perform doggies. Rehabilitation exercises tend to get a tad boring so this mixes things up to keep you motivated!

4. Glute Tenses

This is an isometric (static) hip extension exercise which means you just squeeze your muscles instead of moving your joint. However, it is a very powerful exercise. This is the same as the Pearson glute tension test except this time you hold (squeeze) for a certain amount of time. Lying down is the easiest version to start with, if your glutes are weak. When your glutes feel stronger you can try the standing version and eventually move on to the hardest seated version. Glute tenses can be performed alongside the level 1 clam and doggies/ballet step.

If you have a standing desk you could perform your level 2 glute tenses in your office. Although you may look a bit strange standing in your office while holding onto your bum!

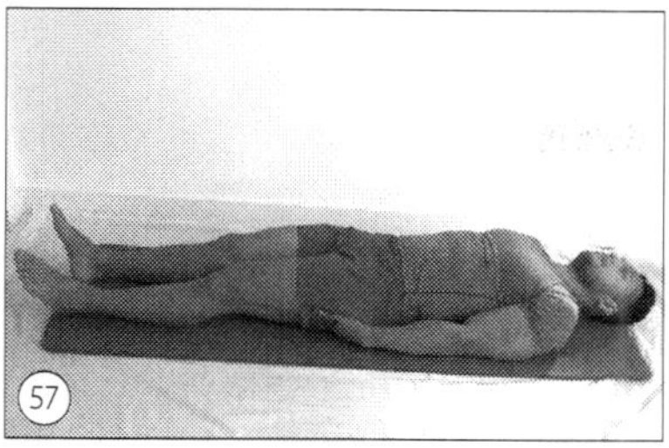

Level 1: Lying down (p57) – Lie down on your back and squeeze your glutes on the left side only and hold for 5 seconds. Try not to squeeze any other muscle. Rest for one second then repeat four more times. Repeat on your right side.

Your target is 5 second holds x 5 repetitions on each side and should be performed 3-5 times a day. Sometimes it's easier to feel a contraction (squeeze) if you bend your knee of the glutes you're tensing. It can also help to place your hand (palm facing) underneath your glutes while you squeeze them because the brain works on senses, try shutting your eyes too. If you feel your quads or hamstrings tense at the same time, try stretching those muscles for 15 seconds and try again. Your glutes are the only muscles that should be tensing/squeezing.

I suggest performing this exercise as much as possible through the day until your squeeze feels the same as the other side or they both feel much stronger before moving to level 2. If you feel you need more time on this exercise, progress to level 2 when you feel ready.

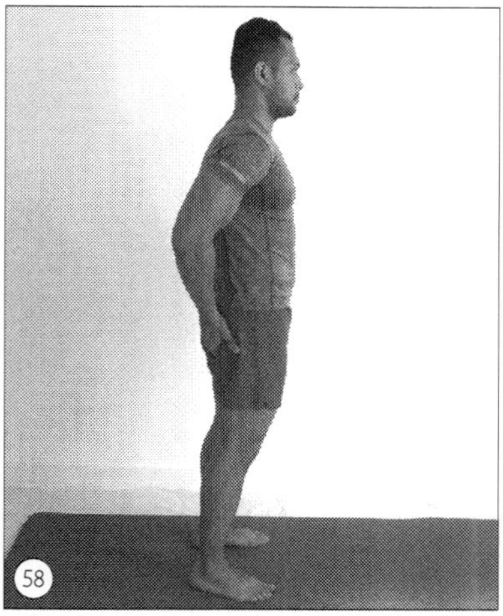

Level 2: Standing (p58) – Stand up and lean your body slightly to the right then contract (squeeze) your glutes on the right side only, hold the squeeze for 10 seconds. Rest for one second then repeat four times. Then lean over to the left a little bit and repeat on the left side.

Your target is 5 x 10 second holds on each side and should be performed 3-5 times a day. You should perform this exercise until your contraction/squeeze feels the same as the other side or until they both feel stronger before moving to level 3 or progress when you feel you are ready.

Sometimes it helps to have your knee slightly bent (the side of the glutes you are squeezing), place your hand on your glutes and shut your eyes while you squeeze.

Level 3: Seated – Sit up straight and lean back on a chair so that your back muscles are relaxed. Squeeze your glutes on the right side only and then hold the squeeze for 10 seconds. Rest for one second then repeat four times. Repeat on the left side.

Your target is 5 x 10 second holds on each side and should be performed 3-4 times a day. You'll get a better contraction if your feet are flat on the floor, not hanging off a table or a chair. Muscles are harder to contract when they are in a stretched position so this is the hardest version of the glute tenses and should only be performed once you are on level 2 of the clam.

5. Single Leg Glute Bridge

This is a level 3 hip extension exercise. It is very hard and should only be performed once you have completed level 2 of the clam. Although I call this a single leg glute bridge the exercise isn't actually performed on one leg but when you push your heel down into the floor it stimulates your glute muscles on that leg, so in effect it is strengthening one leg only.

Level 3 (p59/60) – Lie on your back and bend your knees. Keeping your feet flat press your left heel into the floor then slowly raise your hips to the ceiling and back down for a count of 4 slow seconds

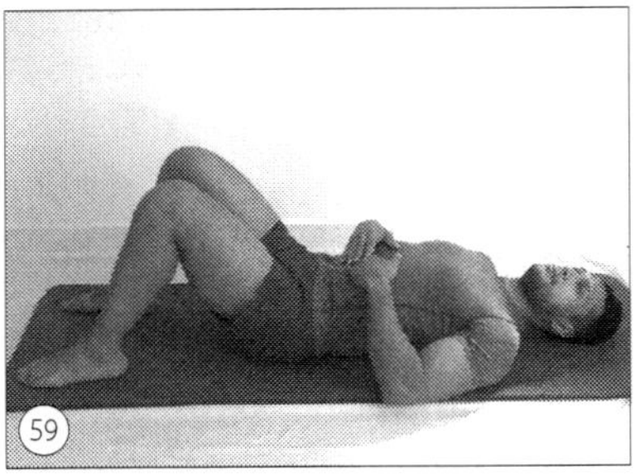
59

60

(1 mississippi, 2 mississippi) up and 4 seconds down. You must keep your feet flat and keep your left heel pressed down throughout the whole movement. Repeat four more times. Rest for 10-20 seconds then repeat.

Your target is 2 x 5 repetitions and should be performed no more than three times a week. If you haven't reached your target of 5 repetitions but you feel a strong fatigue, about 7-8/10 (if 10 is really fatigued) then STOP. Do not push through an 8/10 in fatigue.

It is important that you keep a bend in your hips at the top range. To get the most from this exercise, you must raise and lower your hips slowly. If you go too fast it will be too easy and you won't gain strength. If you feel like you're going to cramp in your glutes, STOP, you've done enough for that day.

When you've reached your target you can increase the repetitions from 5 to 10. You could alternate this exercise by performing one week of single leg bridges and the following week single leg deadlifts.

5. Single Leg Deadlifts

If you are a gym goer, you will be familiar with this exercise except my version is different to the norm because I use it primarily as a glute exercise. This is a hip extension exercise and not an easy one to perform. It takes a fair amount of practice to get it right but it's very good for glute strength.

61

62

Level 3 (p61/62) – Stand up straight, move your left leg back about a foot, bent your left knee and raise your left heel off the ground. Bend your right knee about 5 degrees – just a tiny bit. With a slight duck bum and your chest out, move your upper body slowly towards the floor trying to keep all your weight on your right leg and avoid moving your hips backwards too much. As you lean forwards you should feel your right toes grip the floor as if you are going to fall forwards. As you lean forwards try to keep your duck bum through the whole movement which will keep your spine in neutral. Try to maintain the 5 degree bend in your right knee. Bend as far as you can for a count of 4 seconds then slowly raise your torso for a count of 4 seconds back to the standing position. Rest for 10-20 seconds then repeat.

Your target is 2 x 10 repetitions, alternating each leg. If you haven't reached your target of 10 repetitions but you feel a strong fatigue, about 7-8/10 (if 10 is really fatigued) then STOP. Do not push through an 8/10 in fatigue. If you feel like you're going to cramp (this is very common) in your glutes then STOP, you've done enough for that day. It is normal to only be able to perform a few repetitions of this exercise at first so please be patient. It may be an idea to start with 2 x 5 repetitions until you get stronger. This is a level 3 exercise and should be performed no more than three times a week.

Try to avoid bending your front knee more than 5 degrees throughout the whole movement. This exercise is best performed slowly to gain the most benefit. You could alternate this exercise by performing one week of single leg deadlifts and the following week single leg bridges.

Following the Pearson clam test and glute tension test, if you are only weak on one side of your glutes then it's best to perform exercises on that side only or until it catches up with the other side. If both sides are weak but one side is stronger always start on your weak side first. You can always re-test to feel your strength levels on both sides.

If you are not able to weight train but you are able to perform cardiovascular exercises (bike, cross trainer etc.) because of your back pain, I highly recommend that you perform at least one of the level 1 exercises before a gym or cardiovascular workout even if you're sitting on a bike. More on this in chapter 19.

One thing to note in this chapter with regard to clams and glute bridges: I get asked a lot if you can use bands. If you have back pain and other muscles are overworking and underworking it means your pelvis is unstable. Using bands will aggravate your instability so please avoid using bands until you are fully stable. When you've reached the level 3 target you should be stable; then you can add bands – which are really great for people who do not need this book!

16

Rehabilitation Part 2: Strengthening Your Lower Back

Some of these lower back strength exercises may appear simple and easy. Please do not underestimate any of them. It might take you some time before you reach the target for some of these exercises so please be patient. Always start with level 1 and only move onto level 2 when you have reached the set target or when you feel ready. Every back issue is different so please go at your own pace; you know your body better than anyone else.

1. Swiss Ball Leg Lifts

For this exercise you need a Swiss ball that is appropriate for your height: the taller you are the bigger the ball you require. They usually come in three sizes 55cm, 65cm and 75cm. If you are 5'5" or under then use the 55cm, if you are taller use the 65cm. If you are over 6'0" use the 75cm ball.

63

64

Level 1 (p63/64) – Place a Swiss ball under your pelvis with your hands flat on the floor. Move your hands forwards, rolling your pelvis over the ball until your toes are touching the floor and hands are flat. Keeping your knees slightly bent and fairly close together, lift your legs towards the ceiling. Try not to hyperextend (overarch) your lower back as you reach the top end of the movement. At the top range squeeze your glutes then lower your feet to the floor for a count of 4 seconds. Rest for 20-30 seconds then repeat.

Your target is 2 x 15 repetitions. This exercise should be performed three times a week. If you feel a strong fatigue, about 7-8/10 (if 10 is really fatigued) then STOP. Do not push through an 8/10 in fatigue. This exercise is quite good to do in front of a mirror or have someone with you to make sure you do not hyperextend (arch) your back.

You could perform it over a table but make sure you use a cushion under your pelvis to avoid your pelvic bone rubbing against the table. Try to avoid bending your elbows too much or your triceps (muscles on the back of your arm) will be utilised more than your lower back. When you reach the target you can move on to level 2 Swiss ball back extensions.

2. Seated Good Mornings

The good morning exercise is a gym strength exercise which I converted into a rehabilitation exercise and it's been one of the best rehab exercises I've ever used for lower back foundation strength.

One of my patients, Julie Young, had a chronic back issue when she first came to me. After a couple of treatments, she was doing well with her glute strength but she reported that she was in pain whilst performing the good mornings exercise even after a third treatment. Julie had pain in her weak glute during the whole movement. Only after a whole session of releasing her left hamstrings, lower back and pelvic ligaments with ART was she able to perform good mornings with ease. This is a typical scenario if you've suffered a long-term back issue. I'm happy to report that Julie is now pain free.

For this exercise you need a wooden pole or a broomstick, basically a long pole that is very light to hold. Most patients report they feel better straight after doing this exercise.

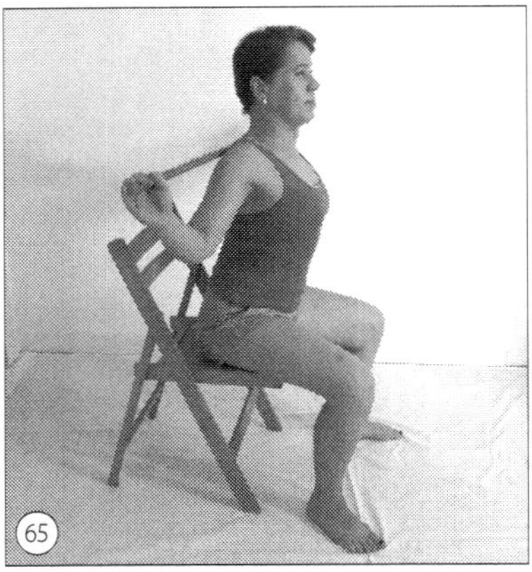

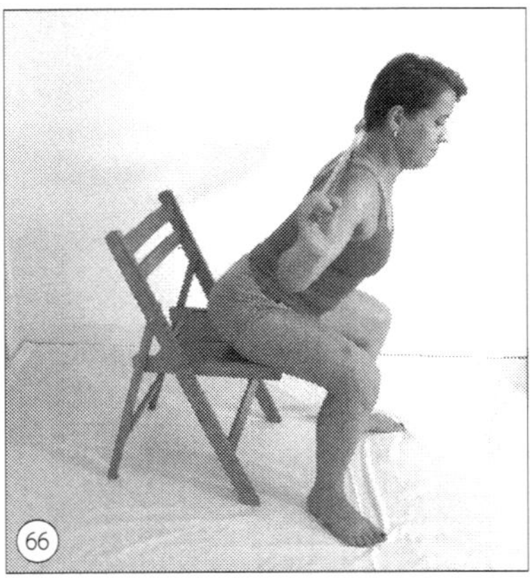

Level 1: seated (p65/66) – Sit on the edge of a chair with your legs wide apart and your feet slightly facing outwards. Make sure your knees are in line with your toes. Put a pole behind your head and rest it horizontally across your shoulders. Hold it at both ends or as wide as you can go comfortably. Keep your head in line with your spine as if you have a rod going through the top of your head down to your bum. Push your chest out a little bit which should help give you a duck bum and a neutral spine. Maintain that position and slowly lower your torso forwards for a count of 4 seconds, keeping your knees in line with your toes. When your spine starts to flatten out (you lose your duck bum/neutral spine) you've reached your end range. Slowly lift your torso for a count of 3 seconds back to the start position whilst keeping your spine in neutral. Rest for 20-30 seconds then repeat.

Your target is 2 x 15 repetitions and should be performed once or twice a day. If you feel a strong fatigue, about 7-8/10 (if 10 is really fatigued) then STOP. Do not push through an 8/10 in fatigue.

This exercise is quite good to do in front of a mirror or have someone with you to make sure you do not overextend (arch) your back. Try to avoid moving your knees inwards and maintain your duck bum through the movement which should help you to keep your spine in neutral. When you reach the target move onto level 2 or progress when you feel ready.

Level 2: standing (p67-68) – Stand with your feet wide apart and slightly facing outwards. Put a pole behind your head, horizontally across your shoulders and hold it at both ends or as wide as you can go. Keep your head in line with your body and push your chest forwards to help give you

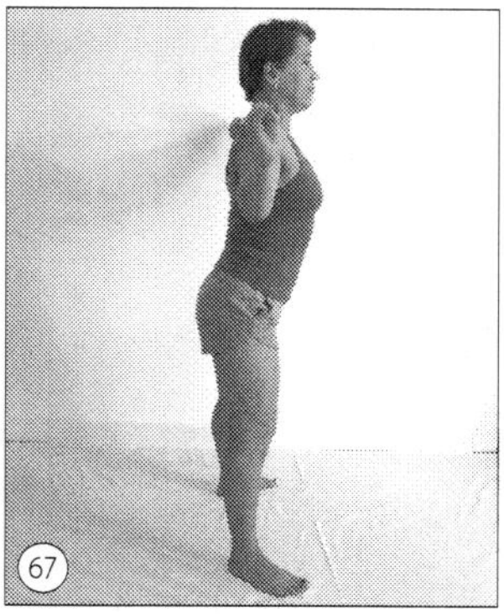

67

68

a duck bum. You may need to accentuate the duck bum a bit more for this version. Bend your knees about 5 degrees. Keeping your spine in neutral, maintain that position and move your hips back as if someone is pulling your bum backwards and so it feels like all your weight is on your heels. This should take 4 seconds. When your spine starts to flatten out you've reached the end of your range. Slowly lift your torso for a count of 3 seconds by pushing your hips forwards back to the start position while keeping your spine in neutral. Rest for 10-20 seconds then repeat.

Your target is 2 x 12 repetitions and should be performed 3 times a week. If you feel a strong fatigue, about 7-8/10 (if 10 is really fatigued) then STOP. Do not push through an 8/10 in fatigue.

The hardest part of this exercise is to keep your knees bent 5 degrees through the whole movement and to move your hips backwards as much as possible. This is another exercise that is good to perform in front of the mirror or with a friend/family member to help make sure you maintain good posture throughout the movement.

3. Swiss Ball Back Extension

This is an advanced exercise and a necessity for anyone recovering from back pain. A good friend of mine Reece Mander is an excellent strength coach who had suffered a long-term back issue before coming to see me as a patient. Even though he is a strong guy he had a fair amount of trouble performing the level 2 part of this exercise which made me realise why a lot of patients with longer-term issues find this the hardest of all the lower back rehab exercises. As a result, I split the exercise into 2 levels to allow your lower back to become accustomed to being put in a position against gravity before movement.

This exercise can be performed on a 45-degree back extension machine in your local gym as well as on a Swiss ball. However, a 90-degree back extension or glute ham raise are too advanced because you have twice the amount of gravity pushing down on you.

69

Level 2 (p69) – Place a Swiss ball underneath your pelvis while bracing your feet against a wall. It is important to keep your knees bent to avoid putting pressure on your lower back. This can take a bit of practice so please be patient!

Place your hands on the ball and lift your torso towards the ceiling with a neutral spine. Place each arm across your chest then hold that position for 10 seconds. Rest 10-20 seconds then repeat 2 more times. To make this harder, place your fingers against your temples and keep your elbows out to the side (p71).

Your target is 3 x 10 seconds and should be performed three times a week. If you feel a strong fatigue, about 7-8/10 (if 10 is really fatigued) then STOP. Do not push through an 8/10 in fatigue. Move onto level 2 when you reach the target or when you feel ready.

Level 3 (p69/70) – Get into the same position on the Swiss ball. Place your arms across your chest keeping your head in line with your body, slowly lower your torso for a count of 3 seconds towards

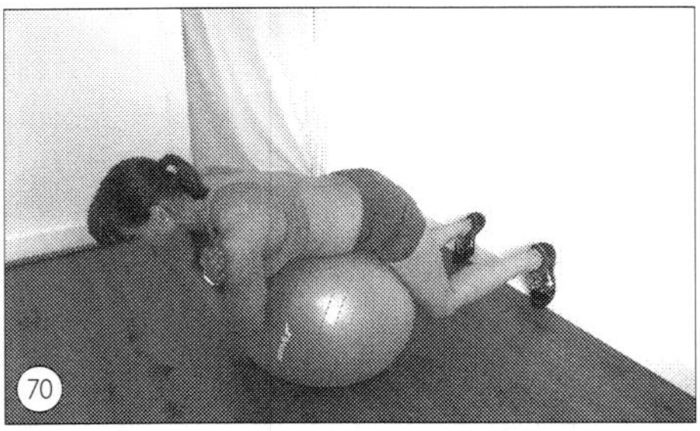

the floor until you can't go any further; this is your end range. Try to avoid lowering your torso to the point that your lower back starts to round (hunch), always try to maintain a neutral spine. Slowly lift your torso for a count of 3 seconds back up towards the start position and perform 12 repetitions. Rest for 10-20 seconds then repeat 2 more times.

Your target is 3 x 12 repetitions. This exercise should be performed 3 times a week. If you feel a strong fatigue, about 7-8/10 (if 10 is really fatigued) then STOP. Do not push through an 8/10 in fatigue. To start with you may want to perform 2 sets of 5 to allow your body to get used to the exercise and then gradually increase to the target range.

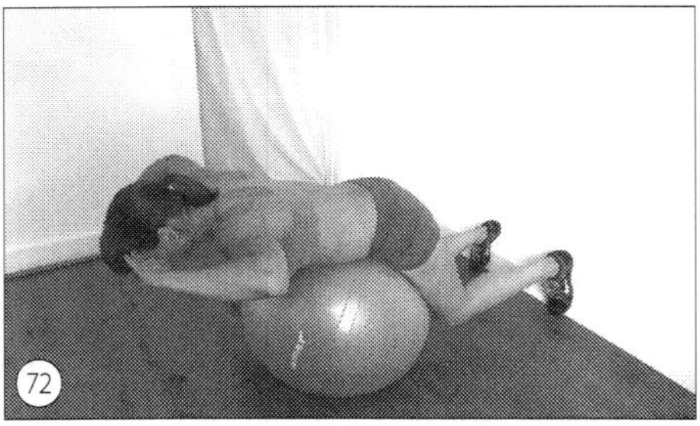

You can make this harder by holding your fingers against your temples and elbows out to the side (p71/72). This is a very hard exercise if you are recovering from a back issue so please take your time.

4. Wall Angels

Wall angels have been around for a very long time and are frequently used by therapists to help patients improve their posture. I was taught this exercise on my first therapy course in 2003 and it is somewhat different to other techniques. Traditionally this is an upper back exercise so if you have kyphosis (rounded shoulders) this will help. Regardless, we all tend to round our shoulders when we are stressed – it's human nature. Your body tends to revert back to the foetal position at times of stress, frustration and exhaustion.

One part of the spine affects the other so if you have rounded shoulders your head is likely to move forward which affects your lower back; it's amazing how much wall angels can help you in this scenario. This is an exercise you can follow for a few weeks and then pick it up again a month later. It is a fantastic preventative exercise you can employ for life.

Level 1 (p73/74) – Stand with your back against a wall and with your feet about a foot away from the wall. Place the back of your hands against the wall at an angle of about 30 degrees away from your waist. Make sure your head, shoulders, elbows, bum and the back of your hands

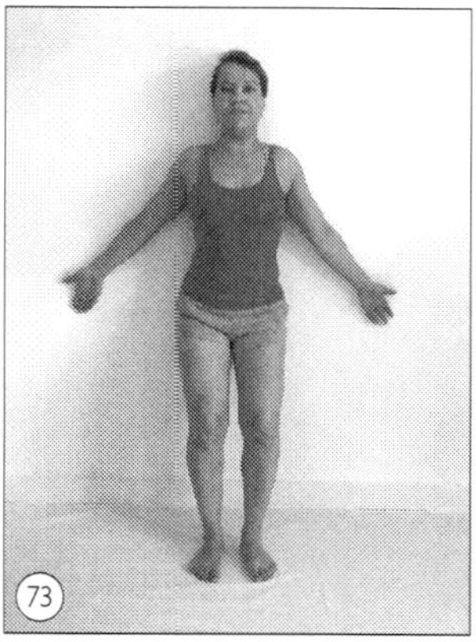

and arms are all touching the wall or as close as you can get. It may not be possible to get every body part against the wall – this is typical for a lot of people. Push your lower back into the wall so you can't fit anything between the wall and your lower back. This will make your head tilt back a lot and might feel uncomfortable at first so please bear with it.

Slowly raise your arms towards the ceiling for a count of 4 seconds whilst trying to keep all your body parts against the wall including your lower back. Try to keep your elbows as straight as possible and you should get to a point where you can't raise your arms any higher, you should feel a bunching of your skin/muscle tissue at the base of your neck. Stop at that point then slowly lower your arms for a count of 3 seconds.

Your target is 1 x 10 repetitions. This exercise can be performed 3-5 times a week. If you feel a strong fatigue, about 7-8/10 (if 10 is really fatigued) then STOP. Do not push through an 8/10 in fatigue.

Remember to keep your lower back pushed into the wall during the whole movement. You may find you fatigue by 4 or 5 repetitions so work up to the target before moving on to level 2.

Level 2 (p73/74) – Repeat the same exercise except this time hold your arms at the top position for 10 seconds which you can build up to.

Your target is 1 x 10 repetitions. This exercise can be performed three to five times a week. I would suggest starting with 5 second holds and work your way up to 10 seconds.

To achieve even more of a benefit from this exercise I would suggest stretching your chest muscles for 15 seconds before you perform wall angels. This helps to loosen off the front (anterior chain) side of your body before you strengthen the back (posterior chain) side. You can find out how to do chest stretches in chapter 18.

*Remember, if you perform any exercise and you feel pain anywhere STOP AND SEEK ADVICE from your doctor or health professional/therapist.

17

Rehabilitation Part 3: Strengthening Your Core

Core work is a very important aspect of resolving back pain. I have treated many patients who attend Pilates classes, which concentrates on strengthening your core, so they already had that aspect covered. Nonetheless, these exercises comprise of advanced versions to help everyone regardless of your level of core strength for back pain.

Please note some exercises should only be performed 3 times a week due to the increased intensity of the exercises so you will need more recovery.

1. Half Plank

There are a variety of levels and positions for all the plank exercises. As always start with the basic ones first. If you are in severe pain, don't be concerned if you can't hold the half plank for very long. At one stage I could only hold the half plank for 3 seconds so don't worry, you will get stronger – take your time.

The plank is traditionally performed with bent arms. However, it can get very boring so I have listed lots of variations to keep things interesting!

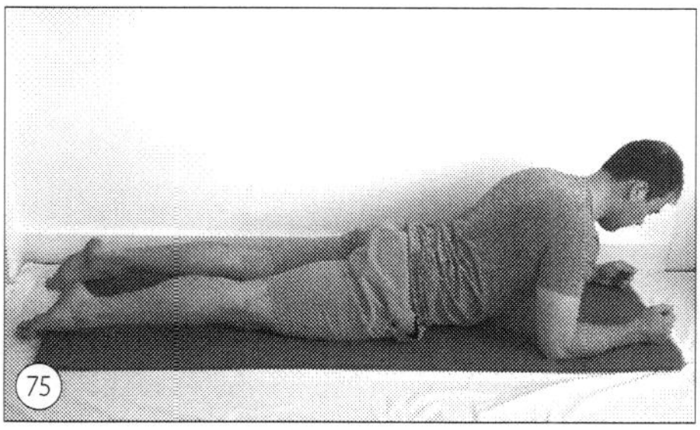

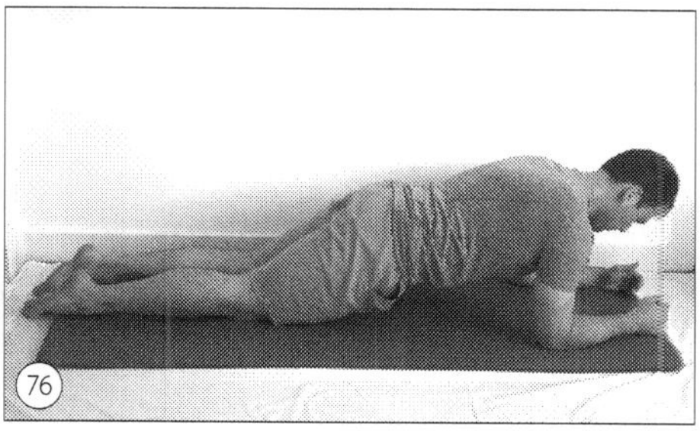

Level 1 – Half Plank (p75/76). Lie on your tummy, raise your upper body and place your elbows (facing forwards) directly underneath your shoulders. Keeping your knees on the floor raise your hips up to the ceiling until your body is straight from your knees to your shoulders then hold that position for as long as you can up to a minute. Rest for 20-30 seconds then repeat.

Your target is 2 x 60 second holds. If you feel a strong fatigue, about 7-8/10 (if 10 is really fatigued) then STOP. Do not push through an 8/10 in fatigue. This exercise should be performed once a day. You may need more rest in between sets initially if you can only hold for a few seconds.

The TVA muscle (the corset-type muscle) attaches into a dense part of fascia (connective tissue) in your lower back called the thoracolumbar fascia. As you fatigue you will feel an ache in your lower back. This is normal, just remember to stop when you hit an 8/10 in fatigue. You will be amazed how much you can progress with this exercise in a week!

Level 1 – Half Plank with straight arms (Half Press up plank) (p77). Get on to your hands and knees. Keeping your shins on the floor, walk your hands forwards until your arms are directly under your shoulders and your body is straight from your knees to your shoulders. Keep your elbows straight as possible. Hold this position for as long as you can up to a 60 seconds. Rest for 20-30 seconds then repeat.

Your target is 2 x 60 second holds. If you feel a strong fatigue, about 7-8/10 (if 10 is really fatigued) then STOP. Do not push through an 8/10 in fatigue. This exercise should be performed once a day. This is an alternative to the half plank.

For both half planks you may need more rest in between the two sets initially. If you can only hold for a few seconds, you could do this exercise twice a day until you reach 2 x 30 seconds then revert back to once a day.

2. Half Side Plank

Level 1 – Half Side Plank (p78/79). Lie on your left side and place your left elbow directly underneath your left shoulder. Keeping your knees bent and on the floor with your feet together, raise your hips up to the ceiling until your body is straight from your knees to your shoulders. Hold that position for as long as you can up to 60 seconds. Rest for 20-30 seconds then repeat.

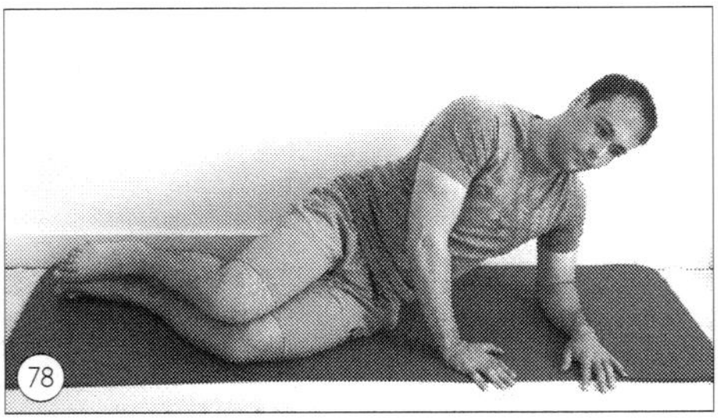

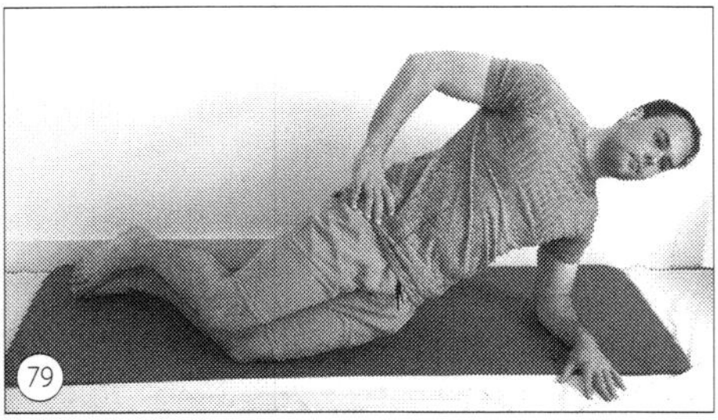

Your target is 2 x 60 second holds on each side. If you feel a strong fatigue, about 7-8/10 (if 10 is really fatigued) then STOP. Do not push through an 8/10 in fatigue. This exercise should be performed once a day. You may need to push your hips forwards slightly to get your body as straight as possible. Make sure your elbow is directly under your shoulder.

Level 1 – Half Side Plank with straight arm (Half Side Press up plank) (p80). Get in the same position as the half side plank on your left side except this time with your arm straight. Keeping your knees bent, raise your hips up and forward until your body is straight from your knees to your shoulders. Rest your right hand on your hip. Hold that position for as long as you can up to 60 seconds. Rest for 20-30 seconds then repeat.

Your target is 2 x 60 second holds on each side. If you feel a strong fatigue, about 7-8/10 (if 10 is really fatigued) then STOP. Do not push through an 8/10 in fatigue. This exercise should be performed once a day. This is an alternative to the half side plank.

3. Plank

81

82

Level 2 – Plank (p81). Lie on your tummy, raise your upper body and place your elbows (facing forwards) directly underneath your shoulders. Tuck your toes under your feet and raise your hips and knees off the floor until your body is straight (without pushing your hips up to the ceiling) from your feet to your shoulders. Hold that position for as long as you can up to 60 seconds. Rest 10-20 seconds then repeat.

Your target is 2 x 60 second holds. If you feel a strong fatigue, about 7-8/10 (if 10 is really fatigued) then STOP. Do not push through an 8/10 in fatigue. This exercise should be performed 3 times a week.

Level 2 – Plank with straight arms (Press up plank) (p82). Get on to your hands and knees. Walk your hands forwards until they are directly underneath your shoulders. Keeping your elbows straight, tuck your toes under your feet and raise your hips and knees off the floor until your body is straight from your feet to your shoulders. Hold that position for as long as you can up to 60 seconds. Rest 10-20 seconds then repeat.

Your target is 2 x 60 second holds. If you feel a strong fatigue, about 7-8/10 (if 10 is really fatigued) then STOP. Do not push through an 8/10 in fatigue. This exercise should be performed 3 times a week. This is an alternative to the plank. You can make both versions of the plank harder by decreasing your rest time in between sets.

4. Side Plank

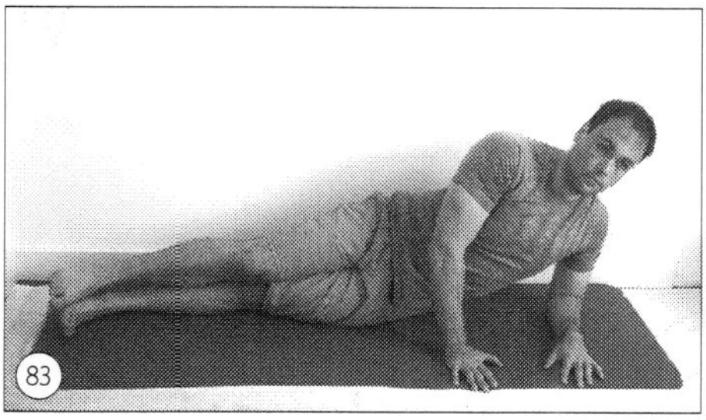

83

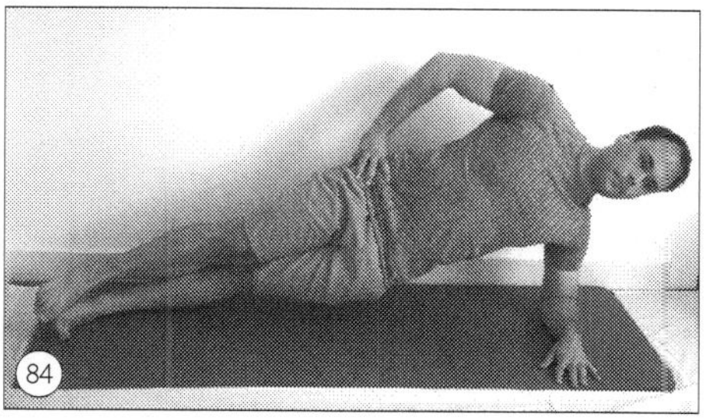

84

Level 2 – Side Plank (p83/84). This is the same as the half side plank except this time, keeping your feet together, raise your hips off the floor until your body is straight from your feet to your shoulders. Rest your free hand on your hip. Hold that position for as long as you can up to 60 seconds. Rest 10-20 seconds then repeat.

Your target is 2 x 60 second holds on each side**. If you feel a strong fatigue, about 7-8/10 (if 10 is really fatigued) then STOP. Do not push through an 8/10 in fatigue. This exercise should be performed 3 times a week.

Level 2 – Side Plank with straight arm (Side press up plank) (p85). This is the same as the half side plank straight arms except this time, keeping your feet together, raise your hips off the floor until your body is straight from your feet to your shoulders. Rest your free hand on your hip. Hold that position for as long as you can up to 60 seconds. Rest 10-20 seconds then repeat.

Your target is 2 x 60 second holds on each side. If you feel a strong fatigue, about 7-8/10 (if 10 is really fatigued) then STOP. Do not push through an 8/10 in fatigue. This exercise should be performed 3 times a week. This is an alternative to the side plank. You can make both versions of the side plank harder by decreasing your rest time in between sets.

**You might have seen a variation of the side plank exercise where your feet are split apart instead of being on top of each other. I do not like this variation because if one or both sides of your hips are extremely tight and weak this can hurt or be very uncomfortable to get into this position which can aggravate you. Remember it's always best to avoid aggravation.

5. Swiss Ball Hip Lift

This is a very basic exercise so it is very good for those people who have had long-term back pain. As always go at your own pace.

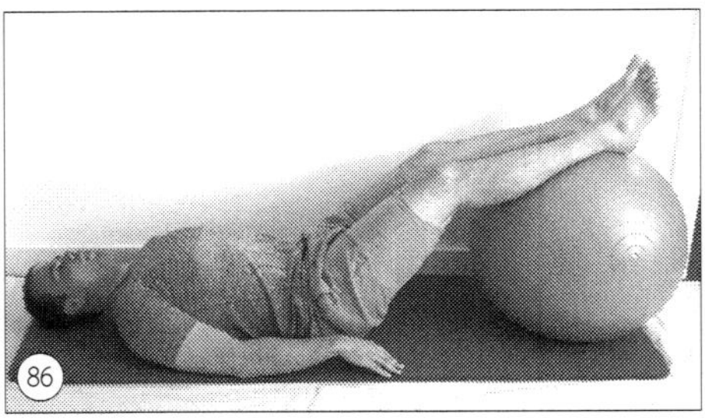

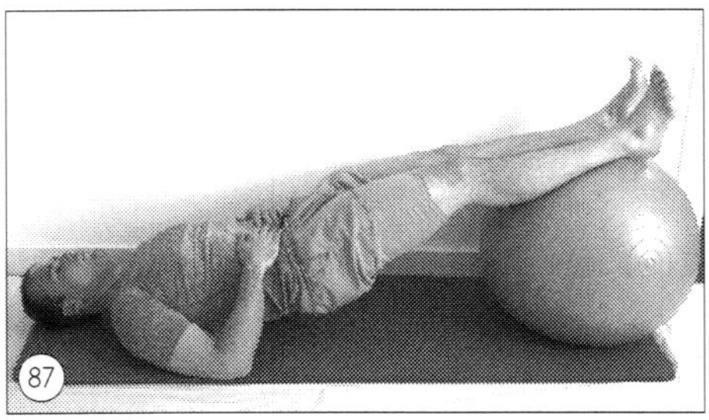

Level 1 (p86/87) – Lie on your back with your heels and calves (back of your lower leg) on a Swiss ball (the taller you are, the bigger ball you need). Rest your hands on the floor and slowly raise your hips to the ceiling until your body is almost straight from your shoulders to your feet keeping a slight bend in your hips. Slowly place your hands on your stomach. Hold that position for as long as you can up to a minute. Rest for 20-30 seconds then repeat.

Your target is 2 x 60 second holds. This exercise should be performed once a day. If you feel a strong fatigue, about 7-8/10 (if 10 is really fatigued) then STOP. Do not push through an 8/10 in fatigue. When you reach the target move on to level 2.

Level 2 (p88) – Perform the same exercise as level 1 except this time place your hands across your chest. Hold for as long as you can up to a minute. Rest for 10-20 seconds and repeat.

Your target is 2 x 60 second holds. This exercise should be performed 3 times a week. When you reach the target move onto level 3.

Level 3 (p89) – Perform the same exercise except this time extend your arms and fingers up towards the ceiling. Hold for as long as you can up to a minute. Rest for 10-20 seconds and repeat.

Your target is 2 x 60 second holds. This exercise should be performed 3 times a week. To make the exercise harder you can move the ball further away towards your heels.

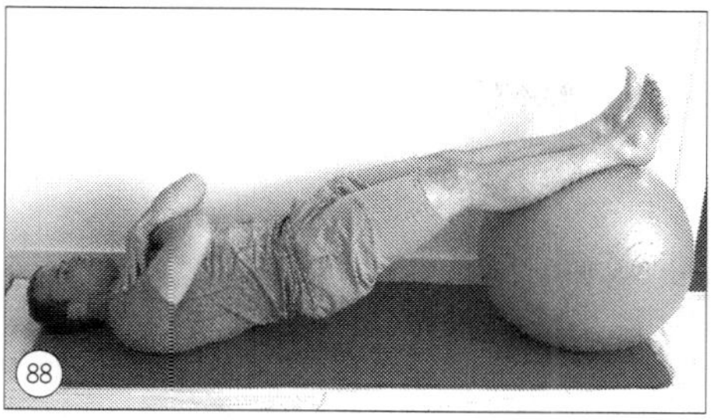

88

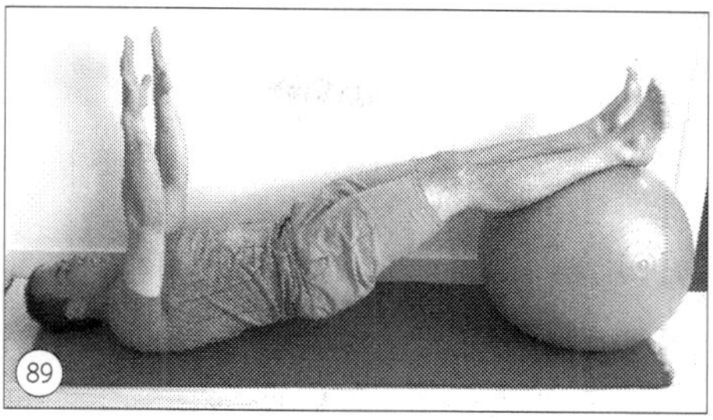

89

6. Superman

This is a very well known exercise otherwise called a bird dog, However, when I was taught this it was called the superman which I prefer because it always made me feel like I was superman when I'd extend my arm out against my head!

90

91

Level 1 (p90/91) – Get on to your hands and knees so that your shoulders and knees are bent at 90 degrees and your back is in neutral. Slowly raise your right arm and extend it out in front of you, as close to your ear whilst trying to keep your body as still as possible. Hold for 5 seconds then repeat on the other arm. Then extend your left leg behind you and raise it to the ceiling as far as you feel comfortable, without overarching your lower back. Hold for 5 seconds then repeat on your right leg. This is 20 seconds in total. Rest for 20-30 seconds then repeat the whole circuit.

Your target is 2 x each circuit (5 second holds twice on each arm and each leg). This exercise should be performed once a day. If you feel a strong fatigue, about 7-8/10 (if 10 is really fatigued) then STOP. Do not push through an 8/10 in fatigue.

The aim of the exercise is to keep as still as possible as you extend your limbs back and forth. Your arm doesn't have to be level with your ear so just lift as high as you feel comfortable. When you reach the target move onto level 2.

92

Level 2 (p92) – Start in the same position as level 1. Raise your right arm up and extend it out in front of you. Maintain than position and extend your left leg behind you without overarching your lower back. Hold for 15 seconds then repeat on the other side – left arm and right leg. Rest for 10-20 seconds then repeat the circuit.

Your target is 2 x 15 seconds holds (twice for each pair of extended arms and legs). If you feel a strong fatigue, about 7-8/10 (if 10 is really fatigued) then STOP. Do not push through an 8/10 in fatigue. This exercise should be performed once a day. The aim of the exercise is to keep as still as possible as you extend your limbs back and forth.

7. Swiss Ball Plank

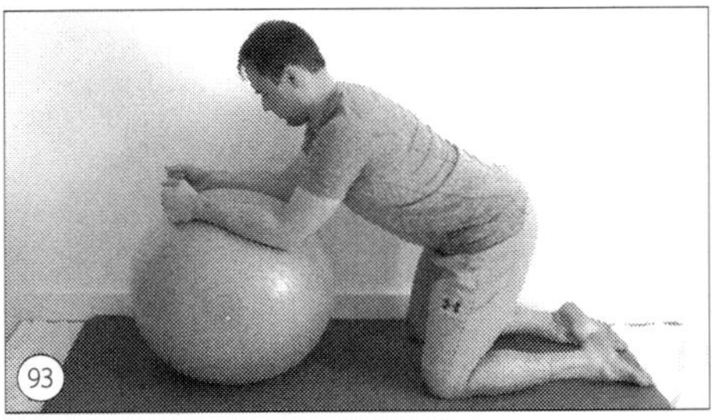

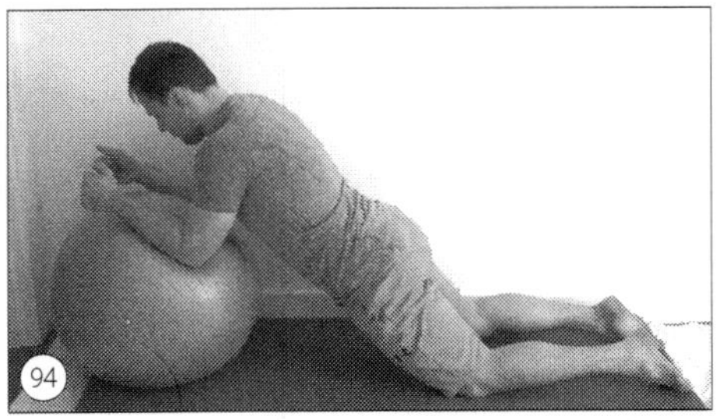

Level 1 (p93/94) – Get on to your knees and place both elbows on a Swiss ball, shoulder width apart with your forearms facing forwards. Make sure your elbows are directly underneath your shoulders. Keeping your knees on the floor, roll the ball forwards, pushing your hips forward until your body is straight from your knees to your shoulders. Hold that position for as long as you can up to 60 seconds. Rest for 20-30 seconds then repeat.

Your target is 2 x 60 second holds. If you feel a strong fatigue, about 7-8/10 (if 10 is really fatigued) then STOP. Do not push through an 8/10 in fatigue. This should be performed 3 times a week.

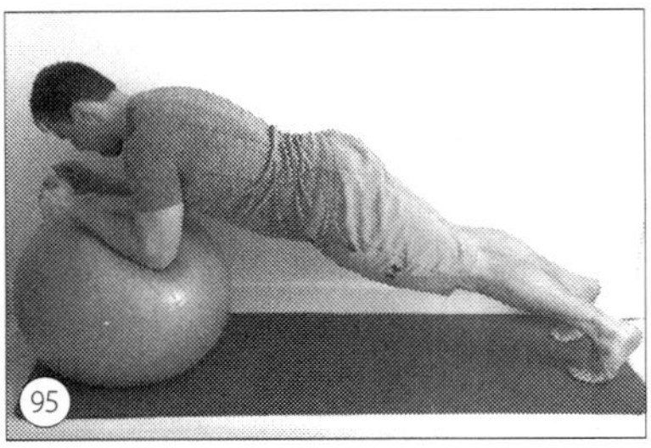

Level 2 (p95) – Perform the same exercise, this time tuck your toes under your feet. Lift your hips and knees off the floor until your body is straight from your feet to your shoulders. Hold that position for as long as you can up to 60 seconds. Rest for 10-20 seconds then repeat.

Your target is 2 x 60 second holds. If you feel a strong fatigue, about 7-8/10 (if 10 is really fatigued) then STOP. Do not push through an 8/10 in fatigue. This exercise should be performed 3 times a week.

8. Swiss Ball Bridge

Level 1 (p96/97) – Sit on top of a ball that is the correct size for your height. Slowly and carefully walk your feet forwards and gently lean back so that the ball rolls backwards towards your head. When the ball is under your head and shoulders, rest your hands on your hips. Raise your hips so that your body is almost straight between your knees and shoulders and your knees are bent around 90 degrees. It is important to keep a slight bend at your hips to avoid putting pressure on your lower back. Hold that position for as long as you can up to 60 seconds. Rest for 20-30 seconds then repeat.

Your target is 2 x 60 second holds. If you feel a strong fatigue, about 7-8/10 (if 10 is really fatigued) then STOP. Do not push through an 8/10 in fatigue. This exercise should be performed 3 times a week. When you reach the target then move onto level 2.

To get off the ball safely, move your feet backwards so that it propels your upper body back to the seated position. Or, gently lower your bum onto the floor and get up from there.

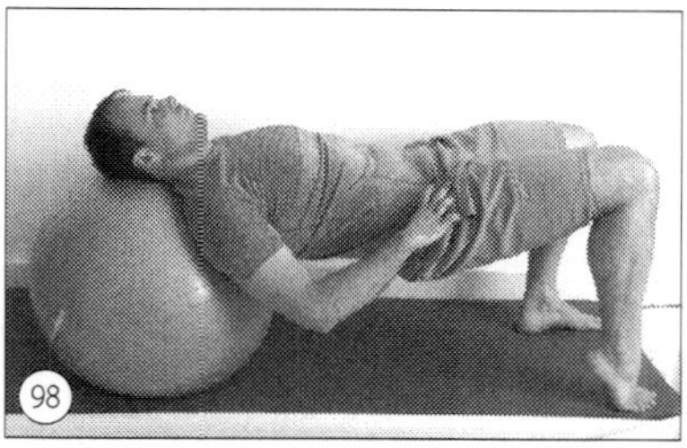

98

Level 2 (p98) – Get into the same start position. This time lift your right heel off the floor keeping your toes on the floor. Try not to sway your body to the right as you do this. Hold this position for 10 seconds then repeat with the left heel off the floor. Lift each heel one more time. Rest for 10-20 seconds then repeat.

Your target is a 2 x each circuit. If you feel a strong fatigue, about 7-8/10 (if 10 is really fatigued) then STOP. Do not push through an 8/10 in fatigue. This exercise should be performed 3 times a week. When you reach the target then move on to level 3.

The aim is to try to keep your body as still and possible as you lift each heel off the floor.

99

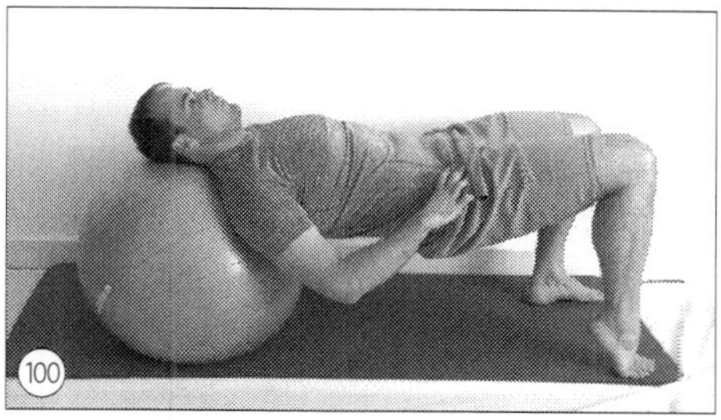

100

Level 3: Raises (p99/100) – This is a combined core and glute exercise. Get into the same start position as level 2 lifting your left heel off the floor. Maintain this position then slowly lower your hips to the floor for a count of 4 seconds and raise back up for a count of 4 seconds. Perform five repetitions in all then repeat on the right leg with the heel lift. Rest for 10-20 seconds then repeat.

Your target is 2 x 5 repetitions. If you feel a strong fatigue, about 7-8/10 (if 10 is really fatigued) then STOP. Do not push through an 8/10 in fatigue. This exercise should be performed 3 times a week. To make this exercise harder you can increase the repetitions to sets of 10.

Rehabilitation programme

Level 1 exercises	**Sets/reps**	**Per day/week**	**Progress to**
GLUTES			
Clam	3 x 1 min hold + 1 x 15 reps	1-2 a day	Level 2 clam
Ballet step (alternate with doggies)	2 x 15 reps	2-3 a day	Level 2 ballet step
Doggies (alternate with ballet step)	2 x 15 reps	2-3 a day	Level 2 doggies
Glute tenses	5 x 5 secs hold	3-5 a day	Level 2 glute tenses
LOWER BACK			
Swiss ball leg lifts	2 x 15 reps	3 x a week	Level 2 S/B back ext.
Seated good mornings (GM)	2 x 15 reps	1-2 a day	Level 2 stand GM's
Wall angels (optional)	1 x 10 reps	3-5 x a week	Level 2 wall angels
CORE			
½ plank bent or straight	2 x 60 seconds hold	1 a day	Level 2 plank
½ side plank bent or straight	2 x 60 seconds hold	1 a day	Level 2 side plank
Swiss ball hip lift*	2 x 60 seconds hold	1 a day	Level 2 S/B hip lift
Superman*	2 x each circuit 5 secs holds each	1 a day	Level 2 superman
Swiss ball plank*	2 x 60 seconds hold	3 x a week	Level 2 S/B plank
Swiss ball bridge*	2 x 60 seconds hold	3 x a week	Level 2 S/B bridge

** Alternate all 4 exercises every day so daily you perform the ½ plank, ½ side plank and only ONE of the other 4 exercises*

S/B = Swiss ball, min = minute, reps = repetitions, secs = seconds, back ext. = back extension

+ rest 20-30 seconds in-between sets

+ always stop when you reach an 8/10 in fatigue (if 0 is nothing and 10 is really fatigued)

+ if 3 times a week, make sure you have one day off in-between e.g. Monday, Wednesday, Friday

Level 2 exercises	Sets/reps	Per day/week	Progress to
GLUTES			
Clam	1 min hold + 3 x 15 reps	1 a day	Level 3 s/l gl. bridge
Ballet step	2 x 15 reps	1-2 a day	Level 3 s/l deadlift
Glute tenses	5 x 10 seconds hold	3-5 a day	Level 3 glute tenses
LOWER BACK			
Standing good mornings	2 x 12 reps	3 x a week	Finish
Swiss ball back extension	3 x 10 seconds hold	3 x a week	Level 3 S/B back ext.
Wall angels (optional for posture)	1 x 10 reps, 10 secs hold	3-5 x a week	Finish
CORE			
Plank bent or straight	2 x 60 seconds hold	3 x a week	Maintenance
Side plank bent or straight	2 x 60 seconds hold	3 x a week	Maintenance
Swiss ball hip lift*	2 x 60 seconds hold	3 x a week	Level 3 S/B hip lift
Superman*	2 x 15 seconds hold each side	3 x a week	Finish
Swiss ball plank*	2 x 60 seconds hold	3 x a week	Maintenance
Swiss ball bridge*	2 x circuit, 10 secs hold	3 x a week	Level 3 S/B bridge

** Alternate all 4 exercises so you perform the plank, the side plank and only ONE of the other 4 exercises*
S/B = Swiss ball, min = minute, reps = repetitions, s/l gl. bridge = single leg glute bridge, back ext. = back extension secs = seconds
+ rest 10-20 seconds in-between sets
+ always stop when you reach an 8/10 in fatigue (if 0 is nothing and 10 is really fatigued)
+ if 3 times a week, make sure you have one day off in-between e.g. Monday, Wednesday, Friday

Level 3 exercises	Sets/reps	Per day/week	Progress to
GLUTES			
Glute tenses	5 x 10 seconds hold	3-4 x a day	Maintenance
Single leg glute bridge (slow up & down)*	2 x 5 repetitions	3 x a week	Maintenance
Single leg deadlifts*	2 x 10 repetitions	3 x a week	Maintenance
LOWER BACK			
Swiss ball back extension	3 x 12 repetitions	3 x a week	Maintenance
CORE			
Swiss ball hip lift	2 x 60 seconds hold	3 x a week	Maintenance
Swiss ball bridge raises	2 x 5 repetitions	3 x a week	Maintenance

** Alternate these two exercises for each session*

+ rest 10-20 seconds in-between sets

+ always stop when you reach an 8/10 in fatigue (if 0 is nothing and 10 is really fatigued)

+ if 3 times a week, make sure you have one day off in-between e.g. Monday, Wednesday, Friday

Maintenance programme

Exercise	Sets/reps	Per week	Notes
GLUTES			
Clam	2 x 15 repetitions	2 x a week	Can use before a workout
S/l bridge (alternate with s/l deadlift)	2 x 5 repetitions	2 x a week	Can use during a workout
S/l deadlift (alternate with s/l bridge)	2 x 10 repetitions	2 x a week	Can use during a workout
LOWER BACK			
S/B back extension	2 x 15 repetitions	2 x a week	Can use during a workout
S/B leg lifts (alternate with S/B back ext.)	1 x 15 repetitions	2 x a week	Can use during a workout
Standing GM's (alternate with S/B leg lifts)	1 x 15 repetitions	2 x a week	Can use during a workout
CORE			
Plank bent or straight*	2 x 60 secs hold	2 x a week	Use at end of a workout
Side plank bent or straight*	2 x 60 secs hold	2 x a week	Use at end of a workout
Swiss ball plank (level 2)*	2 x 60 secs hold	2 x a week	Use at end of a workout
Swiss ball hip lift (level 3)*	2 x 60 secs hold	2 x a week	Use at end of a workout

** Pick 2 of the 4 core exercises to perform twice a week and alternate each week (so you don't get bored!)*

S/B = Swiss ball, s/l = single leg, secs = seconds, GM's = good mornings

+ rest 10-20 seconds in-between sets

18

Rehabilitation Part 4: Static & Mobility Stretches

The general consensus with doctors, websites etc., is it is best to stretch your back when it's stiff and painful. This is true to a point; it will always feel great to stretch your back and it will help to stretch your fascia (connective tissue). However, if you remember in chapter 8, when your lower back becomes tight and weak it leads to a shortening of the muscles at the front of your body i.e. your quads and hip flexors. Hence, it is better to combine stretches on the front of your body (anterior chain) as well as the back of your body (posterior chain). If you sit for long periods in the day or if you travel a lot, it is also extremely beneficial to stretch your upper body too. Your body is intertwined with connective tissue, it criss-crosses everywhere through organs, muscles and over, under and around your joints so stretching your whole body is great for back pain, posture and for general maintenance once you're pain free.

Stretching is a way to elongate your muscles, tendons (the end parts of a muscle) and fascia and should NEVER be painful. When you perform a static stretch you move a joint into a certain position until you feel tension and then hold for 15 seconds. You have to be careful not to overstretch so if you feel pain at any time during the stretch you've gone too far. In that case you need to ease off a bit until there is no pain and you only feel tension, then hold. Every stretch is held for 15 seconds unless you're doing breathing stretching, which I'll come to later.

One other thing to note is ALWAYS static stretch (holding stretch) after exercise, never before. There are exceptions to this but for safety always static stretch AFTER exercise. Static stretching is gentle and tells the brain that you want to relax whereas mobility/dynamic stretches are where you move your joints gently in and out or back and forth. These types of stretches are good to perform before exercise as they tell the brain you want to stretch your muscles to get ready for exercise.

I've found that using deep breathing during stretching has advantages. This is where you breathe in through your nose (with your mouth closed), hold for 2-3 seconds and then exhale through your mouth with pursed lips (described in chapter 12). Doing this twice roughly amounts to the 15 seconds required for each stretch. However, if you're short on time, even doing breathing stretches once will help. As we discussed previously breathing taps into the calming side of your nervous system so you should feel more relaxed while you get a great stretch at the same time, bonus!

Stretching should always be gentle and feel good. When you sit down for long periods, a lot of your lower body muscles shorten which affects back pain, a lot. I've mentioned before about getting into a routine of stretching your quads every time you go to the toilet. This is called association. You associate a task with stretching so it helps you to remember to stretch through the day. Also, staying hydrated is a big factor with back pain so the more you drink means more toilet trips and quad stretching so you get a double whammy!

A lot of people get confused about stretching and strength exercises. A stretch elongates fascia and muscle whereas a strength exercise helps you get stronger. Stretching doesn't resolve injuries but it certainly helps aid the process of recovery and it also helps to prevent your muscles from getting tight in order to stay healthy.

Static stretches

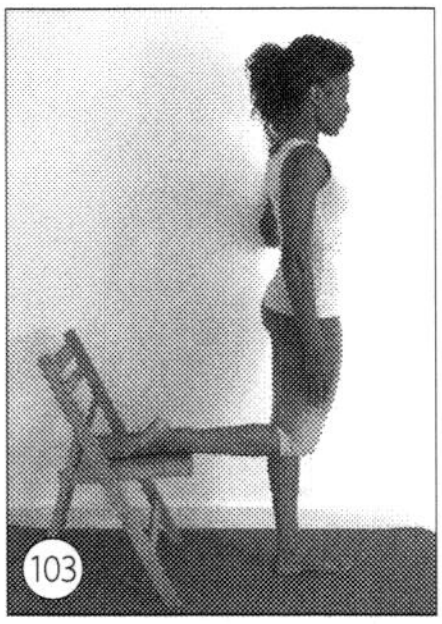

Quads (p101/102/103) – Bend your knee behind you, raise your heel up towards your glutes then grab hold of your mid foot. Keeping your knee fairly close to your other knee, pull your foot towards your glutes until you feel tension at the front of your thigh (quads) and hold. You can also do this lying on your tummy or on your side so it's a great stretch to do before you get out of bed. If you are very tight in your quads and cannot lift your foot high enough behind you, try resting your foot on a chair and slowly sit back until you feel the stretch in your quads, then hold. You may feel the stretch around your knee as well as the front of your thigh. To accentuate the stretch, push your hips forward until you feel tension, then hold. Change legs and repeat.

Calf (p104) – You would be surprised how good your back can feel by stretching your calves. This is because of the fascial (connective tissue) connection from your lower back, down the back of your legs to the underneath of your feet.

Stand up and extend one leg back while bending your forward leg. Straighten your back leg keeping your heel flat on the floor then bend your front knee forwards until you feel tension at the back of your calf/heel (of your back leg) and hold.

Calf bent knee (p105) – This stretch is for your deeper calf muscles. Get into the same position as the calf stretch except this time bring your back leg forwards so that the toes of your back foot are a few inches away from your front heel then bend both knees until you feel a stretch at the back of your calf and heel (of your back leg), then hold. You might feel a stretch in both calves, this is ok!

Side hip (p106) – Stand up with your hips shoulder width apart and your right palm facing the right side of your hips with your knees slightly bent. Lean your upper body to the right and slowly reach your right hand down your leg. As you lean to the right, bring your left arm out to the side and up towards your ear. Stop when you feel tension on the left side of your upper body, then hold.

107

108

109

Chest (p107) – Stand against a wall, side on. Place your left forearm on the wall about 4-5 inches higher than shoulder height, keeping your left palm flat on the wall. Slowly take a step forward with your left leg while keeping your forearm completely still until you feel tension in your left chest muscles around the front of your shoulder and hold.

Upper back (p108) – Clasp your hands together as if you are giving someone a huge hug, with your palms facing you. Gently push your upper back away from your hands (backwards) until you feel a stretch across your upper back and hold.

110

Lats (p109) – This stretch is for your lateral back muscles otherwise known as the V part of your latissimus dorsi muscles, lats for short. Grab hold of a door handle with your left hand, walk your feet backwards, bend your knees and push your bum backwards so that you lean forwards. Keeping your back in neutral, push your bum backwards and a little to the right until you feel tension in the left side of your upper body then hold.

Hip flexors (p110) – Get on to your knees and place your left foot forwards. Keep your body upright, move your hips forwards until you feel tension at the front of your right hip, then hold.

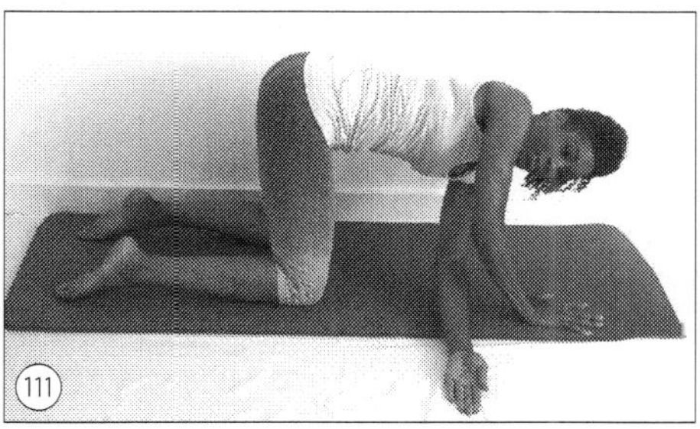
111

112

Back: single arm (p111) – This is my preference to the side lying torso twist (described later) because it is more stable on your spine. Please go slow with this stretch. Get on to your hands and knees. Place the back of your left hand on the floor then slide it under your right shoulder between your right arm and hip. Move as far as you can until you feel tension in your upper back, then hold.

Glutes (p112) – Lie on your back and bring your right knee up towards your left shoulder. Bend your right knee bent around 90 degrees and pull your right knee and foot towards your left shoulder until you feel a stretch in your right glutes then hold.

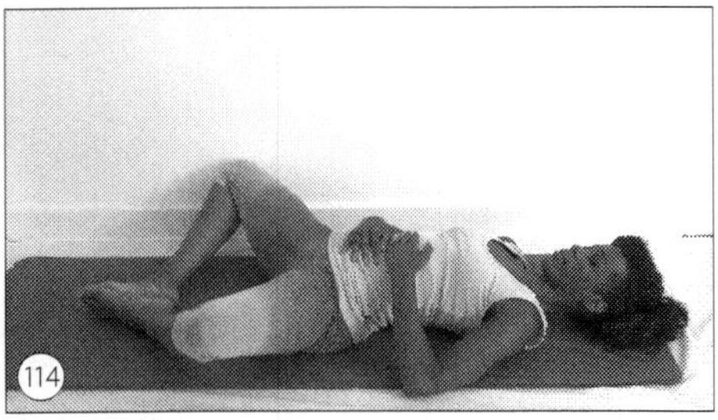

Deep glutes (p113) – Lie on your back, bend your left knee and place your right ankle on your left thigh just above your left knee. Grab your left thigh (place your right hand in between both legs) and lift your left thigh towards your chest until you feel tension in your right deep glutes, then hold.

Lying groin (p114) – This is an adductor (inner thigh) muscle stretch and is very good to open up your pelvis for easing back pain. Get on to your back, bend your knees and keep your feet together. Very slowly allow your knees to lower towards the floor until you feel tension in your groin. Take your time with this stretch, it may take up to 10 seconds just to get into the stretch, then hold. This is a great stretch to use the deep breathing technique.

Seated groin (p115/116) – You have both short and long adductor muscles so you can do this stretch in two different ways. First, get on to the floor and sit against a wall. Keeping your feet together slowly allow your knees to lower towards the floor until you feel tension in your groin (like a seated version of the lying groin stretch). Go slowly as it may take a few seconds to get into the stretch before you hold. To stretch your long adductors: this time sit against the wall with your legs straight and move them as wide as they will go before you feel a stretch in your groin.

To accentuate this stretch, keep your back upright, lower your upper body towards the floor while placing your hands on your thighs. Stop when you feel a stretch in your groin. You must keep your lower back straight and try to avoid hunching forward.

Lower back (p117) – Lie on your back and lift your knees up to your chest. Place your arms around your legs like you are hugging them and gently pull them towards your chest until you feel tension in your lower/mid back then hold. Be careful if you have just been diagnosed with a disc bulge, stenosis, a herniation, spondylosis or spondylolisthesis. This is a great stretch to take the pressure off your lower back first thing in the morning so I suggest doing this before you get out of bed.

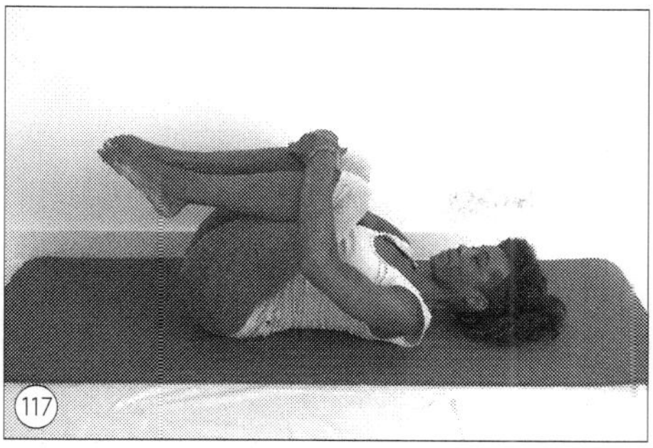
117

118

Hamstrings (p118) – Stand up and place your left foot on a low step or chair. I would suggest making sure you are near a wall in case you lose your balance. Relaxing your left foot slowly lean forward with your hands on your left leg, keeping your spine in neutral, until you feel tension in the back of your hamstrings then hold. You can also do this seated as described in the 3D stretch.

119

120

Hamstrings 3D (p119/120/121/122) – I learnt this stretch from Charles Poliquin many years ago and I have found it to be the most efficient stretch for your hamstrings because you stretch all of them. Get on to the floor and extend your left leg forwards. Bend your right knee behind you (like a hurdler) (p120) or bend your knee in front of you placing your right foot against your left leg (p119). Place both hands on your left leg and slowly lean forward. Slide your hands down your leg maintaining a neutral spine, until you feel tension in your hamstrings, then hold. Try to avoid hunching your back.

121

122

Slowly come back up to the start position, twist to your right and move your left arm 6-8 inches to the right of your left leg (p121). Slowly lean forward and push your left arm as far forward as you can until you feel tension in the back of your left leg then hold. You can use your right arm to stabilize you by placing it either in front or behind your hips.

Slowly come back up to the start position, twist to your left and move your right arm 6-8 inches to the left of your left leg (p122). Slowly lean forward and push your right arm as far forward as you can until you feel tension in the back of your left leg then hold. You can use your left arm to stabilize you by placing it behind your hips.

Slowly come back up to the start position and repeat the first step. This time you should find you can lean forward much further. I highly recommend performing deep breathing during each section while performing this three dimensional stretch.

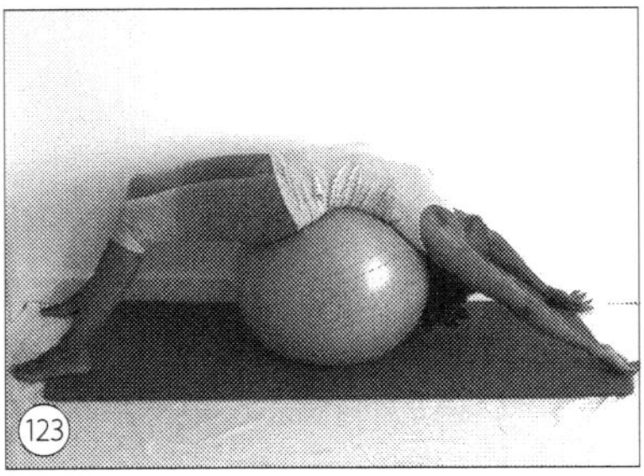

123

Swiss ball back/abs stretch (p123) – Sit on a Swiss ball and, very slowly, start walking your feet forward as you lower your back on to the Swiss ball. When your whole back is on top of it, keeping your knees bent allow your whole upper body to relax. When this is comfortable try lifting your arms above your head, one at a time to increase the stretch. You can hold this stretch for up to a minute. To get off the ball, bring your arms back to your waist first then use your feet to walk backwards to propel your upper body back to the seated position.

Mobility stretches

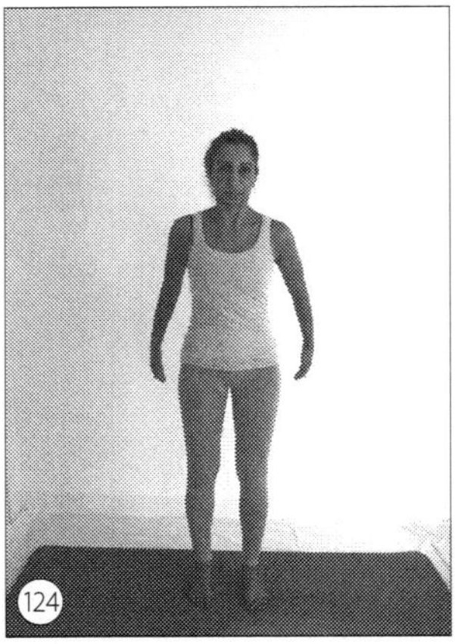

124

125

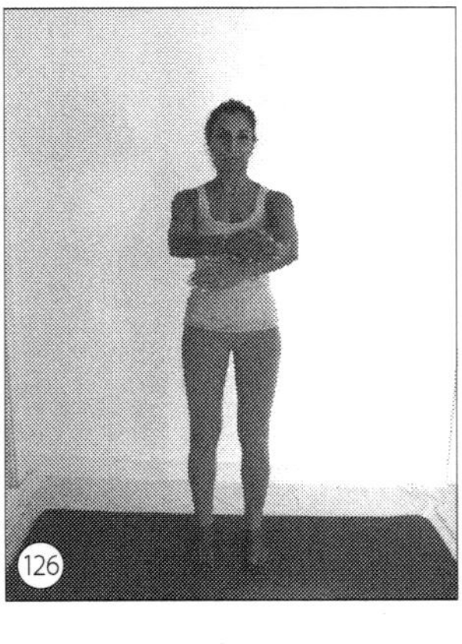

126

127

Mobility stretches are controlled movements to stretch your muscles. They involve joints moving back and forth, left and right and pulsing movements. They are great to perform before a workout or at any time of the day. Any of these stretches can be performed 2-5 times a day.

Arm swings up (p124/125) – Stand up with your arms at your side with the palms of your hands facing your body, gently swing your arms forwards up to the ceiling and then backwards. Try to keep a slight bend in your elbow so your arms don't fully lock out. Perform 15 swings.

Arm swings out (p126/127) – Extend your arms out in front of you to shoulder height then gently swing them in and out horizontally. Gradually increase your range of movement. Try to keep a slight bend in your elbows so your arms don't fully lock out. Perform 15 swings.

128

129

130

131

132

133

134

135

Body twist (p128/129) – Extend your arms out to shoulder height and out to each side. Gently twist your body to the left allowing your arms to swing to the left and then repeat to the right. Try to keep a slight bend in your elbows so your arms don't fully lock out. Perform 15 swings to each side.

Hamstring swings (p130/131) – Hold on to a wall with your right hand and place your left hand on your hip. Standing on your right leg gently swing your left leg forwards and backwards a few inches off the ground. Gradually increase the height of your swing as high as you feel comfortable. Perform 15 swings on each leg.

Pulsing hip flexor (p132/133) – Get in to the same position as the hip flexor stretch except this time place your hands on your thigh and gently pulse your hips forward and backwards. Perform 15 pulses on each leg.

Cat stretch (p134/135) – Get on to your hands and knees, shoulder and hip width apart with a neutral spine. Push your belly towards your spine, curving your back towards the ceiling. Then

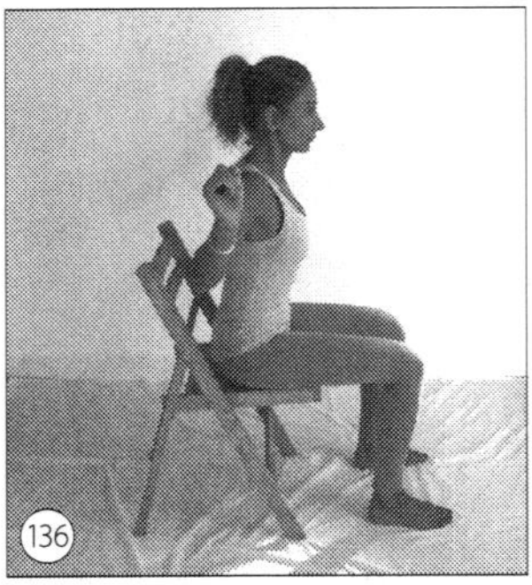

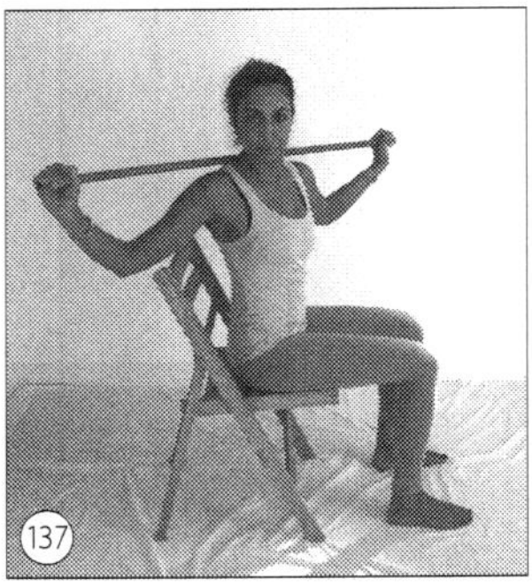

lower your spine back to the neutral position and repeat this 5 times.

Seated twist with pole (p136/137) – Sit forward on a chair with a pole horizontally across your shoulders. Grab the pole at both ends and keeping your body upright gently twist slowly left and right 15 times.

Stretches for work

These stretches are designed for you to do at your desk or if you are sitting/working a lot at home and are very gentle and very simple to perform.

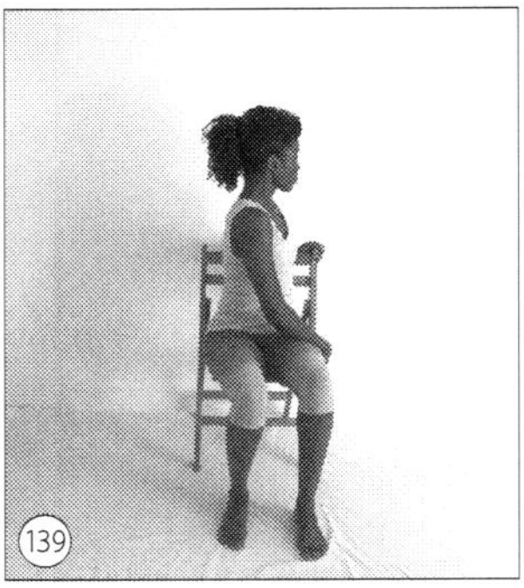

Seated lat stretch (p138) – This is an alternative to the side hip stretch. Sit on a chair and place your left hand on the chair beside your waist. Raise your right arm out to the side, over your head and over to your left. Lean your body over to your left; when you feel tension in the right side of your upper body, stop and hold. Repeat on the other side.

Seated twist (p139) – Sit upright on a chair and twist your upper body to the left. Place your left hand behind you and brace your right arm against your left leg. When you feel tension in your mid back, stop and hold.

You could also perform chest, calves, quads, standing hamstrings and lat stretches at work. I did all of them for a few years at work, I got some funny looks but I felt great for doing them!

Rolling

Foam rollers

Another way to release fascia and tight muscles is by using a foam roller. They come in all shapes and sizes and can be used on a variety of body parts (p140).

For back pain I would suggest make your priority foam rolling your quads, calves and your IT band (iliotibial tract/band). The IT band or ITB is a thick band of fascia that runs from the outside of your knee up to the top, side of your hip (p141). The biggest glute muscle attaches into your ITB so you will feel a good release in your glutes by rolling your ITB (p142).

Most people with back pain are dominant (overworked) in their quads so they are always good to release. If you sit all day your calf muscles are put into a shortened position and if you stand all day your calf muscles do a lot of work so stretching, foam rolling or tennis ball rolling them can help a lot for your back pain.

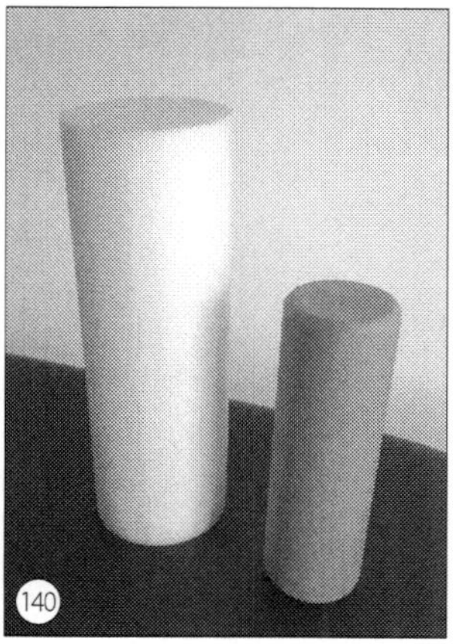
140

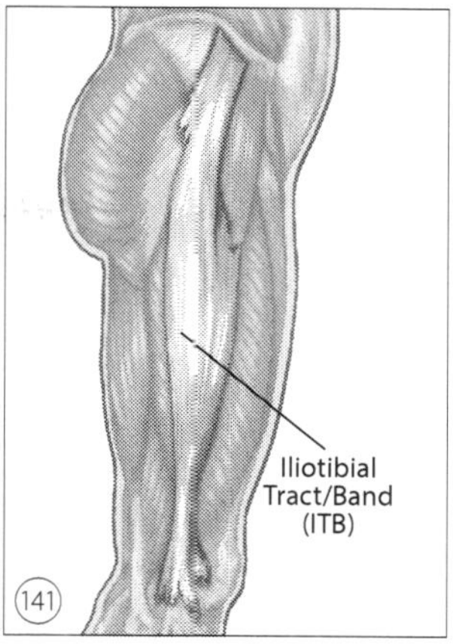

141

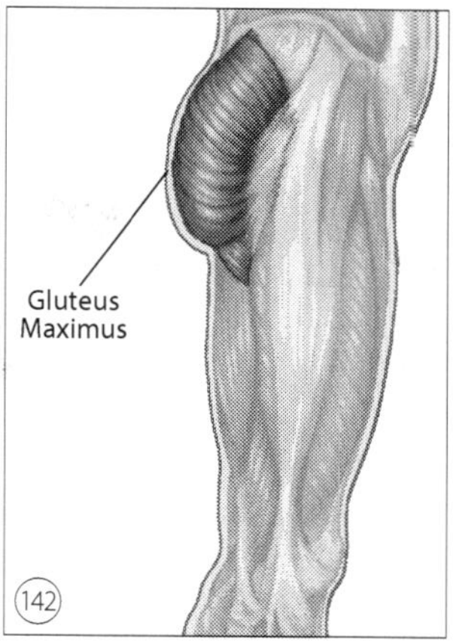

142

143

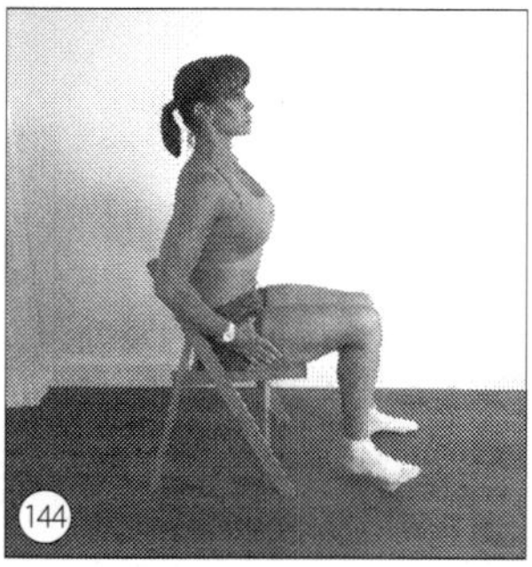
144

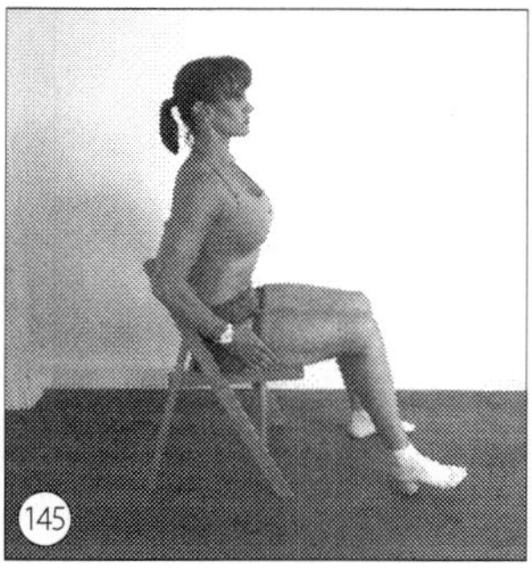
145

The best way to roll is allow your body part to sink into the foam roller, move a few inches along your muscle then for hold a few seconds and repeat until you've rolled the whole muscle*. Or, allow your body part to roll very slowly (in one direction) over the roller* (p143).

Tennis ball rolling

I am a huge fan of using tennis balls for releasing the fascia underneath your feet. Walking and moving all day with a bad back can cause a lot of extra load on your feet, especially if you are limping, leaning to one side or walking in an unaccustomed fashion. The tennis ball roll is the best stretch for your feet and helps to release the connective tissue on the back of your legs all the way up to your lower back.

To roll your feet, sit on a chair and place a tennis ball under your heel (p144/145). Apply enough pressure on the ball so that you do not feel any pain, then slowly move your foot backwards and forwards as far as you can go at each end of your foot. As you move the ball you should feel a stretch underneath your foot. See if you can tilt your foot slightly inwards and outwards to cover all areas of your foot and only roll forward and backwards, never side to side.

I am not a fan of using the tennis ball for rolling your glutes. I have seen many patients do this so much that they either cause their muscles to switch off and become even weaker or they actually trap their sciatic nerve. It is much safer to use a foam roller for your glutes as I explained earlier. Using a tennis ball for your calves is very good but you must be careful not to apply too much pressure; if you feel pain, you need to ease off.

*Performing any type of stretch and/or foam rolling should be gentle so please remember that if you feel pain during any type of stretch or rolling technique STOP and seek advice from your doctor or health professional/therapist.

Stretches to avoid

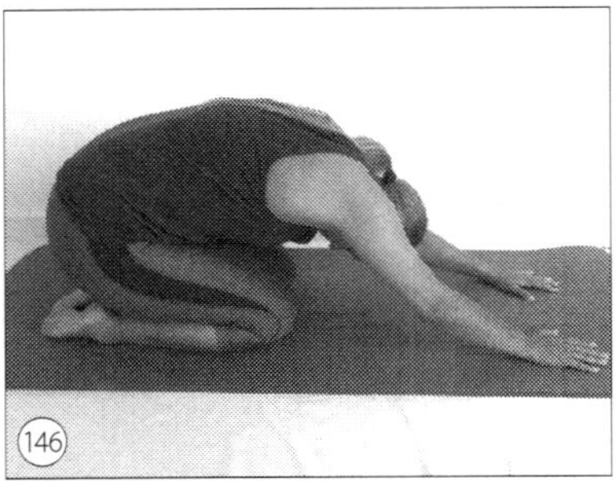
146

Until you are out of pain and your back is strong and stable I would avoid stretches that flex your spine, especially if you have a newly diagnosed disc or bone issue (disc bulge/herniation, stenosis, spondylosis, spondylolisthesis).

Whilst this is a simple stretch (p146), it can aggravate your lower back if you're weak and unstable.

Instead of this lying torso twist (p147) the single arm back stretch (p111) is a much better stretch as it doesn't put pressure on your lower back.

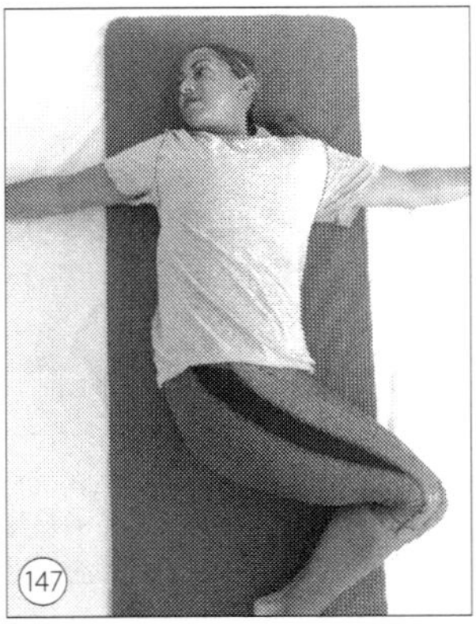
147

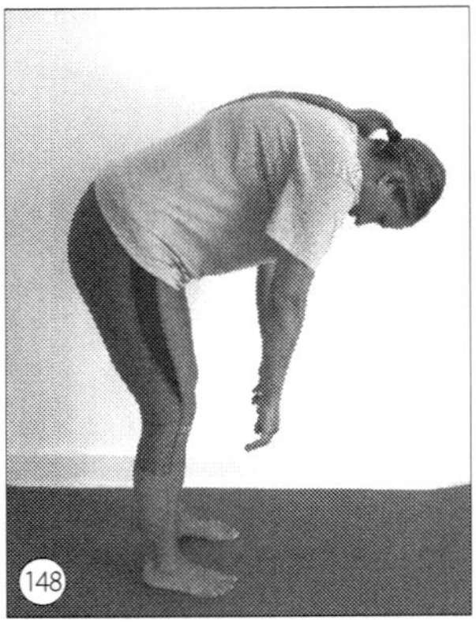
148

149

Touching your toes (p148) is a stretch that everyone wants to do, but I would perform the lower back stretch instead (p117), it's a safer bet plus you can do it before you even get out of bed!

I showed you this stretch earlier but with your foot and head relaxed (p118). If you flex/tilt your head to the floor and move your foot up to the ceiling (p149) this puts a lot of strain your sciatic nerve, this is a very bad thing to do for anyone with a back issue especially for those who already suffer from nerve entrapments.

Mobility/dynamic stretches are great to warm up your joints especially if you are feeling stiff, and they are great to perform before a workout even if you are only sitting on a bike for 10 minutes. This is the same for rolling which can be performed at any time of the day.

Any static stretch can be performed multiple times through the day as long as you have zero pain and hold for 15 seconds. I've been known to stretch my quads and hip flexors 10 times in a day! Remember to ALWAYS stretch and roll until you feel tension, NEVER to pain.

19

In The Gym

Gyms and health clubs are more popular than ever – they literally are popping up all over the place. I think it's awesome that so many people want to keep fit and stay healthy. However, if you have back pain, how do you know if you can exercise, when you can exercise and what exercises will help or hinder you?

Even if you don't go to a gym for weight training, swimming or cardiovascular work (bike, cross trainer etc.) you may still find some tips to help you in this chapter.

Adductor machines

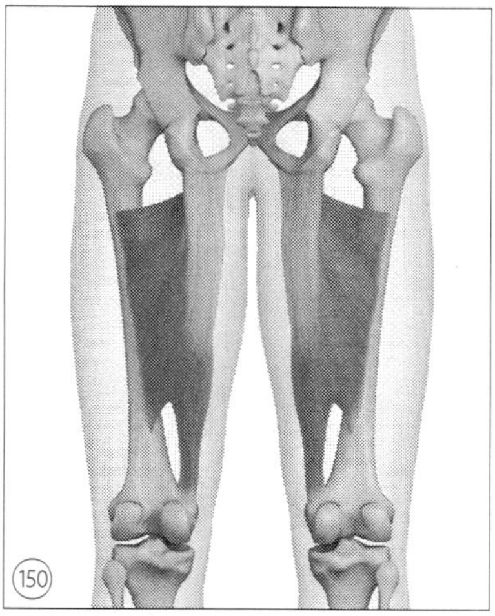
150

151

As you already know, your glutes, lower back and core muscles are top priority when it comes to resolving back pain. Part of the issue may also involve a lot of other muscles that can end up overcompensating. One group of muscles that tends to overwork a lot are your adductors, otherwise known as your groin or inner thigh muscles (p150). Groin muscles can also become weak although it's not as common.

So far, most people I have treated who were experiencing adductor pain have had one or both weak glutes. If your adductor muscles are overworking, using an adductor machine (p151) (the one where you bring your legs inwards) in the gym is best avoided. When your lower back is healing it is better to do single leg exercises to strengthen your adductors, like split squats (p154) for instance.

Split squats work your adductors to full range and train all your leg muscles at the same time so that they work together in unison. They are an awesome alternative to squats. I'll come to this in more detail shortly.

Muscle atrophy prevention

If you have to stop training because you are in pain, you'll notice that your muscles start to atrophy (muscle wastage) – in other words they get smaller.

One of the best ways to prevent muscle atrophy is by using branched chain amino acids (BCAA's). They are proteins that can help prevent the breakdown of your muscle cells while you are taking time out from the gym. My schooling has taught me that taking 5g a day of BCAAS in powder form (in half a glass of water) can help prevent your muscles from wasting away.

Muscle memory

Ever heard of muscle memory? It literally is the memory of your muscle cells (Gundersen, 2016). The beauty of this scientific discovery is that when you train you encourage new nuclei (the most important part of a cell responsible for growth and activity) to your muscle cells which give them the ability to grow, replicate and then combine to form muscle fibres. Smaller cells then start to form around these nuclei that help to create bigger muscles.

If you have to stop training, due to pain, your smaller muscle cells disappear but your recently attained nuclei (from regular weight training) continue to hang around, so that when you start training again you still have more nuclei in your muscle cells that are ready to recruit the smaller cells again – they contain a 'memory' of your previous strength. This means your muscles can grow again but this time much quicker. Think of it like a tree that grows new branches: in the winter the leaves may fall off but the new branches stay intact so the when spring occurs, new leaves grow again but more leaves grow this time because there are more branches. It's quite amazing to see how quickly a previously trained gym goer with back pain can gain muscle again once they are pain free.

Is it safe to squat?

152

153

One of the most common things I get asked by a gym goer suffering with back pain is "Can I squat?" (in a gym with a dumbbell, barbell or kettle bell) (p152/153) and my answer is always the same, "No you cannot, not even with bodyweight!" A squat is a bilateral exercise which means both of your limbs are working at the same time. If one side of your body is underworking and causing an imbalance of your hip, performing a squat (even with just your body weight) will make that situation worse. Having muscles that do not work in harmony will not only continue to worsen but this time you're adding weight to the equation.

A lot of people who are imbalanced in their hips will weight shift when they are under load (weight) due to weakness on one side of their glutes. Hence, why I don't even recommend body weight squats when you're healing from a back issue. The best thing to do is take time out from doing squats and perform unilateral exercises (single limb exercises that strengthen one limb at a time). When you are in recovery from back pain, single limb exercises recruit more muscle fibres so they allow your weaker leg to catch up with your stronger leg. It is always a good idea to perform more sets on your weaker leg (glutes) with unilateral (single limb) exercises while you are still performing rehab strength exercises.

It is the same principle as I talked about in chapter 14. If your glutes aren't firing properly and the signal between your brain and your glutes has significantly decreased, gym exercises will not strengthen your glutes, that goes for any group of muscles. Remember gym strength is completely different to rehab strength. In this instance, training with weights in the gym may keep your issues at bay but the only way to get your muscles to fire and strengthen properly to resolve your pain is to get treatment and follow the rehab programme.

Hip thrusts

Hip thrusts otherwise known as bridges, hip raises and glute bridges have been around for many years but as therapy exercises (on the floor or on a Swiss ball), and in recent years they've become very popular in the gym using weight plates on your tummy, with a ball between your thighs or with a heavily weighted barbell. Whilst I have no problem with this exercise being performed with high repetitions and very low weight I do not favour a very heavily weighted hip thrust especially a heavy barbell and certainly not with a ball between your legs which overworks your adductors. In fact, I ask all my patients – including athletes – to avoid them.

Our bodies were not meant to be put into any EXTREME position with that kind of heavy resistance. If you look at gymnasts, they can contort their bodies into all types of positions. I am an ex competitive gymnast myself, I remember getting into some very strange positions with my spine! However, gymnasts use body weight only. Nevertheless, I've treated a lot of ex gymnasts who have had severe issues with their spines later in life.

When you're at the top range of a hip thrust (your hips are pushed forward towards the ceiling), your lower back is forced into a hyperextended position (overly arched). The sheer weight of gravity resisting you in this position can compress the vertebrae (bones of your spine) in your lower back. Using heavy weight in this position can not only accelerate wear and tear of your bones but you could also risk damaging one of your intervertebral discs, especially if you already have an excessive anterior tilt of your pelvis (duck bum).

It doesn't stop there. I've seen very fit, strong patients of mine become so tight in their quad muscles from doing excessive heavy hip thrusters, they've been borderline suffering a tear. Some patients have developed knee pain because of the dominant forces on their quads due to a lack of rehab strength in their glutes. This defeats the object of performing a glute exercise to strengthen your posterior chain which ends up giving you a problem in your anterior chain (quads). The other thing to consider is your hip flexors. One of your quad muscles is also a hip flexor, one group of muscles affects the other. Your hip flexor muscles attach to the bones in your lower back so if they are affected in a bad way, it has a huge impact on your lower back. Hence, if your glutes are weak and you have a poor connection between your brain and muscles, your quads and hip flexors are likely to over work. So performing hip thrusts can aggravate this ten- fold. The only way to resolve this issue is with treatment and rehab strength then change the way you perform the hip thrust.

I prefer to perform them on a Swiss ball or a bench (p159/160). They are the same as the level 3, Swiss ball bridge exercise in chapter 17 but start with your feet flat. You can make this harder by lifting each heel making sure your hips stay parallel to the floor. I would try body weight first then you can use a 2.5-5kg weight plate. The idea is to use multiple repetitions with a slow eccentric (lowering your hips to the floor) and slow concentric (raising your hips up to the ceiling) which means you lower and raise your hips slowly. My preference is 5 seconds down and 5 seconds up. I would suggest 3 sets of 10 reps when you are strong enough to do so assuming your glutes are firing on all cylinders at this point. Always try body weight first. When using weight plates the single leg glute bridges (level 3 glute exercise in chapter 15) are my preference, even though it's less range of movement up and down the exercise uses less core strength and focuses more on your glutes.

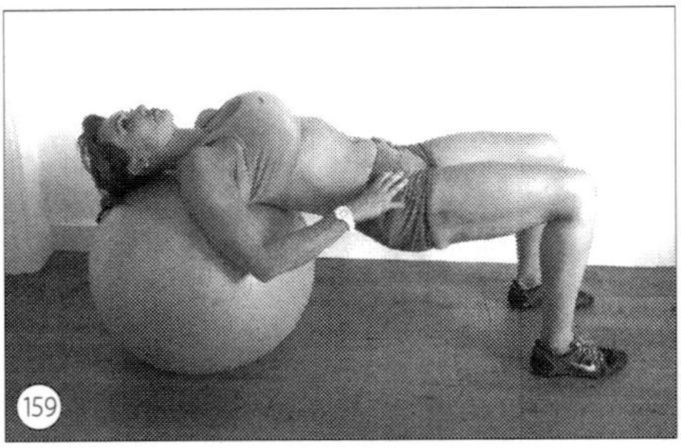

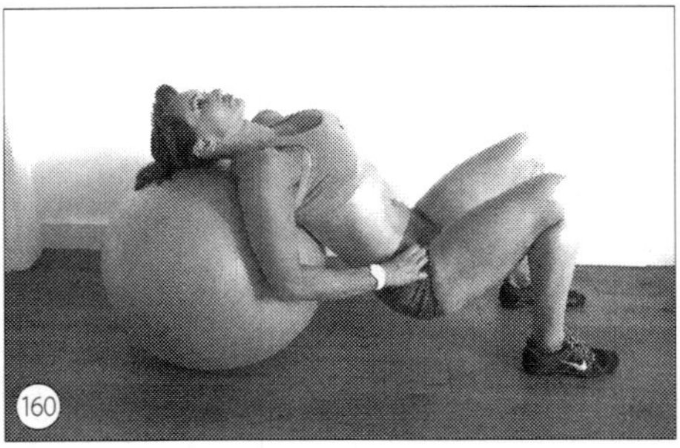

Remember ALWAYS leave a bend in your hips when you raise them to the ceiling, NEVER push your hips all the way up or you will compress the bones in your lower back. You may think a 2.5kg plate sounds very light but when you perform high repetitions, with a 5 second eccentric and concentric, trust me, 2.5kg starts to feel very heavy!

Only last year, I trained with one of my best friends Peter Nesden when he was in the country for a few days. Peter has been weight training for many years so he is very strong and muscular. After we finished our legs workout I suggested we finish off by doing some glute bridges (the floor version of hip thrusts). He wanted to use weight on his pelvis so I agreed. However, when I suggested he use a 5kg plate he looked bewildered and said, "But normally I use over 100kg with a barbell for a hip thrust". I replied, "That's OK, just trust me!" We did 3 sets of 15 with a 5 second eccentric and concentric tempo with one heel raised to make it harder. Let's just say we both felt the burn, in a good way! Higher repetitions with little or no weight are very safe with any back issue but it is best to go through every progression of bridges first before using weight.

Incidentally, I would never use heavily weighted hip thrusts for an athlete as I do not believe that they translate to any sport. However, I do use glute bridges with multiple repetitions and body weight as a warm up/glute activator or with a light weight as a post workout exercise for a lot of my athletes and personal training clients. If you'd like to read more about exercises for athletes with back pain, you'll have to wait a bit longer for my next book, Back Pain Free for Athletes.

Bands

As I mentioned previously, bands for glute exercises should only be used when you're pain free and stable. If you have back pain and other muscles are overworking and underworking that means your pelvis is unstable. Using bands will aggravate your instability. When you've reached the level 3 targets of the rehab programme and you are pain free, you should be fine to use bands as long as you maintain your glute strength especially pre-workout.

Deadlifts

When you return to the gym after time out for being in pain I always suggest two things. As long as you are on level 2 of the glute rehab, before performing deadlifts (p161), I would suggest introducing rack pulls for 3 sets of 10 repetitions for at least 3 weeks at the start of your workout. A rack pull is a partial deadlift otherwise known as a pin pull. You set up a barbell on a power rack or steps and risers so the barbell is level with the top of your knees which means you perform less than half the movement of a standard deadlift, the top part. This encourages your lower back, glutes and hamstrings to work in unison after you have regained balance and rehab strength. Rack pulls are also great to enhance confidence when you eventually return to performing full deadlifts. It is normal to have some insecurity when returning to any leg exercise after suffering with back pain.

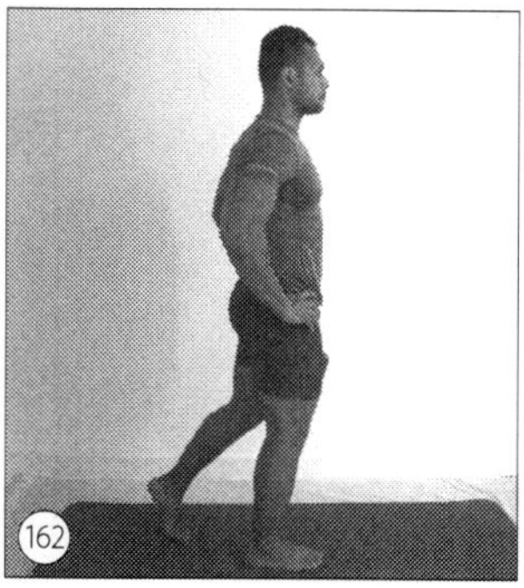
162

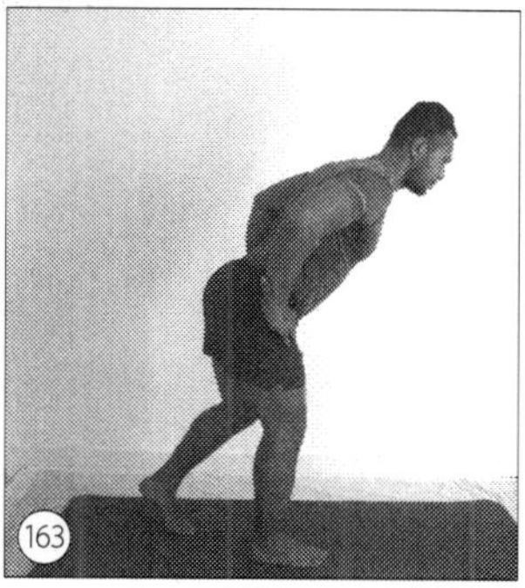
163

Another alternative to deadlifts is the single leg deadlift which is described in chapter 15 (p162/163). It's best to start this exercise with body weight for 3 sets of 10 repetitions then then start using 2kg dumbbells and increase the weight by 1kg as you get stronger. Lower and raise your upper body slowly for a count of 4 seconds using the same sets and repetitions. I would avoid trying to jump from 3kg to 6kg. You'd be surprised how hard this exercise is using a light weight and slow repetitions, even for a 100kg man!

Weight training for beginners

If you are a beginner in the gym, please do not be put off by people who tell you that weight training caused their back injury. I often find those people acquire injuries because of either bad technique, training when they are fatigued or they already had a pre-existing issue. For beginners, when you train with weights for the first time, it is very common to experience niggles or twinges or even suffer an injury within the first 12 months, regardless of whether you have a really good personal trainer. I view this as the weight training shows you where your weaknesses are.

I have seen this occur so much over the years and it often happens to people who either don't sleep well (lack of recovery), or people who have had sedentary jobs and have probably never stretched or worked out before. Having a poor diet can add to that too. This can lead to a dysfunctional body from a lack of movement but without suffering many or any symptoms. Following the Pearson Method within your first year of weight training can resolve niggles and twinges and prevent injuries from developing. Then you can move on to the maintenance programme (chapter 17) for prevention. Honestly, prevention is so much better than cure.

Exercise prescription

One of the biggest mistakes I see with gym goers is performing core work at the beginning of their workout. It is dangerous and slows down your ability to grow muscle because it tires you out. You need your core muscles for exercising with weights full stop, especially with exercises such as squats and deadlifts so you do not want to tire out the muscles that you require for those types of lifts. ALWAYS perform core work at the end of your workout. The only exception to this is if you are doing a circuit/HITT/tabata class where the weights are extremely small and the reps are very high. Either way, if you have back pain you still need to be careful.

You may be in a position where you cannot lift weights at all and you can only sit on a bike. I remember that feeling very well. If that's the case, I would suggest performing your glute rehab first, cycle for 10-30 minutes, perform your lower back and core exercises then have a good stretch until you're able to start trialling using weights again. It's better to do something, you'll feel better for it, I can guarantee that!

If you are a gym goer who prefers working out by using cardiovascular (CV) equipment I would suggest following the same regime. It is much better to activate your glutes first before utilising them on a CV machine like a bike or cross trainer. For most people with back pain, the cross trainer (preferably without using the arms) and the bike are the safest machines to use but you may have to trial both of these. I've seen patients who have felt aggravated after using the bike until they have reached the level 2 stage of glute and lower back rehab.

Please do NOT run, row, skip or jump while recovering from a back injury. All of these can aggravate you beyond belief. Ideally, if your back pain symptoms have gone, you feel stable but you still have stiffness you should be OK to start doing impact work again; providing you are on level 3 rehab exercises. Just because you are pain free does not mean your muscles have been fully restored to full function so it is best to trial these exercises once you are pain free. I would suggest to start off with five minutes of running/skipping etc., then gradually increase the amount of time by five minutes every session.

As you will see on the maintenance programme (chapter 17) there are exercises you can use pre, during or at the end of your workout. I have also listed a variety of core work so you only need to pick two exercises out of the six listed (both planks and side planks have two variations) so that you don't get bored!

Recovery and prevention

Recovery after a workout is a major priority for every gym goer who is healing from back pain. If you don't recover you won't heal properly and you won't allow for muscle growth. When you train any group of muscles you need to allow 48 hours' rest before you train those muscles again. In layman's terms after you weight train, your muscles are broken down and then re-built, that process takes 48 hours after your workout. So if you train your legs on Monday you can train them again on Thursday. If you train the same muscles while you are still re-building you risk regression.

(164)

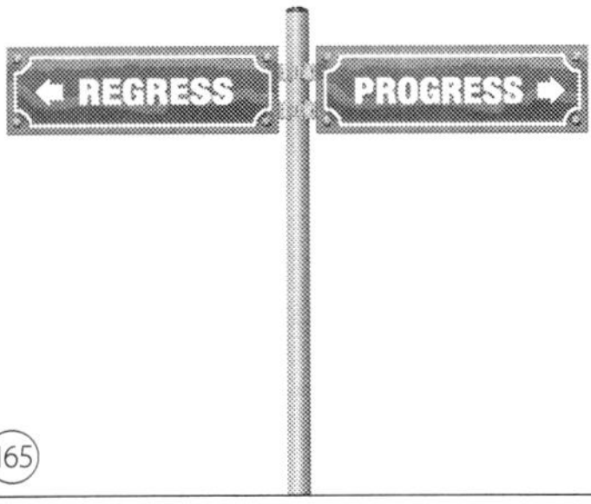

(165)

Upon your return to training following a back issue it is normal to feel extremely achy for longer than two days for the first two weeks, this is just from a lack of conditioning. I would suggest using hot and cold showers in the morning and Epsom salts in the evening (described in chapter 10) to help you recover quickly. Make sure that you have no muscle ache in your lower back/legs before you perform your next session to avoid regression.

Once you are pain free, maintaining strength in your posterior chain is a priority so I highly recommend using glute exercises pre workout as a preventative method as per the maintenance programme in chapter 17. As I mentioned earlier I would also suggest adding lower back exercises into your workout at least once a week, as a lot of people seem to neglect their lower backs in the gym. This will help your pain from coming back.

On a side note; if you weight train when you are very fatigued from a long day's work or if you are sleep deprived it can lead to regression (p164) and further injury. If you feel really tired have a day off! You want to progress not regress! (p165).

Last note

My last and most important note on this subject is: please remember you CANNOT go back into the gym and perform the same weight you were using for each exercise before your back issue. The best advice I can give you is to train yourself like you are a complete beginner. Stick to higher repetitions for at least six weeks to allow your body to re-condition and let your muscle memory do its job. Use single leg exercises for six weeks, remember to perform your glute rehab pre-workout and continue to follow the rehab programme. Follow the maintenance guidelines and you should be able to re-build your foundation steadily and safely.

20

The Whole Package: Your Door To Freedom

This is the last chapter of the book. I have more tips and advice for you along with reiterating some important aspects of your healing process and how to put them all together in a package to get you to your finish line!

At work

If you sit at a desk during your working day you may want to consider using a headset instead of a handset or mobile phone (p166). Leaning your neck to one side to talk on the phone is not a good idea if your lower back is stiff and in pain. Remember: one part of your spine affects the other. Using a headset is a very safe option at home as well as at your work place.

166

167

I already discussed ergonomics in chapter 10 but sitting at your desk with bad posture is something that happens every day and I feel needs to be reiterated. Remember all your joints should be bent around 90-100 degrees including your elbows, hips and knees so you may need to adjust your chair accordingly. Your feet should be flat with your ankles bent around 90-100 degrees so you might need a step for your feet if they are dangling around to avoid putting undue pressure on your spine. Try to avoid slouching as much as you can. The more you are aware of your posture the more you will self-correct yourself. If you've been sitting for more than 2 hours, try going for a walk around your home or office for a few minutes and stretch your quads. Stretching your chest is also a good idea if you sit a lot during the daytime.

An adjustable standing desk may be of use to you (p167). I would not suggest using it as an alternative to a chair but as a great addition so you can alternate between standing and sitting. As a bonus, you could do your glute tenses while you stand, although be prepared for some funny looks!

I do not favour backless chairs. I know they are supposed to help people with back pain but I found that they made my pain a lot worse, same for some of my patients. They may suit you if you are more stable but if you're in a lot of pain I would suggest you would be better off with a conventional chair that can adjust your back position and seat height until your symptoms improve. It's not the chair that's the issue, it's your spine that needs correcting and strengthening.

Posture at your desk is extremely important, here's a useful suggestion to correct your posture and sit up straight. This exercise is very simple and the more you use it the better (p168/169/170/171). Sit on a chair, clasp your fingers together, palms facing you then move your arms up to the ceiling (the backs of your hands should be facing the ceiling) and allow your spine to straighten. This should push your chest forward and pull your head slightly backwards. Stay still in your new position then relax your arms. You should be sitting up straight. You can use this easy exercise throughout the day to correct your posture while sitting or standing.

168

169

170

171

172

Whether you work in an office, a factory or you drive a van and deliver packages, always bend your knees when you lift boxes, bags and cases.

If you carry a lot of books, files or a laptop, using a trolley case is much easier than using a rucksack or carrying a case with a handle (p172). A lot of laptop cases come with four wheels now and they are small enough to carry on buses, trains and planes.

Remember that stretching your quads for 15 seconds each through the day is a great way to release your anterior chain (the front side of your body) to help your back pain. Stretching your chest and calves can help too especially if you sit a lot. Remember I talked about associating your stretches with going to the toilet, it really is an easy way to remember to do them! Having a BPA free (toxin free) water bottle is great to have on your desk to remind you to stay hydrated. I recommend getting one in your favourite colour as you're more likely to drink from it!

Stretching

Remember that stretching* is gentle and should NEVER be painful. For some people just a few stretches will be enough to start with; it totally depends on what type of back issue you have and the level of your severity. If in doubt, wait until you are in the company of your health practitioner/ thrapist or even a friend, partner or family member to perform your first few stretches. This will help you feel confident and supported. Once you're able to perform one or two stretches you should be on a roll. It may feel better to stretch after a hot bath or shower while you are warm, just be safe and make sure you have non-slip mats and that you are fully dry first!

Rehabilitation programme

Rehabilitation exercises* are also gentle so you should NEVER EVER feel pain performing them. You may feel a very strong ache (from weakness) which is often confused with pain. Regardless, if you get to a point where you feel a strong ache around 8/10 (if 0 is nothing and 10 is agony) you need to STOP, do not work through fatigue. Some exercises take longer to achieve. This is ok and very normal. Please allow yourself time to build strength and remember to use your symptoms chart, that's a really good way to help motivate yourself to continue with your exercises.

As long as you are doing the exercises steadily you should see progress; please don't be in a rush. Some of the exercises may seem really hard at first so remember the phrase, 'Rome wasn't built in a day'; it took time. Please bear in mind that having treatment can be a very quick release but rehab strength takes time to gain, so please be patient.

In 2007 a trainer friend of mine called James asked my advice about a personal training client of his who had back pain. The lady in question was in pain when trying to perform certain exercises in the gym, so I suggested certain rehab exercises and that she start with a half plank exercise for the core aspect. My friend's client couldn't perform the half plank for even 10 seconds. James was amazed at how weak she was and he couldn't understand how someone couldn't do a half plank for even 10 seconds especially as he could hold a plank for 5 minutes. When I explained how pain and weakness worked, he realised that he had been pushing her too hard. After a few weeks, he observed the progression of her core, glutes and lower back rehab strength and within three months she was able to perform every exercise in the gym without pain. The client in question was a mother of two children and had suffered back pain ever since she had first given birth six years before she started training in the gym with my friend.

The moral of the story is: please be patient and go easy, doing too much too soon can hinder your progress. Trust me: relapsing is the worst, physically and mentally; it can be horribly depressing. Some of my patients stopped doing their rehab because their pain disappeared, even though they were only on level 1 exercises. They thought they were healed. Within a few weeks or months their pain came back. Even if you are pain free this does not mean your back has fully recovered. The Pearson Method gets results but only if you are consistent and go through each level of the rehabilitation programme. As soon as your pain has disappeared the first thing you want to do is stop doing the boring rehab exercises! This has even happened to professional athletes I've worked with. If you have not reached level 3 and you stop performing your rehab exercises you risk going backwards. Once you've reached the targets for level 3 exercises move onto the maintenance programme and you should prevent re-occurence.

If you relapse for whatever reason, it's really important to try and stay positive. If you have already reached a stage of less pain but you relapse and take a few steps backwards, remember that you have muscle memory. If you've been there before you can get back there again and go beyond. Fear is the one thing that will hold you back from recovering. Staying positive is by far the hardest part of labouring through a relapse – that's when you really need friends and family and a lot of positivity tools. Relapses could also mean that you've just done a bit too much and your body wasn't quite ready for it and that's OK. Take your time, you will progress. Be consistent and above all, stay positive.

*Stretching and rehabilitation exercises are gentle so please remember that if you feel pain during any stretch or exercise STOP and seek advice from your doctor or health professional/therapist.

Travelling

Travelling on planes and in cars/coaches can aggravate back pain a lot, for some of you it can't be helped due to your work or home situation. This is especially true if you're travelling/driving for long hours at a time and changing time zones.

Car seats these days are not too bad as they can be adjusted but some seats on planes are poorly designed, some of them are just awful. As suggested previously, packing a mini hot water bottle can help while you're on a plane. Most cabin crew are happy to give you some hot water especially if they know you're in pain. Just remember to make sure the hot water bottle is completely empty before you go through security for your flight. Hot patches are ideal if you're on the go particularly if you're doing a lot of driving. If you have heated seats I would definitely use them on long drives. If it's a hot day I would suggest whack the air conditioning on too or open your windows all the way. It might seem a bit weird to have heat and air conditioning on at the same time but it works!

173

One of the advantages of travelling by train and plane is that you can get up, walk around and stretch (p173). I always get an aisle seat for that reason. I have no qualms about doing my hip flexor stretches in the aisle next to my seat and doing standing hamstring stretches on my seat! If you're driving for a long period, make sure you have enough breaks to stop and walk around and have a good stretch at the other end. You'd be surprised how much this routine can help you as a preventative when you're pain free. I would employ this for life.

Hydration is very important when travelling for long hours. Of course this is harder if you're driving rather than flying but if you need to visit the toilet it's a great excuse to make a stop at a service station and have a quick stretch. It's important to stay hydrated when you fly full stop and is a necessity for back pain. I would suggest buying one or two bottles of water before you board (after security) so you know you'll have enough water for your flight. Once again, the more you visit the toilet the more you can stretch!

The weather

174

For many years I could wake up first thing and tell you how cold it would be for that day. Cold weather is a huge aggravation for back pain. Moisture and cold can get right into your bones or at least seem to. Make sure you wrap up warm and always use a scarf if the weather deems you should. Shivering makes you tense which can exacerbate your pain.

If the weather's good and you're stable enough to walk your dog, please be mindful especially if they are big and strong (p174). If your dog suddenly pulls you, not only will it hurt but it can hinder your recovery. It may be worth asking your partner or a friend to walk your dog initially until your pain lessens and you feel stronger.

Is surgery for you?

The requirement for back surgery depends on what issue you have and how severe it is. Often enough people with bone issues such as spondylosis or spondylolisthesis and disc issues (herniations, bulges) can avoid surgery. Nevertheless, to rule out surgery you would usually need an X-ray to check for broken bones or degeneration/deformation and an MRI (magnetic resonance imaging) to confirm or rule out any other disease or condition. If you have an MRI, the report, along with your specialist's opinion, should show whether you need surgery or not. In some severe cases, spinal bones may need to be fused together, sometimes there is no other option.

This may also be the case for some herniated intervertebral discs (the spongy discs in between your vertebrae that act as shock absorber) that may have been ruptured (torn) so badly that they need surgical repair. A typical repair would be a discectomy where they remove part of the disc that is protruding on your spine and affecting your nerves. It is a fairly quick surgery but it can have consequences. Most of the time with this sort of surgery your glutes, lower back and/or core may become weak as a result. Plus, the surgical scars can become very thickened as well as the build-up of fascia around a scar. Hence, treatment and rehabilitation should be your key to recovery. The quicker you start this process the better.

Without question the most common condition I get asked about regarding surgery is with intervertebral disc issues (bulges, herniation, thinning, degenerative) (p175). Whether mild or moderate, and in some cases severe, disc issues can be treated with manual therapy and rehabilitation exercises. I view the onset of a disc bulge/thinning disc as a warning sign that one of your intervertebral discs has become unhealthy and it's a big hint that you need to resolve the issue, by strengthening certain muscles around it, release others and then maintain it. With treatment and rehab strength you should be able to get yourself pain free.

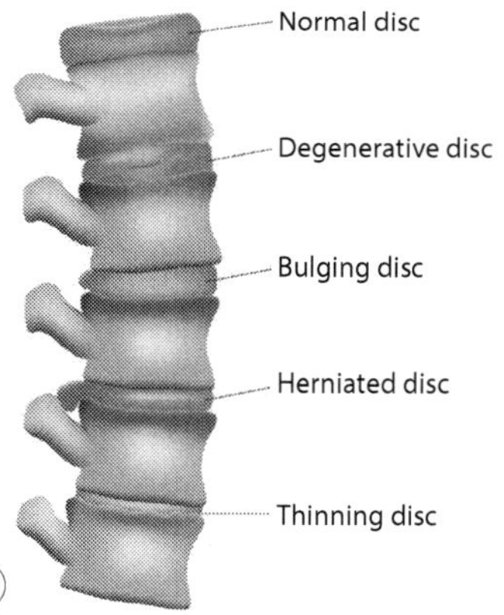

175

This may not be the case for everyone but certainly for most of the cases I have seen, actually for every case I have seen except two. It turned out that one patient had cancer, I was thankful I referred him for an MRI when I did (they caught it just in time), and the other patient needed surgery. Once you have a disc bulge you need to maintain your strength otherwise you can relapse. In that instance you just need to follow the maintenance rehab programme. To reiterate that, maintenance of a disc bulge is for life.

A few years ago, Mark Coles, a good friend of mine in my industry, called me one day and asked if I knew a good surgeon. When I asked why, Mark told me he had suffered a disc bulge four weeks prior to our conversation and was told by two osteopaths, a physiotherapist and a specialist that he needed surgery. I was confused. Mark said his MRI report showed that he had a mild disc bulge. This didn't make sense; I'd never heard of a mild disc bulge that needed surgery. I cancelled my afternoon appointments later that week and drove two hours to his workplace to see him. When Mark came out to greet me he was limping, it was clear that he was in a lot of pain and he had lost a lot of muscle (atrophy) on the affected side of his glutes. His atrophy was visible even though he was fully dressed. One set of his glutes was pumped and the other side was half the size. Typically, when you have a disc issue it affects one side of your glutes which immediately starts to atrophy (waste away).

I treated him with ART for about 45 minutes and then gave him most of the level 1 exercises in this book for his glutes, lower back and core. He questioned the amount of exercises I had given him because he had been categorically told by all of the aforementioned therapists and specialist that he should not be doing ANY exercises in or out of the gym. Mark was also told that he would never squat again by the specialist. I told him I would get him pain free and back to performing squats if he followed my guidelines.

After treatment of his sciatic nerve, lower back and hip muscles I got his weak glutes firing properly and when I left he was walking normally. He became pain free very quickly. Over the following two months I saw him twice more and I wrote him a weight training programme so he knew what exercises he could and couldn't do in the gym while he was recovering. I wanted him back in the gym the following week after my visit using light weights and high repetitions of specific exercises. The quicker you deal with this type of situation the quicker you heal. I am happy to report that Mark got back to performing squats and within 6 months he'd beaten his personal best. He has since become one of the most highly respected figures in the fitness industry in the UK.

This is a common situation. However, there are a lot of good surgeons out there that will insist on the use of manual therapy before going under the knife. Not all cases are that straight forward and occasionally surgery is the only option. Regardless, if you are in any doubt you are always entitled to a second opinion.

MRI scans

I see so many lower back patients that have had MRI scans and their MRI report shows no abnormalities or issues of any kind. That patient may then be told their pain is in their head; it makes my heart sink. Every single time I hear this I feel like someone has punched me in the chest. I remember being told my back pain, multiple trapped nerves, travelling pains down my legs, numbness and whole body pain and dysfunction was all in my head. I was told time would heal me, well it doesn't, that's just ludicrous. I will never forget that debilitating, crippling feeling when I was told 'I don't believe you're in pain.' PAIN IS THERE FOR A REASON. Trust me, you are not going crazy.

You have special sensory receptors that send a signal to your brain so you can feel things like temperature, vibrations and pain. The receptors for pain are called nociceptors and are a way of telling your brain that something is not right – as I said pain is there for a reason. Lower back pain is often caused by a hip imbalance, whether short or long-term. For whatever reason, muscles become weak and others become overworked as a result. Fascia gets tight and 'bunched up' and over time twinges develop that gradually turn into pain. I have NEVER EVER seen this type of issue show up on an MRI. The problem is that some therapists and specialists do not understand fascia, nerve entrapments or imbalances so your life can end up turning upside down because you have no idea what is wrong with you or how to resolve it.

However, MRI scans are excellent at ruling out other diseases and conditions and X-rays are very efficient at ruling out bone conditions. With back pain it is always beneficial to use a process of elimination. Once your scan and X-ray are clear of abnormalities, it's likely that your issue is a hip imbalance and/or trapped nerve and your muscles not doing what they are supposed to. Fascia is always involved too. That is why I created my own guided diagnosis of what muscles are involved with overworking and underworking along with specific protocols on how to re-build your rehab/ foundation strength.

Whiplash – what does it really mean?

For those of you who have been involved in any type of car accident, fallen off a horse, fallen down the stairs and hit your head or suffered a sporting injury involving head trauma, you were probably sent for a neck X-ray. Whiplash is categorised as a neck injury and although you may suffer neck tightness or pain, it is extremely common for the rest of your spine to be affected too. Almost every patient who has been diagnosed with whiplash, has also suffered issues to their upper, mid or lower back as well as their jaw. Another issue related to whiplash is lockjaw – this is where all your jaw muscles go into spasm and tighten up so much that you can't open your mouth properly and it seizes/locks if you open it too far, or just eat food. I had lockjaw intermittently for about three years after my accident and I've had to have a lot of treatment on it (ART, cranial osteopathy) due to severe, chronic tightness.

All of these muscular issues are not talked about with whiplash. I would love for this to change. If I had undergone an X-ray of my whole spine, a doctor may have seen multiple fractures and been able to do something about it. Just remember if you're involved in any type of incident/fall get your whole spine checked out: in my experience whiplash is NOT just a neck injury. With a lot of these issues I see on a daily basis – not all, but a lot – patients are not treated to the full extent and therefore their muscular tightness increases over time which leads to a bigger issue years later in life. Prevention is so much better than cure!

Should you rest?

A lot of patients ask me if they should rest. It depends. It always depends, on a variety of factors. My answer to this is if you've been involved in some type of accident where you physically cannot walk and it hurts just to stand up, you will need to rest and take some time off work. The first doctor I saw the day of my car crash said I should keep moving and avoid pain medication; that was absurd. At that stage I most definitely needed pain medication and I certainly needed a lot of rest. However, what I really needed at that time was rehab strength. The stronger you get, the more your pain should lessen, the less rest you'll need.

If you're in pain but you can walk easily, then I would advise you to rest only when you feel you really need it – which is likely to be at the end of the day. As long as you avoid aggravating your condition you shouldn't have to take much time off work if at all. However, remember in chapter 11 (on sleep) I discuss why rest is important when you're coping with pain because your body has to work so much harder from the stress and moving in a way you are unaccustomed to. Well, you may not need to take time off work but you most certainly need good quality sleep.

Pregnancy and pain prevention

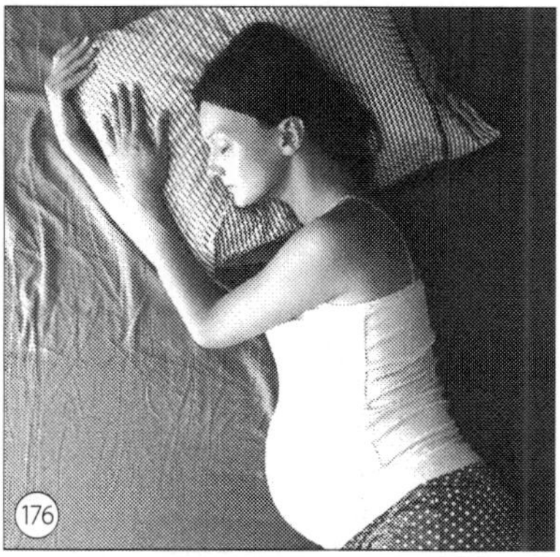

As I discussed earlier I see a lot of pregnant women and mothers who suffer with horrific back pain. During pregnancy a handy tip would be to perform daily clam exercises but just doing 2 x 10-15 repetitions or as many as you can muster for that day. For each trimester it is usually easier to lie on your side to rest and sleep which is perfect for doing clam repetitions (p176). The doggies and the ballet step are also great preventative tools for pregnant mothers.

My friend Emma Stanley recently had her third baby. Clam exercises have been a big part of her life to maintain her back strength while being pregnant as well as post pregnancy. I treated her for back pain during her first pregnancy, she was pain free soon after giving birth. During her second pregnancy she applied all the relevant rehab strength and never suffered any back pain. However, about six months into her third pregnancy she started experiencing back pain again. Admittedly she had forgotten about doing her clam reps as a preventative tool, but within a week of me reminding her to perform daily clam reps, her back pain disappeared.

This is a great way to alleviate the heavy pressure on your lower back caused by your pregnancy bump. Keeping your core and glutes strong you can help avoid pain during and post pregnancy. A lot of mothers still need lower back strength post-baby, all the exercises in the rehabilitation chapters (15-18) can help with that.

Sex

I see a large amount of back injuries caused or aggravated by sex! Annoyingly, it is part of life that can make your back pain worse. The best thing to do is find a position that doesn't aggravate you. Through personal experience, I have determined that it's best to be on your back regardless, whether you're male or female, so one of you will have to do more work than the other! That said, if you both of you are in pain try experimenting to see which positions cause the least amount of discomfort and stick to them until you're both feeling better.

The good leg

With any back issue, one or both sides of your glutes will be weak. Often if you have a chronic, longer term back issue it's likely that your 'good' leg will have been doing a lot of work. That type of overcompensation can become a problem of its own.

I frequently see patients who have a groin strain or extremely tight quads on their good leg that's often caused by weak glutes on their other leg. The way I view this is if your left glute is weak your body can weight shift on to your right leg which can end up doing so much work that the muscles on your 'good' leg start to tear or strain. When muscles overwork they get so tight that one day your brain says, right that's enough and before you know it, you have a tear or a muscle strain, on your good leg. I believe this is your body is telling you there is a bigger problem at stake.

177

In this picture (p177) imagine the boat is your pelvis and there are 10 people (muscles) working on either side to keep the boat balanced. If the strongest member on the right side (glutes) decides they have to rest the other 9 (lower back/leg muscles) people have to work harder to keep the boat balanced. The right side becomes the weaker side of the boat and out of those 9 people, 3 (specific muscles) may work harder than the other 6 but the problem is the boat is now leaning to the left side. So the people on the left (the good leg) have to work harder to keep the boat balanced. The people on the right side of the boat become exhausted because there are only 9 of them and 3 of them (specific muscles) are now terribly over worked while the 10th person is suffering from complete exhaustion. The left side (the good leg) gets forgotten about because they always had 10 people on their side but ends up working twice as hard to keep the boat from tipping and eventually over time one will suffer complete exhaustion.

Some people may have no symptoms whatsoever on their 'good' leg (the left side of the boat) until their back is fully functional and months or sometimes years later the good leg starts aching and getting stiff because those specific muscles that were over worked still need releasing. Overworked muscles don't suddenly release on their own, they need help via treatments and stretching. There is a LOT of crossover in the fascia of your pelvis from one leg to the other which means whatever muscle you release on one leg WILL affect the other. It is very good practice to ALWAYS look at both legs for treatment purposes.

PLEASE TAKE NOTE: I have to reiterate this as it is one of the most important facts in your rehab programme. If you are pain free and ALL your symptoms have disappeared but you are only on level 1 exercises, especially the clam, your back issue has NOT resolved. Please complete all levels of the rehab programme. ONLY when you have completed level 3 exercises can you move on to the maintenance programme; otherwise it is highly likely your back pain will come back. I have treated a lot of patients who do not finish their suggested rehab and their pain returns.

Pearson clam test

While performing the Pearson clam test if you do not feel anything in your left glutes while lifting your left knee, it is highly likely that your left glutes are not firing properly (p178/179). If you feel tension in your right glutes while you're lifting your left knee you probably have a fair amount of overcompensation in your right leg. In this instance, stretching your right hip flexors, quads, glutes, hamstrings and calves can help but treatment on your right leg is key to helping your left glute muscles fire. This is indicative of a long-term issue and could take a few treatments to resolve. This happens a lot and can be resolved with patience and adhering to your rehab programme.

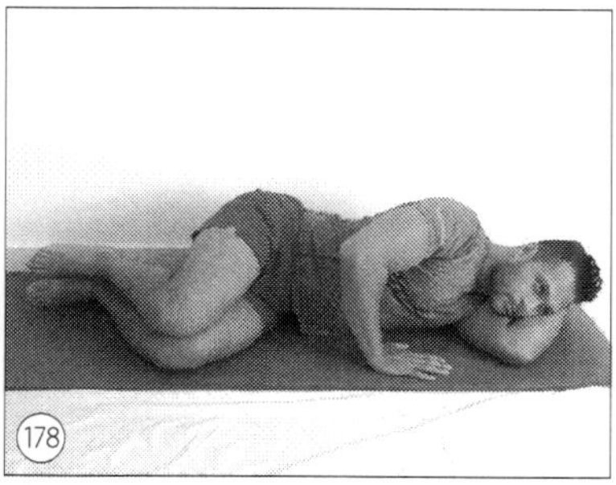
178

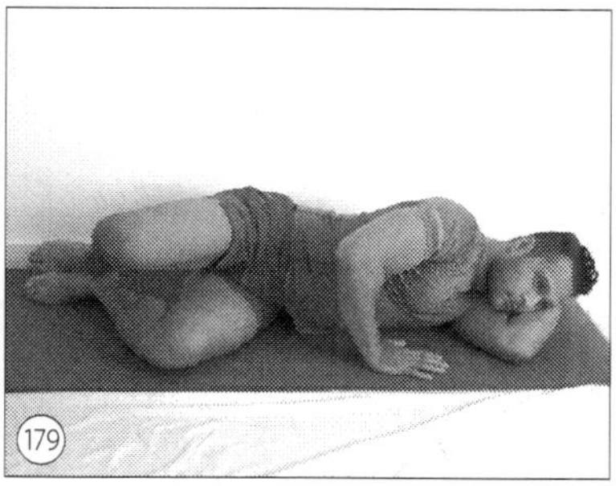
179

Occasionally you may perform the Pearson clam test and not feel any tension anywhere. This could give you a false positive. You should always feel something in your glutes of the knee you are lifting. In this instance you may need to release your hip flexors, quads, glutes, hamstrings and QL's and then re-test. Sometimes your body can recruit other muscles to overwork but they won't show up in the test. It doesn't happen that often but it's good to know just in case, you should ALWAYS feel something.

Sometimes after you've had treatment, maybe a few days later, you may feel like your pain has moved. It could move from one side of your hip to the other or maybe feel like a large area has moved into a smaller area of pain. This is called adaptation and is very normal. It's not that your pain has moved, it means that you already had dysfunction or tightness in that particular area but as other muscles heal, your body highlights other areas that require work. If you've had long-term back pain this can happen a few times until there is no pain or discomfort left.

What do symptoms mean?

When back pain is an intermittent (comes and goes) and insidious issue (gradual onset), you may notice how symptoms change, they might become more frequent and more intense. Back pain that comes and goes usually becomes more frequent, and for a lot of people it ends up being a permanent fixture until you seek help – I see this a lot. In fact, some patients suffer intermittent back pain for over 20 years before they seek help.

Regardless of what back issue you are dealing with, understanding your symptoms can help to know that your recovery is moving in the right direction.

Symptoms severity list

This chart can give you an idea of where you are at with your back issue. Remember with imbalances although you may wake up with pain one day, looking at the symptoms chart, I bet you would have been experiencing mild symptoms on and off for a while. Think of it like a snowball the size of a pea falling from the top of a mountain. It could take 3 months to reach the size of a golf ball, then you might feel an ache. It may take another 6 months by the time it's the size of a tennis ball and by then you might have the occasional twinge. By the time it's the size of a football, a year later, you experience pain for the first time.

MILD	MODERATE	SEVERE	EXTREME
Slightly stiff	Increased stiffness	Constant back pain	Extreme constant back pain
Slight ache	Painful twinges	Travelling pains	Inability to walk
Mild twinges	Intermittent back pain	Shooting pains	Severe restricted movement
Back discomfort	Low intensity ache	High intensity ache	Constant numbness
Glute discomfort	Intermittent glute pain & back stiffness	Constant glute pain quads, knees, calves, feet	Severe pain, glutes, hips
Pain with movement	Intermittent numbness	Severe constant throbbing/ache	

On the symptoms severity list above, when your symptoms start to go from right to left you know you are improving and moving in the right direction. Left of the mild column is pain free!

One of the ways I like to help my patients is to remind them of the symptoms they've experienced but in a positive way as a progressive marker to see how much they have already recovered. Some people know their body really well so they know how far they have come, whereas for others pain is pain. Even if they are 50% better they have no distinction between a 4/10 or an 8/10 in pain, to them it is the same.

As I mentioned in chapter 12 sometimes it can be beneficial to mark down every symptom that you have such as pain turning over in bed, discomfort standing from a seated position, stiffness bending forwards, aching first thing in the morning etc. Then give each symptom a number out of 10, if 0 is no pain and 10 is agony.

Symptoms chart	Wk1	Wk2	Wk3	Wk4	Wk5	Wk6	Wk7	Wk8
Pain turning over in bed	8	7	5	3				
Discomfort tying up shoelaces	5	5	4	2				
Pain getting out of bed 1st thing	9	8	6	4				
Pain sitting for long periods	6	6	4	3				
Discomfort getting out of the car	5	4	4	1				

If you look at your chart once a week (not daily), you should see your numbers start to decrease and eventually your symptoms should disappear altogether. When pain goes away, your brain forgets it was there in the first place. It's amazing when I see a patient and ask if they can tie their shoes up without pain and they can't remember even having that particular symptom, that's a lovely part of the process. This is a really good way to mark your progress and motivate you to move forward with the rehab programme.

Therapy

I have already mentioned that ART treatment is the best soft tissue release in the world in my eyes, however, I do appreciate you may live miles away from your nearest therapist. If this is the case, then try to find someone nearby who at least practises some sort of fascia release.

Your Pearson clam test will usually show you what muscles are overworking but don't be surprised if your good leg feels tighter during a treatment than your weaker leg. Remember overworked muscles may not show up on the test so if in doubt ask your therapist to release your quads, hip flexors, glutes, hamstrings and QL's (quadratus lumborum) on both legs.

Your QL's (p180) attach to your bottom rib, diaphragm and pelvis and are pivotal with stabilising your pelvis. They are almost always shortened if you suffer back pain so will need releasing at least

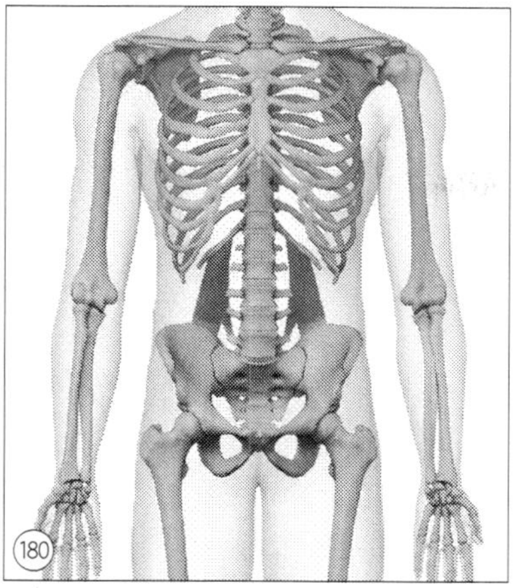
180

once. Most therapists are happy to work on what muscles you would like releasing but they can advise you on which muscles are tighter than others during treatment. After treatment you should notice a difference with your glutes: you should feel them engage much stronger during your rehab exercises. For some people this may take multiple sessions and others only a few. You might feel sore after a first treatment, you may feel nothing at all. Just bear in mind if you do, this is normal.

Good therapists should be happy to refer you to another specialist therapist if they cannot help you. Everyone has their specialities, some more than others but no one therapist can do every therapy out there. Unfortunately, some therapists have egos and won't even consider referring you to another therapist who specialises in a modality that they do not cover. You will often find a community of therapists and trainers/coaches that work in conjunction with each other; this is a sign of great minds thinking alike and they usually help their patients recover way quicker

Beware of therapists who ask you to buy a block of sessions. If your issue could be resolved within four to six sessions why would you buy a block of 10 or 12? If your issue is mild you may only need two to three sessions or less. Occasionally, I've treated patients once and their pain has gone within 2 weeks of performing the rehab exercises. It's the most priceless feeling in the world! I believe that intention has a lot to do with healing people. I think that therapists who have good intentions make a huge difference to the speed of your recovery.

Self-diagnosis

Without doubt the hardest part of a therapist's job is going into battle with the internet's assumptions of diagnosis. I ask every patient to avoid searching the internet for 'clues' as to why they are in pain. That's what therapists are for! Therapists (sports therapists, physiotherapists, osteopaths and chiropractors) are trained to diagnose injuries so let them do their job and try not to self-diagnose. As I've mentioned before, I always suggest to go with recommendation. Trusting your therapist is a huge part of recovery.

Healing gently

Just because you're older doesn't mean you will heal slower than others – you might heal quicker than someone 10 years younger than you. Speed of recovery can be helped by adhering to a healthy food regime, having good quality sleep and a healthy gut. A 'to do' list like this can help.

To do list - daily	Mon	Tue	Wed	Thu	Fri	Sat	Sun
Drink 2 litres water	✓	✓	✓				
Do glute exercises	✓	✓	✓				
Do stretches	✓	✓	✓				
Do core work	✓	✓	✓				
Take bone broth	✓	✓	✓				
Do lower back work	✓	✓	✓				
Meditate/visualise	✓	✓	✓				

There does come a stage when you're feeling better that you have to try activities again or as I like to say they need to be 'trialled'. This is for all exercises that would have previously aggravated you and especially applies to activities such as swimming, yoga, running, jumping and weight training.

It is impossible to predict how quickly you will gain strength or heal with treatment. The main thing is that you remember to follow all the guidelines, both emotional and physical. There is no one size that fits all so please go at your own pace and be patient. Making a daily 'to do' list can help you to stay on course.

More positivity tools

Mantra statements

One thing that really helped me cope with depression and motivation was using mantra statements all over my house. I printed 'I am' and 'I can' positive statements (avoid using negative words like pain, agony, discomfort etc.) in bold capital letters on A4 pieces of paper, laminated them (this is optional) and put them up in places I would see regularly like on my fridge or next to the mirror in my bedroom. It's a really easy way to help you stay motivated to recover.

I AM HEALTHY – I CAN RUN 5 MILES – I AM SUPER STRONG

Write-ups/letters

Pain is physically exhausting, mentally debilitating and affects everything in your life. However, it is invisible so bear in mind that people who have never suffered pain in any way, shape or form may have a hard time understanding what you are going through and find it difficult to empathise. Try to be honest with them about how you are feeling, as I suggested previously by asking them to read this book may give them some idea of what it's like to suffer pain on a daily basis. Then ask them to support you. Remember how important your support network is. Talking about how much you're suffering helps to get negativity out of your body and is a very positive tool.

There are other ways to rid yourself of negativity. I talked previously about muscle memory; you also have cellular memory from emotions. When we suffer traumatic events or stress of any kind, we carry memories in our cells. This may sound a bit weird but you have cells in your brain and all over your body that contain memories. This is the foundation of many holistic therapies. Along my journey as a patient and a therapist, I have found that releasing negative energy on a deep level is an extremely efficient way to really accelerate the healing process. I mean really accelerate it.

Crying is a great way to release pent up emotions regardless of your age or gender. Talking to a counsellor or friend/family member, meditating and visualisation are also very effective tools at eradicating negative emotions. Another exceptional alternative is something called write-ups or simply, letters. They are a very powerful psychological tool that you may have heard about through your religion or via a psychologist. The idea is to write down a negative situation you've experienced from start to finish like you are telling a story to someone then burn it.

Start the write-up/letter with how or why did your pain start, was it through giving birth or a traumatic event or did you wake up with it one day? Start at the very beginning of the situation and finish your letter/write-up to the present day including every negative, painful emotion you experienced along the way. Then your burn your letter, safely, and ask for those negative emotions to be removed from your body and instantly to be replaced with positivity and love. If you are religious, you may want to ask your negative emotions to be sent into the universe and replaced with God's love.

Dear Me,
One day 2 years ago I fell over and hurt my back...

This cannot be typed, it has to be written with a pen and paper and it needs to be written and burned on the same day, ideally in a safe container outdoors. The reason you write it and burn it on the same day is because you don't want negative emotions hanging around. The notion is that negative emotions hanging around could manifest into pain elsewhere. Plus, when you remove something from your body i.e. negative feelings, you need to replace them with something positive, instantaneously. That's the way I was taught, by a very close, spiritual friend of mine. My brain doctor also told me that writing letters will target one important part of the brain but it is important to speak your words as you write them too so that you target another specific part of the brain to deal with the emotions properly.

This may sound a bit wishy-washy but I assure you write ups/letters have a very, very powerful effect on emotional wellbeing and healing pain. I have recommended these write-ups to many of my patients and they have described the after effect as having a weight lifted off their shoulders (they didn't even know was there) and immediately feeling emotionally lighter. Their recovery was accelerated for sure. Try it – you have nothing to lose and everything to gain!

Your door to back pain free

The whole point of writing this book is to help YOU, the reader, to know that you DO NOT have to suffer in silence or live in pain, there is a solution to being free of pain and it comes in a package. Some of these elements are costly but a lot of them are inexpensive, simple and free. Healing back pain takes time and effort, you just have to make time. Regardless of whatever back issue you are dealing with, there is ALWAYS something you can do to help you feel better. I refuse to think otherwise, as long as you're willing to put the effort in and call on friends, family and colleagues to help you. Remember that performing your exercises takes time and adherence so please stick with them and use the tools in this book to help you.

If you have doubts or thoughts of rumination like "What if I'm in pain forever?" or "What if this exercise doesn't work for me?" or "What if I still can't sleep?", remember – visualisation, write-ups/letters, counselling and meditation can help you with positivity, hope and belief that you will recover. Surrounding yourself with positive people whether its friends, family or colleagues or all of them. Positivity is one of your main keys to your door to freedom.

181

If you relapse, remember it is temporary, try to stay as positive as you can, you have lots of tools now to cope and to get yourself back on your path to healing. Even if you're out of pain but still feeling stiff and achy use heat, do not and cold treatment/showers and breathing stretches. Get your family and friends to stretch with you, they will feel the benefits too. Use your symptoms chart, your 'to do' list and mantra statements to help you stay on course with your rehab programme, stretches, hydration and nutritional work. Feel AMAZING every time you tick a box and be PROUD of yourself that you are achieving things every day to help yourself recover. When you're pain free and have performed level 3 rehab exercises, maintenance will be your new door. Once you are free of pain you want it to stay that way.

I hope you find all the information helpful with your recovery; your application then your outcome will be your proof. A new door is opening. One of my favourite sayings is "The proof of the pudding is in the eating" which means you can only judge something after you have applied and tried it. After all, "It's all about the result!"; the Pearson Method gets results. My car accident was a blessing in disguise... Ultimately this is how I was able to write this book, experimenting on myself for well over a decade and observing similar patterns in my patients to create this method. Now I can share all of it with you – this is your time.

I wish you the best and most positive journey for your recovery. I wish to shower you with positive dust sprinkles to help you heal. I hope that I have given you enough inspiration and motivation to put your trust in me to help you. If you recall my story from the beginning of the book and how messed up I was, remember...if I can do it, so can you.

It is my whole intention that each and every one of you will be able to enjoy life as it is meant to be, back pain free.

With love

Heather x

Definition of trust:

Firm belief in the reliability, truth or ability of someone or something

Definition of belief:

An acceptance that something exists or is true

Definition of hope:

A feeling of expectation or desire for a particular thing to happen

If you have enjoyed this book please feel free to leave a review on www.backpainfree.me

Acknowledgements

First and foremost, I have to thank my dad, Neil Pearson, for teaching me, "there is no such word as can't" and that I should always believe in myself. Those thoughts have always inspired me through some really hard times. He also taught me to always put 100% effort into everything. He used to say "If you're going to do something, do it to the best of your ability". He suffered back pain for years and always used to ask me to walk on his back to help his pain when I was young! If he was alive today I would make sure he was pain free and he would be very proud of me for writing this book.

At the time of writing *Back Pain Free* my very dear childhood friend Deckstar Pereira passed away. I would like to thank him for his friendship, compassion, support and 'brotherly' pep talks during some very low periods. He was a role model and inspirational mentor to many and would be super proud of his 'lil sis' for writing this book to help others.

Thank you to Warren Baker, Mark Coles, Peter Nesden, Emma Stanley, Julie Young, Reece Mander and James Guiney for allowing me to share your personal stories. I am extremely appreciative.

Thank you to all my family, friends and colleagues for your love, support and for being there when I've needed you most.

Thank you to Dr Josh Berkowitz and all at IV boost for helping me with chelation therapy and providing me with the most professional medical service whilst writing this book.

Thank you to BMW for making such sturdy cars, had I been in a smaller car during my accident I may not be here to tell the tale!

Thank you to all my models: Marcia Sharp, Jana Matouskova, Karim Badawi, Maralyn Ragg, Ridhi Sharma, James Guiney, Caroline Labourdette and Peer Sharma (my Doberman doggy godson!) for your help, effort, sense of humour and patience; you are all fabulous!

Thank you to all my friends, patients and colleagues who took the time and effort to write such wonderful testimonials for this book. I am humbled and extremely grateful to all of you.

Very special thanks to:

Neil Mason, for your fantastic service, your integrity, honesty and for setting me on the right path of treatment.

Amanda O'Connor, for your amazing treatments, support, advice and for suggesting I change career, it changed my life!

Sharma Pillay, for being the most amazing, supportive friend over so many years, I literally owe you my life! Thank you for keeping me sane and balanced whilst writing this book.

Jana Matouskova and Chris Griffiths, for your many efficient and excellent ART treatments through some tough times and whilst writing this book especially keeping my spine healthy!

Pali Cooper and Patty Leahy, for inviting me to teach ART which has enhanced my soft tissue skills and made me a much better therapist. Teaching has been one of the most rewarding parts of my career. I am so grateful to you both.

The ART Europe Instructing team, especially Shane Lawlor, for helping me be the best instructor I can be and for your constant support and great sense of humour when I've really needed it!

Luke Webb, for always believing in me and asking me 1,000 questions I had to search the answers for! You have helped me develop so much as a sports therapist and strength and conditioning coach, thank you for allowing me to gain a huge amount of experience with your elite football team at Bradfield College. I am extremely grateful to you.

Dave Pickthall for being an extraordinary supportive friend and the best boss anyone could ever ask for at one of the worst times of my life. You have always been a rock for me and as good as family. I cannot thank you enough, you are amazing!

My family: Virgina Roebuck, Johnny Roebuck, Simon Pearson, Dorothy Pearson and Malcolm Breganza for your love and support, always.

Extra special thanks to:

Charles R. Poliquin, for your knowledge, wisdom, 19 of your awesome courses and for introducing me to ART. I feel extremely privileged to have been taught by you so many times. I cannot express how much you have helped with my career goals, my athletes, my nutrition and my injuries. You have and always will inspire me to be the best at what I do. I am humbled that you agreed to write a testimonial for this book. Such a shame you didn't get time to write one before your passing but I'm sure you would have been very proud of me. I am honoured to have known you. You will always be in my heart when I beast my athletes in the gym! You are a legend.

Dr Leahy, for continually resolving so many of my injuries even to the present day! Thank you for your friendship, love and support and for teaching me the best, ever evolving, soft tissue modality on the planet. ART has changed my life; I am truly honoured to practice and teach such an awesome technique.

Dr Serrano, for your care and concern and helping me with so many aspects of my health. Thank you for your awesome internships, knowledge, friendship, love, treating me as a member of your family, honesty, multiple treatments and always continuing to inspire me with your knowledge and crazy amount of scientific research papers!

Dr Peter Jaillet, for your amazing skills, passion, love and commitment to heal my brain injury especially at the time of writing this book. I do not think I would have been able to do such a good job had it not been for you and your caring son David. You've helped me get my life back. The 'real' Heather is finally returning and I know there's more to come!

Richard Hammerton, for your amazing skills; you really are a superstar editor and photographer. I am so lucky! I am extremely grateful for your constant tips and suggestions with this book; you have worked so very hard to help me adhere to such tight deadlines! Thank you your support, your love, praise, encouragement and 25 years of a fabulous friendship.

Keith Voles, for your amazing creativity during my whole career in this industry. You are the most talented, innovative designer on the planet, I am so lucky and grateful to you. Thank you so much for your seriously hard work particularly with my deadlines to go to press and for your support, love, lifelong friendship and constant ingenuity throughout this process!

Ken Kinakin, for introducing me to Dr Peter Jaillet, for your help, praise, love, support and for kicking me up the butt, constantly encouraging me to finish writing *Back Pain Free*. I am so grateful for your awesome friendship and providing me with your solid 'brotherly' shoulder whilst writing this book. Thank you for your constant words of wisdom, you truly are Obi-Wan!

References

Chan, S, W. (2012). Panax ginseng, Rhodiola rosea and Schisandra chinensis. *International Journal of Food Sciences and Nutrition*, 63(1), 75-81.

Gundersen, K. (2016). Muscle memory and a new cellular model for muscle atrophy and hypertrophy. *The Journal of Experimental Biology*, 219(2), 235-242. https://doi.org/10.1242/jeb.124495

Jerath, R., Barnes, V. A., Crawford, M. W. (2014). Mind-body response and neurophysiological changes during stress and meditation: central role of homeostasis. *Journal of Biological Regulators and Homeostatic Agents*, 28(4), 545-54. Accessible at: https://philarchive.org/archive/RAVMRA-2

Normal Stock vs. Broth vs. Bone Broth: Is There a Difference? (n.d.). In KettleandFire. Retrieved from https://blog.kettleandfire.com/difference-between-stock-and-bone-broth/

Pratte, M., Nanavati, K. B., Young, V., Morley, C. P. (2014). An Alternative Treatment for Anxiety: A Systematic Review of Human Trial Results Reported for the Ayurvedic Herb Ashwagandha (Withania somnifera). *Journal of Alternative and Complementary Medicine*, 20(12), 901-8. https://doi.org/10.1089/acm.2014.0177

Sigthorsson, G et al. (1998). Intestinal permeability and inflammation in patients on NSAIDs. *GUT*, 43(4), 506-511.

Xie, Z et al. (2017). A review of sleep disorders and melatonin. *Neurological Research*, 39(6), 559-565. https://doi.org/10.1080/01616412.2017.1315864

Zampi, D. D. (2016). Efficacy of Theta Binaural Beats for the Treatment of Chronic Pain. *Alternative Therapies in Health and Medicine*, 22(1), 32-8.

Index

About the author

In 2001, Heather Pearson was involved in a very traumatic car accident. She was in crippling pain throughout her body – severe back pain was by far the worst. For many years Heather could not walk properly without pain. Eventually she decided to change career from working in TV, so she founded 1body4life and began a lifelong journey in the health and fitness industry to help herself and others in pain. In the years that followed, Heather attended courses around the world, learning from the most elite professionals in strength training, physical therapies, nutrition and sports psychology. For over a decade she experimented, using her own injuries, and after seeing patterns develop with her patients she created her own formula of diagnosis and a methodology for resolving back pain quickly and efficiently.

Heather has become one of the leading injury specialists in her field and is recognised as such, not just by her patients but also her peers in the UK and worldwide. She has earned herself a reputation for resolving the most complicated cases of back pain. She is known for her specific and structured rehabilitation exercises, advanced soft tissue skills, psychology work, in-depth knowledge of biomechanics and the unusual speed and lasting effect of her work with injuries especially complex back issues.

Heather teaches biomechanics to personal trainers all over the UK. Her successful creation of the Pearson Method has attracted patients and athletes in the UK and across Europe. She liaises with personal trainers and coaches all over the world to help them and their clients. In 2011 she began to teach ART® (Active Release Techniques) an advanced soft tissue technique to chiropractors, osteopaths, sports therapists, physiotherapists, sport massage therapists and strength coaches including elite medical staff in the Premier League, the highest level of English football. Heather is Europe's only female ART® Lead Instructor and she recently won ART® Instructor of the year award.

Heather has worked with a range of professional athletes including various world champions, elite weight lifters, physique competitors, football players and Ironman athletes in the UK, Europe and USA. She has worked extensively for football teams for 14 years working pitch-side, sports injury diagnostics, rehabilitation and fitness testing. Since 2010 she has helped produce arguably the best schools/scolleges football programme in Europe, with Bradfield College being crowned the 2018 ISFA cup national champions as well as consistently producing the highest quality players, as shown with a recent graduate signing professional terms with Premier League Burnley FC.

As an educator, Heather has been a guest on podcasts around the world, presented at conferences in Europe, Canada and the USA and over the last decade she has presented at various sports schools and colleges around the UK on a voluntary basis. It is her way of giving back to help others develop in her field of expertise. Heather holds a Master's degree in Nutrition and Sports Science, nine diplomas and is certified in 36 modalities of treatment, nutrition, sports psychology and strength coaching.

Heather applies the Pearson Method daily in her clinic in West London and still continues to travel internationally, learning from the best of the best. She says "When it comes to resolving injuries, there are always improvements to be made – you never stop learning."

29976965R00099

Printed in Great
Britain
by Amazon